Perestroika 1989

Editor-in-Chief

ABEL AGANBEGYAN

CHARLES SCRIBNER'S SONS
NEW YORK

First published in Great Britain in 1988 as *Perestroika Annual* by
Futura Publications, a Division of Macdonald & Co (Publishers)
Ltd.

Charles Scribner's Sons
Macmillan Publishing Company
866 Third Avenue, New York, NY 10022

ISBN 0-684-19117-2

Macmillan books are available at special discounts for bulk
purchases for sales promotions, premiums, fund-raising, or
educational use. For details contact:

Special Sales Director
Macmillan Publishing Company
866 Third Avenue
New York, NY 10022

10 9 8 7 6 5 4 3 2 1

*Printed in Great Britain by
Hazell Watson & Viney Limited
Member of BPCC plc
Aylesbury, Bucks, England*

Foreword

ROBERT MAXWELL

One of the greatest of the achievements of President Gorbachev, which illustrates his world stature, is that he has made the two words *glasnost* and *perestroika*, which are at the heart of his policy of renewal for the Soviet Union, into household words which have entered into the everyday vocabulary of the West.

The policy of *glasnost*, which may best be understood as the willingness without fear to throw open long-shuttered windows on Soviet life, is by comparison easier to implement. It requires courage and determination; but beyond that it is no more than releasing a natural force.

The policy of *perestroika*, the restructuring of Soviet society and its economy, is far more difficult. It is not just a release of natural forces. Indeed, it has to override many natural forces, especially those of historic Russian inertia and habit and of entrenched vested interests, in order to accomplish its goals of change, efficiency and economic revival.

The purpose of this yearbook, to be published regularly, is to monitor and explain the progress of this great change, both in thought and in action.

It has long been one of my personal objectives to improve the flow of communications between peoples. The more the inhabitants of this globe understand each other, the less likely are war and the misery associated with it, the more likely is material and cultural progress for us all. I was therefore delighted when Professor Abel Aganbegyan agreed to become editor-in-chief of a series of volumes on *perestroika*. The yearbooks will provide the world with a detailed picture of the progress of *perestroika* each year.

FOREWORD

The essential characteristic of this series is that it brings to the world the thoughts and writings of very distinguished Soviet citizens. This is Soviet society seen from the inside, in a way that would have been impossible before *glasnost*. Some of the contributors are well-known throughout the world. Abel Aganbegyan and Gary Kasparov are obvious examples. Others are not yet as familiar to non-Russian speakers. All are important in Soviet society; and the composite picture they give of the year's progress is a fascinating commentary on what history may well regard as one of the most important developments of the late twentieth century.

November 1988

Robert Maxwell
Publisher

Contents

CONTENTS

Introduction: The Language of Perestroika

Soviet theoretic papers as well as popular social and political literature are permeated both with new terms and concepts and with familiar concepts filled with new meaning. In fact, perestroika has created a new and rich language. The *Perestroika Annual* includes the key ideas reflecting the most important events and happenings of perestroika to date; future yearbooks will include definitions of further terms and concepts. For this reason, the material presented here is in no way exhaustive.

Unlike the constant revolutionary process of perfecting Socialism, perestroika is a package of radical measures involving the revolutionary transformation of society and providing for qualitative shifts in all its spheres. Perestroika is by its very nature comprehensive, with democratization and glasnost as its motive force.

One of the major tasks of perestroika is to combine the achievements of the scientific-technological revolution and the planned economy, to bring into action the whole potential of Socialism. Perestroika provides for priority development of the social sphere, meeting the demands of Soviet people for good living and working conditions, education, medical services and opportunities for recreation, as well as permanent concern for the spiritual and cultural enrichment of each individual and society as a whole. The ideological aspect of perestroika is no less important. Society has been undergoing a cleansing; Stalinism and its consequences have been given an open evaluation for the first time, and the reasons for the 'period of stagnation' have also been stated and analysed. Perestroika entails society energetically getting rid of distortions of Soviet morality; it means persistent realization of the

1

principles of social justice; actions matching words and obligations matching rights; the rise of honest, good-quality work and the fall of wage-levelling.

The sovereign power of the Councils of People's Deputies

The sovereignty of the Councils of People's Deputies – the basis of the Soviet system of State Government and self-government – will be restored in the process of reforming the USSR's political system. The slogan 'All Power to the Soviets' is much older than Soviet power itself. But before 1917 and after the late 1920s it was no more than a slogan; and under Stalin, although power was officially in the hands of the Soviets, in actual fact it was usurped by a narrow stratum of the State and Party bureaucracy. The 19th Party Conference, held in June 1988, found it necessary to consolidate the legal, managing and controlling functions of the Soviets, to turn over to them all the important questions of state, economic and socio-cultural life, and to restore the leading role of electoral bodies with respect to the executive and its apparatus.

Political system reform

The political system of 'administrative Socialism' has sent the country down a blind alley and brought it to the verge of crisis. The party had discovered the negative aspects of the period of stagnation and raised the question of restructuring the political system.

The reform of the political system scheduled by the 19th Party Conference presupposes the following:

● Maximal development of public self-management, including full development of citizen initiatives and full development of the representative bodies of power and of public organizations and working collectives.

● Building up a mechanism for democratically revealing and shaping the interests of the classes and social groups and for their coordination and realization.

● Providing for free development of each nation and ethnic group.

● Radically strengthening the Socialist legal system and procedure so as to exclude the possibility of abuse and usurpation of power, ensure the constitutional rights of citizens and build up safe defences against bureaucracy and formalism.

● Creating an effective mechanism for self-renewal of the political system as the current situation demands.

New political thinking

This concept appeared in the process of perestroika as a reflection of the need for radical changes in the evaluation, doctrines and concepts of domestic and foreign policy both in the USSR and other countries. In Soviet domestic policy the new political thinking has found its realization in the reform of the political and economic systems and social and legal institutions, and also in radical changes in all aspects of the life of the Soviet people. The main principles of this new political thinking have been formulated in Mikhail Gorbachev's book *Perestroika and the New Thinking for Our Country and the World*. They are as follows:

● Nuclear war cannot be a means of attaining political, economic, ideological, or any other aims.

● General human moral and ethical norms must serve as the basis for international politics, their aim being to make relations between countries more human.

● Political decisions and total disarmament are the only means of providing equal security – which is to be guaranteed by a constantly dropping level of strategic balance and the total exclusion of nuclear arms and other weapons of mass destruction from military arsenals.

● Security is an indivisible category affecting all parties equally. It must be based on admitting the interests of all nations and states and recognizing their equality in international life.

- Military doctrines must be of a purely defensive nature.

- Each nation must have the right to choose its own form of social development and must opt for non-interference in the internal affairs of other states. Respect for others goes hand in hand with an objective, self-critical evaluation of one's own society.

- The freeing of political stands from ideological intolerance.

- The solving of all global problems, including those of economic development and ecology, as a necessary condition for providing a lasting and just peace.

- The use of resources freed as a result of disarmament for the development of human civilization.

Democratization

This concept ostensibly accompanied all the stages of the USSR's development – but in reality the revival of democracy and its increase in all aspects of Soviet society started only recently, after the famous April plenary meeting of the CPSU Central Committee in 1985. In the economic sphere democratization is aimed at persistently entrenching self-management in the life of working collectives; at having enterprise heads elected and enabling people to influence industrial and social processes. With this aim in view councils of work collectives have been set up at enterprises and conglomerates, and given full authority regarding a wide number of production and social issues.

Democratization of social and political life means overcoming bureaucracy and corruption, taking public opinion into consideration and providing conditions for every Soviet citizen to express his or her position openly and to take an active part in discussions and make decisions concerning the most acute problems of our society. We regard democratization as the driving force of perestroika.

Glasnost

Glasnost is one of the major democratic principles of the Socialist system. In accordance with that principle the Soviet people must have a real opportunity to express their opinion on any problem in public and political life. Until recently, for the majority of Soviet people the reverse was the case. Now the situation has changed dramatically. The press have suddenly opened the floodgates. Magazines compete for sensational news. Newspaper circulation has rocketed. But could all these changes just be temporary?

As was pointed out at the 19th Party Conference, the CPSU regards extension of glasnost as a key political objective. Without glasnost there can be no democracy, no mass political creative activity and no participation by the people in management.

Social justice

While determining the possible measure of social justice under Socialism, Karl Marx and Vladimir Lenin pointed out that: (a) during the first stage of Communism, justice and equality find their expression in the fact that private ownership of the means of production and exploitation of man by man have been abolished; (b) all people have equal rights; and (c) their social position must be determined first and foremost by their work. However, for many years, theory and practice here in the USSR did not go hand in hand. It was precisely social injustice that people had to face so often. And these problems were the object of deep and special analysis in the materials for the 27th Congress of the CPSU and other Party documents for a reason. It was pointed out that social justice presupposes struggle against 'wage-levelling', against unearned incomes and against unjustified privileges; it implies improvement of forms of moral stimulation and a decisive improvement of material stimulation. Social justice implies equal access for all members of the society, without exception, to the socio-economic benefits our country can provide at the present time. It also implies equal responsibility before the law, with no areas exempt from criticism. It is a full realization of human rights. The principle of social justice being realized to its full in all spheres of social relations is one of the major goals of the CPSU's social policy.

Socialist pluralism

Over sixty years ago the official press proclaimed conformity of thought and unanimity the most important achievements of Socialism. Dissidence, any opposing point of view, any expression of doubt or opposition to the official interpretation of any event were nipped in the bud and proclaimed to be anti-Party and anti-State. The 19th Party Conference of the CPSU called upon the people to restore Lenin's principle of Socialist pluralism. Socialist pluralism implies a variety of opinion, organizations and directions of social thought within the framework of the Socialist system of values and within the framework of the Socialist system itself. And this is not just ideology. In the course of the preparations for the 19th Party Conference and at the conference itself the principles of Socialist pluralism were strengthened, their further development was stimulated and their consolidation as the basis of Socialist political life was promoted. A wide discussion of the most urgent problems of economic and political life has allowed the Party to work out a concrete strategy for the next phase of perestroika – to adopt political decisions on a truly democratic basis.

Radical management reform

This became essential when it was apparent that the Soviet economy was slowing down dramatically. Briefly, it involves a transition from bureaucratic orders to performance-based management. The radical reform of management is aimed at the reorientation of economic growth from intermediate to final results. Today attention is focused on meeting demands for a natural combination of national, group and personal interests, harmonious human development and a new, higher, level of prosperity for the Soviet people. The consumer has become the top priority in economic relations, and now has the right and opportunity to make choices in the market place.

Comprehensive cost-accounting

The economic system must allow enterprises to cover all the expenses of simple as well as expanded production and to pay for raw materials out of their own pockets. At present we have hundreds of such enterprises, although just a few years ago this kind of economic management was unthinkable. Briefly, the principles of comprehensive cost-accounting are as follows. The enterprise is responsible for its payment obligations to the State budget, Ministry, banks and suppliers. The money earned by the enterprise is used to finance R & D, modernization, incentives and social programmes: and the amortization charges and profit remaining after the State budget and the Ministry get their share is at the disposal of the enterprise.

Cost-accounting income

This is a new economic category resulting from the radical reform of the economic mechanism. From the point of view of political economy, full cost-accounting income is a new created value consisting of the cost of the product necessary for the enterprise plus the cost of a part of the surplus product, less amortization of the fixed assets. In short, it is the share of the enterprise income which remains totally at the disposal of an enterprise working under the new economic conditions. Full cost-accounting income cannot be taken away or redistributed among other organizations. It is lower than the gross output income (i.e. money received as a result of realization of production, labour and services, minus expenses). The difference consists in the sums the enterprise has to pay to the budget, to the higher body (Ministry) and to the bank. Full cost-accounting income includes the means assigned to pay for labour and income that is to be used by the enterprise for whatever needs it may have. This kind of income is only guaranteed if the major principles of comprehensive cost-accounting are all complied with completely – if the enterprise is profitable and has full material responsibility, for example.

Informal associations

These are all kinds of groups organized spontaneously, mainly by youth. The associations deal with practically anything: cultural creativity, use of leisure time, community work and political activity, social issues and educational or ecological problems. As traditional organizations do not offer enough opportunities in the field of communication, relaxation, recreation and cultural activity, young people are now looking for new means of self-realization through various groups, societies and companies. The need for such associations has been felt for a long time, but earlier informal groups of this kind were forbidden and their membership punished. Now the situation is different. The level of young people's education and awareness has risen, which has led to non-traditional forms of communication springing up and individuals finding new means of self-fulfilment.

Speed-up

One strategic aim of the CPSU is the qualitative transformation of all aspects of life in the USSR. The speed-up programme put forward at the April plenary meeting of the CPSU Central Committee in 1985 became a cornerstone of the CPSU's programme and received a detailed foundation in the decisions of the 27th CPSU Congress. The speed-up policy presupposes far-reaching changes in economics; a well-grounded social policy; consistent entrenchment of the principle of social justice; improvement of social relations; renewal of political and ideological institutions' forms and methods of working; further development of social democracy; and decisive elimination of inertia, stagnation and conservatism. The main idea behind the speed-up programme is to reach a new level of economic growth through multiple intensification of the production process and by means of scientific and technological progress, economic restructuring and effective forms of labour organization, management and incentives.

Individual enterprise

Individual enterprise on the part of Soviet citizens aimed at meeting demand for goods and services is socially useful, since it increases employment and offers them opportunities to receive additional income in accordance with their efforts. There was a time when people involved in activities of this kind were persecuted and regarded as rogues and cheats. Today we are witnessing 'a second wave of NEP'.[1] The law allows individual enterprise in domestic industry and every-day services, as well as other kinds of activity based exclusively on the work of citizens and their families, without restoring hired labour. People involved in this kind of activity pay tax on their income.

Orthodoxy and Socialism

A millennium ago medieval Russia adopted Christianity. This was not only a religious event – it provoked a great political and social response and so became a notorious landmark on the centuries-long road of Russian history, culture and development. In the words of Mikhail Gorbachev, General Secretary of the CPSW Central Committee: 'Working people, both believers and non-believers, made a Socialist revolution, the first in history: they worked together, side by side, building Socialism, and in the years of the Great Patriotic War they fought at the front lines and worked heroically on the home front. The peace-loving work of the religious organizations of this country and their role in the struggle for nuclear disarmament deserve the highest commendation. The same is due to the clergy for their support of humanism and just relations between

---

[1] NEP – New Economic Policy, introduced by Lenin in 1921 and later denounced by Stalin.

peoples and for their support of the domestic and foreign policy of the Soviet States.'

The Millennium of the Baptism of Rus was widely celebrated – not only by the Orthodox Church, but by the whole Soviet people. A Church delegation was received by the head of the Soviet State, Andrei Gromyko; a number of Soviet science centres held symposia, conferences and exhibitions on history, culture and art; meetings, discussions and concerts were organized; and the foundation on a new cathedral was laid in the Moscow suburb of Tsaritsino. Indeed, the Millennium of the Baptism of Russia has turned out to be a nationwide celebration. At present, thanks to democratization and glasnost, relations between the State and the Russian Orthodox Church have largely improved. The Church supports the positive changes happening in the life of society and calls upon believers to take an active part in the transformation, to sped up the process of spiritual renewal, to work honestly to love their fatherland, protect the environment and fight for peace.

The cooperative movement

Not long ago economic executives were afraid of the concept of 'cooperation' as if it were seditious. Today, it is a widespread form on business. Indeed, full-scale development of the cooperative movement is today regarded as the embodiment of Lenin's vision of Socialism as a state system of civilized cooperators.

Socialist cooperatives are a permanently developing and progressive form of socially useful activity. The cooperative movement opens up great possibilities for citizens to apply their skills and knowledge in productive work in accordance with their likes, dislikes and abilities, and for each to receive an income depending on quality and quantity of labour and on his or her share in the final results of the cooperative activity. It also offers a means of meeting the cooperative members' needs. In June 1988 a law on cooperatives was adopted with the aim of discovering the vast potential of cooperation, giving it an increasing role in speeding up both the country's social and economic development and the process of democratization in the economic field and giving kolkhoz[1] development a real boost.

---

[1] Kolkhoz – collective farm.

A Who's Who of Perestroika

A leader who failed

Construction worker, team-leader, manager, Secretary of the Sverdlovsk Regional Committee of the CPSU, Secretary of the CPSU Central Committee, First Secretary of the Moscow City CPSU Committee, candidate for the Central Committee Politburo membership, Soviet minister, First Executive Chairman of the State Construction Committee – these are the milestones in the career of Boris Nikolayevich Yeltsin.

Boris Yeltsin's first steps as the political leader of Moscow were inspiring and gave reason for optimism. He won the hearts of Muscovites with his mobility and energy; he was always on the go and constantly meeting people.

Yeltsin had been promoted to the post of First Secretary of the Moscow City Party Committee as a man of experience and vigour, capable of being critical, since the situation in Moscow was grave and the Party's City organization needed serious improvements. Yeltsin got down to work immediately, improving the situation and helping Moscow get rid of the accumulation of negative factors. But when it came to turning the ideas of perestroika into reality and applying its ideas, which demanded hard and persistent work, Yeltsin failed to display the qualities needed to be an effective Party leader. Instead of looking to the Party organization and workers for support, he resorted to arbitrary decisions and commands; and there followed endless shuffles of Moscow District Party Committee personnel. Nor did he respond to criticism from Politburo members.

At the October 1987 plenary meeting of the CPSU Central Committee Yeltsin handed in his resignation; and in November the plenary meeting of the Moscow City Party Committee relieved him of his post. Subsequently, at the 19th

Party Conference, held in June 1988, Yeltsin asked the delegates for political rehabilitation, but did not find any support.

Freedom of thought; the main thing in perestroika

The Soviet newspaper *Moscow News* stands out as a herald of perestroika. The credit for this goes to Yegor Yakovlev – born in 1930, when the newspaper was founded. Although that is considered symbolic, he did not regard himself as a born editor and for thirty years went through all kinds of professions within the sphere of journalism, with the exception of photography.

Yakovlev's career as a reporter was not an easy one, as he always tried to tell people the truth and the truth was not always welcome. As a result, he was often fired – which, he says, acted as a stimulus. The last time this happened was when he was dismissed as Editor-in-Chief of the magazine *Journalist*, which he himself had founded. The magazine, so popular in the 1960s, tried to fight conformity, pompousness, bureaucracy and group irresponsibility. However, Yakovlev was so thoroughly suppressed during the period of stagnation that he did not even get into the *Literary Encyclopaedic Dictionary* published in 1987, despite the fact that he had written over thirty screenplays and some twenty books during the past eighteen years.

'In the Soviet Union,' he says, 'it is traditional to be proud of having come from tractor-driving stock.' Yakovlev himself is proud of his journalistic dynasty. His mother was a journalist; his children, Vladimir and Alexandra, are both journalists; and his wife, a historian by profession, is co-author of the majority of his books.

After Yakovlev came to *Moscow News*, it became one of the most widely read newspapers in the world. Today it is published in five languages in 140 countries and has broken through the conformity which became obligatory during the period of stagnation. Through his newspaper Yakovlev teaches his readers democracy, offering space to foreign as well as Soviet correspondents so they can give their view of life in the USSR. *Moscow News* is no sensation-seeking sheet

13

out to spread gossip; it sweeps the veil of mystery from taboo and shows the reader that he or she is a free citizen of a great country, with a right of his or her own.

Doing away with the personality cult for ever

The Children of the Arbat has set passions seething in the Soviet Union, ranging from utter disparagement to almost religious adulation. We have not witnessed such a reaction to a literary work for years. This is a novel about the generation of the 1920s to 1930s, with their unlimited belief in the ideals of Socialism, whose devotion to Soviet power and sincere Komsomol enthusiasm were thwarted by the monstrous system of reprisals entrenched by Stalin and his colleagues. The novel – which deals with the dictator's psychology and the motives and stimuli that prompted Stalin to adopt decisions and take action – is Anatoly Naumovich Rybakov's *chef-d'œuvre*, accomplished despite obstacles from the very beginning. Born in 1911 in Chernigov, Rybakov spent his childhood and youth in Moscow, on Arbat Street, and studied at the Exemplary Moscow Lepeshinsky School together with children 'from the Kremlin'. His father, a prominent Soviet engineer, abandoned the family when Anatoly was quite young, leaving them in a hard way financially, so Anatoly took his mother's name and had to start work at an early age.

At the end of 1933, when he was in his last year at technical college, Rybakov was arrested and sentenced to three years' exile under Clause 58/10 for counter-revolutionary activities. He was sent to Siberia, as was then the practice, and after the end of his exile in 1936 spent four years wandering all over Russia before settling in Ryazan in 1940.

From the beginning of the war he was at the front, first in a field-engineering squad then in a motorized battalion. He fought near Moscow, at the Kursk Bulge, in Warsaw and Berlin, and came out of the war a battalion commander in the First Guards Army under Chuikov. Rybakov's coming home to the Arbat after thirteen years gave the first impetus to his urge to write. In the following thirty years he achieved his goal brilliantly. He wrote a trilogy for children, a trilogy for

14

teenagers and five novels for adults; he also wrote stories, which were later adapted for the screen, television and stage; and his novels have been translated into over forty foreign languages.

The Children of the Arbat was to have been published by *Novy Mir* in 1966, and by *Octyabr* in 1978. But it was only finally published – twenty years after it was written – thanks to perestroika.

A scientist's responsibility

In such closed societies as dictatorships, the majority of people become conformists. This phenomenon appeared in the Soviet Union during the Stalin personality cult and in the period of stagnation. Indeed, only a few scientists were courageous enough not to sign the letter denouncing the views and actions of Andrei Sakharov, which was published in *Literaturnaya Gazeta* and other organs of the official press. Among those few was Renat Sagdeyev – despite the fact that in those years so defiant a position could have cost him his highly successful scientific career – and in June 1988 he boldly defended Sakharov in *Moscow News*, demanding that the scientist's honours and decorations, illegally taken from him during the period of stagnation, be returned.

In 1961, at the age of 31, Sagdeyev became a Doctor of Sciences in Physics and Mathematics; at 32 he was elected a corresponding member of the USSR Academy of Sciences, and at 36 he became a permanent member. In the years to come many universities and academies elected him an honorary member, among them the USA National Academy of Sciences. In 1973 Sagdeyev became the head of the Institute of Cosmic Research at the USSR Academy of Sciences. He has headed a number of unique research projects on the Cosmos, Prognoz, Venera, Meteor and Intercosmos space vehicles and orbital complexes, and is the scientific adviser for the major international projects Vega and Phobos.

As a scientist, Sagdeyev has an acute feeling of responsibility for the fate of the world. Since he could foresee, perhaps more clearly than anyone else, a disastrous end to civilization as a result of the nuclear arms race, he founded and headed The Committee of Soviet Scientists Against the Nuclear Threat. He is known for his honest and principled position on many problems pertaining to perestroika, democratization, science and society; and often speaks out, giving an open and impartial evaluation of Soviet science and outlining its position in world science today.

A rostrum for civic truth

Playwright Mikhail Shatrov wants the Soviet theatre to be a rostrum for the truth. A mining engineer by education, in the late 1950s Mikhail Filippovich Shatrov became one of the youngest playwrights in Russia. His professional credo soon became evident: he was always of the opinion that history was much more interesting than fiction, that history itself was the best playwright.

Shatrov sees Lenin as the leading theme in his writings. He has been developing documentary drama, a genre introduced by him in his treatment of the Lenin theme as far back as in the mid-1960s, beginning with his play *July 6th*.

Mikhail Shatrov's plays *In the Name of the Revolution, A Quiet Day, A Revolutionary Sketch, This Way Will Win, Dictatorship of Conscience, Bolsheviks* and *On . . . and on . . . and on . . . !* have become extremely popular. They have been staged in the Leningrad and Moscow youth theatres, the Lenin Komsomol Theatre, the Moscow Art Theatre and others; some of them have been shown abroad, some made into films. For his productive work Shatrov was awarded the Order of the Red Banner of Labour, the Order of the People's Friendship and the USSR State Prize.

Things did not always go smoothly for him, however. Even in the time of stagnation, when the truth was not honoured, Shatrov tried to tell the whole truth and nothing but the truth. His writings were too documentarily exact for literary officialdom and for those writers who not only told the people lies or half-truths but did not want to know the historic truth themselves. They were carefully whitewashing the truth, internationally leaving blank spaces. In Shatrov's plays there are historic personalities who had been carefully erased from our memory for years. And what about the image of Lenin? Shatrov's Lenin, living, fighting, hesitating, suffering, making mistakes and rising above them, differed so much from the sugary, powdered image offered to us by many writers and playwrights. Of course, such a position, such an uncompromising approach, did not make life easy for Shatrov. For during the stagnation period, to many the truth seemed too seditious to tell so as to be heard. Many of his plays, such as *This Way Will Win, The Brest Peace Treaty, On . . . and on . . . and on . . . !*, were criticized – and the critics tried to make the author smooth out all the sharp points.

But all the discussions about Shatrov's plays essentially boiled down to one simple question – to speak or not to speak the truth. However, Shatrov's readers and his audience had long since decided for themselves. That is why every play of his raises acute interest, besides sparking off debate. His authority is great in the literary community, too. Shatrov has been elected Secretary of the USSR Union of Writers, and today historical documentary drama, Shatrov's own genre, is acquiring an ever-growing audience.

An artist, not an official

For over two years, Elem Germanovich Klimov, the new leader of the Cinema Workers' Union, together with his supporters, has been fighting for a new system for managing cinematography. But each step meets with immense resistance and is hampered by ambitions, disputes and endless scandals. The Union has been trying to defend the rights of talent, but mediocrity does not want to give in and resorts to demagogical arguments and fashionable 'democratic' slogans. Yet where is democracy to be found in art if the numerical majority persecutes talented loners? Nevertheless, Klimov has managed to create a system that provides for the well-being of the working group, making it no longer dependent on the bosses' tastes or the 'importance' of the theme but on the artistic result, on whether or not the film is a success with the audience and the critics. Since the restructuring of cinematography under Klimov is now in full swing, he has decided 'I am not an official. I am an artist, and it is high time for me to return to filming.' And he has plenty of ideas. He wants to film Bulgakov's *Master and Margarita*, for example, although his main subject is Stalin and Stalinism. To reveal the nature and the consequences of the political phenomeon, to penetrate its very depths, would mean the restoration of our freedom and would cure us of the myths that have taken us prisoner.

Klimov became a director at 31. In the twenty-five years he has been in the movie industry, he has made six full-length films and several documentaries. That may not seem many, but there were years of forced silence, when it was impossible to make films the way he wanted; and Klimov was unwilling to compromise with top management, nor was he capable of doing so. But if we speak about his films, about their screen-life, about their relevance, their truthfulness and concern for the people, about his great experience as a producer, six films do not seem so few.

Klimov's films have been awarded prizes at many international festivals, but his popularity and his authority are, above all, the result of his civic position and his courage as the head of the USSR Union of Cinematography. There is good reason for the world's interest in Soviet cinema of late. In Klimov's own words: 'We have tried to create a new atmosphere in our cinema, an atmosphere of frankness and justness. We have taken films off the shelves, we have tried to help talented people as much as we can, to support them. And we must go on, we should not deviate or slow down.'

In 1987, in recognition of his role in cinematic art and his public activities, Klimov was made a member of the American Academy of Cinematographic Arts and Sciences, and also an honorary member of the British Cinematography Institute.

The indefatigable Fyodorov

Svyatoslav Nikolayevich Fyodorov is often called the first Soviet 'capitalist' for his total economic independence and

18

indefatigable Socialist enterprise. But fame was a long time coming to him.

Fyodorov's origins were quite ordinary, but in 1938 a big black car came and took away his father, a division commander. He never returned. After the war, Fyodorov studied at a medical institute and conducted his first experiments on transplantation of the crystalline lens. Although his first patients got back their sight, he was often forbidden to work in his chosen field and was not given a laboratory or money or equipment.

After 1974, when the Americans also started working seriously on the problem of an artificial crystalline lens, Fyodorov's enemies were forced to admit defeat. Having received the 20 million rouble Institute of Eye Microsurgery on lease, Fyodorov literally put the treatment of sick people on an industrial basis. 'To treat the sick quickly and effectively,' he stresses, 'is more profitable for the State than gold mining.'

Now, after thousands of people in practically all countries have had their sight restored thanks to the artificial crystalline lenses, the widespread publicity seems well-deserved. Today Fyodorov is a prominent scientist, an honoured inventor, a professor, a corresponding member of the USSR Academy of Sciences and General Director of an inter-industry scientific-technical complex that has branches in twelve other Soviet cities and will very shortly have branches in other countries as well. He emphasizes that the main investment must go not into production expansion, but into man: we must start believing in man, we must stop talking about the human factor and start speaking about development of the individual and the harmonious development of the personality, which is the main aim of the Revolution and of Socialism. And his credo finds expression in his actions; doctors in his clinics make 600 to 700 roubles a month, and his personnel have the best living and working conditions of all the USSR Ministry of Health's subordinate organizations and bodies.

At the 19th Party Conference Fyodorov offered a new standard for the evaluation of State management: 'The main criterion of our management system is people's happiness.'

Victor Bossart's credo

For about seventy years there has been a rule in effect in the USSR that any director, even the director of a small factory, can only be appointed by a ministry after coordination with the Party. Victor Bossart was the first to become a director in violation of this rule. At 38 he was elected General Director of the industrial association 'RAF'. Bossart's father had been a kolkhoz chairman unjustly arrested and punished in 1938; but Victor's life went on and, after graduating from the Kazan Aviation Institute, he became an engineer. After 1975 he worked as a shop superintendent at the gear-box plant, and at 31 became the plant director. He then graduated from the Economic Institute by correspondence. In his opinion, an enterprise director should be twenty per cent engineer and eighty per cent economist.

The relations between the young plant director and the General Director of the Industrial Association were complex. At several meetings Bossart spoke about bureaucracy, about endless sittings, sluggishness and wage-levelling, and named names; he made many enemies, and was no longer given the floor at meetings. Not everybody liked his being a man of principle. But that was possibly why he got special attention among other candidates for the post of General Director, and today the first successful steps of the enterprise after its many failures may be ascribed to the new course of its leader. His main ideas include complete self-financing in all the association's shops and plants; election of all management, from team-leader to director; and glasnost in everything that concerns the association. Now all the personnel of enterprises and organizations elect their directors, thanks to the new law on industrial enterprises introduced as a result of Soviet management reform.

Always up front

The life of Vladimir Pavlovich Kabaidze, General Director of the Fiftieth-Anniversary-of-the-USSR machine tool factory in Ivanovo, has not been easy. Like all those born in 1924, he went to fight in World War II when he was 17. He was wounded three times and suffered severe contusions twice, but each time returned to his unit despite the doctors' insistence that he was not yet fit enough to do so. The spring of 1945 and victory found him on the Oder River, where the Allied Armies met. Now the whole country knows about the Ivanovo factory and its director: it is in the mainstream of scientific and technological progress. And Kabaidze is no ordinary man, either as a personality or as a leader; he is one of those we call 'the foremen of perestroika'.

One of our major troubles is that our machine tools are swiftly becoming obsolete. Indeed, it would be wise for dozens of plants to stop producing outdated tools, which could bring the country to ruin and will keep us behind in the future. Kabaidze sees modernization as a major factor in machine tool building. At Ivanovo, production has been expanding every year under the five-year plans in the following manner: in 1986, 8·2 per cent; in 1987, 25 per cent; in 1988, 81 per cent; and in 1989 it will reach 92 per cent. Not a single machine-building plant in the USSR can boast such a rate. As Kabaidze himself puts it, if the machine-tool industry lags behind, the rest of industry will automatically lag behind, too.

The General Director has to fight bureaucracy and sluggishness for his right to think and act independently as a leader and an effective manager. Kabaidze sees two major difficulties blocking the way of perestroika: 'Everybody wants to rule, but nobody wants to part with his power, with the privilege of deciding for us what we can do ourselves. And, secondly, we are in the habit of latching on to any innovation which may look to be a panacea, but when there are no quick results we either forget about it or find fault with it and pick up something else.'

Well, we shall overcome – following the example of enterprising leaders such as Kabaidze.

A bomb for bureaucrats

A worker has been sitting around with nothing to do but smoke – for a whole shift, for a month, for two months – since there are no materials to be used at his workplace; but he continues to receive his salary. That's how it was before Travkin came to the work site. He was the first to suggest and to introduce a new principle of work organization and remuneration named 'team contract': the whole team works with one purpose, to hand the project over to the client on time and in good shape. Construction has found a new type of teamleader – since his personal earnings and the workers' pay in the team depend only on the final result.

Nikolai Ilyich Travkin has been working in construction since he was 16. He began as a bricklayer. He has been a Communist for eighteen years. He finished college and then completed an institute course by correspondence. Quite an ordinary beginning for a biography. But Travkin turned out to be a talented, original builder and leader. In 1977 he became a leader of a multi-skilled team and then head of a Mobile Motor Team.[1] He was the first to introduce a teamcontract in his MMT and provide its advantages in practice. He was always full of initiative and searched for new methods, constantly fighting the bureaucratic obstacles in which our construction industry abounds.

In 1984 Travkin became the head manager of a construction company. He was then 38 years old. While a team-leader he was awarded the Order of the Red Banner, and in 1986 became a Hero of Socialist Labour. Since 1986 he has been the head of a State industrial enterprise embracing nine construction companies.

Travkin has been generous in sharing his experience with other construction workers. His suggestions for improving the economic system are of interest for all industries. He is one of the most ardent supporters of team contracts and of complete self-financing in all industries and spheres of activity. He often writes to the central press. 'A Bomb for Bureaucrats', the headline of one of his articles in *Izvestiya*, is characteristic of Travkin's style.

[1] Mobile Motor Team (MMT) – a unit within the Soviet construction system providing construction sites with machinery.

22

A muzhik from Archangel

Nikolai Semyonovich Syvkov lives in the Archangel region. He has no titles, no awards, no special education. He is a farmer through and through, a man of the soil. But many people in our country know about him today, and he is often mentioned on television and in the press.

The sovkhoz on whose land Syvkov lives and works is not one of the best: production costs are high, management is bad, losses are great. Syvkov did not want to work with idlers and earn the same salary. Besides, he couldn't stand incompetent management. He therefore decided to work independently, on a contract, and started to breed cattle independently, with bull calves being supplied by the sovkhoz. First he took five bull calves and raised them, then twelve. The meat cost was three times lower than that in the sovkhoz. The daily weight gain was half as much again. Syvkov then decided to organize a team on contract and raise a hundred bull calves at once.

The local authorities in the sovkhoz, the district and the region should have been happy to see Syvkov's initiative and to support him and spread his ideas. But nothing of the kind. Syvkov's independence, his economic progress and his high income as a hard-working farmer prompted a storm of protest and real persecution. He was accused of all sorts of crimes by the local authorities. They marked him as 'suspicious', after central television shot a documentary about him and his experiments: he was even called a 'kulak'. Yet he was just a farmer desiring a decent standard of living for himself and producing useful revenue for the country. It is estimated that his three-man team provides meat for eighty-seven of his compatriots annually. Syvkov might have done much more had he not been forced to devote so much time and effort to fighting bureaucrats and conservatives. Syvkov himself has no doubts about the validity of his approach: 'The sovkhoz of the future must be a group of teams working on contract. And livestock experts as well as agronomists must lend them a hand in growing crops and raising cattle.' This point of view has gradually

23

been making its way and is now becoming the official position of the State.

A life of contradictions

It is as difficult to get into Yuri Nikolayevich Afanasyev's lectures or speeches as it is to obtain tickets for a superstar's concert. The largest Soviet newspapers and magazines feel honoured if they manage to get an article out of him. However, his enormous popularity has earned him as many opponents as supporters. His candidacy for the 19th Party Conference, when put forward, caused a real fight; and when he was elected a delegate to the conference, three days later *Pravda* published a crushing criticism of one of his articles.

Afanasyev comes from the Ulyanovsl region. He studied at Moscow University from 1952 to 1957 – years that promised a turning-point in our history which failed to materialize. That was when Afanasyev made his first steps in science and first attempts at public activity – when he learned his first bitter lessons, though the feeling of irretrievable personal loss was to come to him later. He spent several years in the Krasnoyarsk region as a Komsomol worker, finally becoming a leader of the Soviet Young Communist League, and joined the CPSU not long before the 22nd Party Congress. At that time angry speeches about the personality cult were still ringing from the rostrums, yet the borderline between truth and pseudo-truth was blurred, revision of the past could already be traced in eulogies and bureaucratic lip-service was evident in bombastic economic reports.

After four years on the staff of the Young Communist League Central Committee (1964–8), Afanasyev became a teacher and scholar. He took a postgraduate course at the USSR Central Committee's Academy of Social Sciences, then at the Sorbonne in 1971 and 1976. His research interests were foreign history (mainly French history); the historiography of the October Revolution; intervention and the Civil War; the October Revolution and French public opinion; ideological struggle and historical science; and modern trends in French history. In 1981 he defended his Doctor's thesis on French

24

history, which was later published in the USSR and in Bulgaria. He has produced over 1,500 pages of research papers, books, essays and reviews. He also prepared for publication a book by Fernand Braudel, a prominent modern historian, on the world's material culture in the fifteenth to eighteenth centuries, and wrote the commentary for it.

April 1984 saw the release of his social programme, on which he had been working for many years. Afanasyev is now Rector of the Moscow History and Archives Institute, a post he has held since 1986, and his social programme is well known from his public speeches before audiences in Moscow, Leningrad, Obninsk and Baikonur, and also from his statements and interviews in the press and on TV and radio both in the USSR and abroad. He is an energetic advocate of consistent and comprehensive democracy without exception and of glasnost (openness) in our society. The restoration of the Communist Party's leading role in Socialist society (as opposed to past and present attempts to see it as a ruling party), a decisive struggle against the Stalinist legacy in social science, a turn to creative Marxism and the true cognizance of world and domestic history are among the key ideas in his speeches, which have played their role in creating the social atmosphere of perestroika.

The road to unity a millennium long

Not long ago parents wanting to have their children baptized were risking their careers: the Church and Socialism were looked upon as incompatible concepts. Perestroika has brought about a significant improvement in Church–State relations in the USSR – and religious workers also have something to give perestroika.

Pitirim (Konstantin Vladimirovich Nechayev), the Metropolitan of Volokolamsk and Yurievsk, is the Chairman of the publishing department of the Moscow Patriarchy, Editor-in-Chief of the *Journal of the Moscow Patriarchy*, head of the editorial board of *Theological Studies* and a professor at the Moscow Theological Academy.

He was born in 1926 into a clerical family, with the dynasty of priests going back as far as the seventeenth century. In 1951 he graduated from the Moscow Theological Academy, with a Doctor of Theology degree, then became a deacon and later a monk named Pitirim. Later he was made Archbishop and then Metropolitan.

Metropolitan Pitirim has been the head of the publishing department of the Moscow Patriarchy for more than twenty-five years. He directly supervised the publication of five editions of the Bible, and of a great number of magazines and books on theology. He was the principal editor of the following books: *The Russian Orthodox Church* (1982), which was published in Russian and English; *The Russian Icon* (an illustrated book) in Italian; and a number of books in English, French, German and Polish.

Metropolitan Pitirim has visited many countries, the USA among them, in the course of more than one hundred journeys abroad. He is active in international Church organizations, and frequently speaks at Church conferences on the dangers of war and the need for a non-nuclear world. The international conference 'Theologists and Publicists: a Call for Peace', which took place in Moscow in January 1988, was his initiative. During the world conference of religious workers on 'Saving the Sacred Gift of Life from a Nuclear Catastrophe', which was held in Moscow in May 1982, Metropolitan Pitirim headed the press centre.

Pitirim is a board member of the Soviet Culture Fund, a member of the Board of Directors of the International Fund for the Preservation and Development of Humanity, a member of the Central Council of the Union of Friendshiip Societies, Vice-President of the USSR-Italy Society, and a member of many other Soviet friendship societies.

Metropolitan Pitirim has received honorary doctorates from the Preshov Theological Faculty in the Czechoslovakian Socialist Republic and from the Comensky Theological Faculty in Prague, and has been awarded the highest honours of the Russian Orthodox Church and of other Churches. For his patriotic activities and work for peace, in 1986 he was awarded the USSR Order of People's Friendship and the Jubilee Medal of the World Peace Council.

He has stated, in an interview with the press, that 'New relations under the conditions of glasnost and perestroika impose even greater moral responsibility upon Church members in their service to the people.'

The whole truth . . .

Not long ago the name Shmelyov didn't mean anything to anyone. Then came an article that provoked widespread debate, followed by a novel and a number of stories. As a result, Nikolai Shmelyov suddenly found himself ranked among the most talked about writers and publicists. Nevertheless, he is not a professional writer. He graduated in economics at Moscow State University; four years later, in 1962, he defended his Candidate's thesis (which corresponds to a PhD) and in 1969 defended his Doctor's thesis. He has written over twenty books, among them *Economic problems in the Developing Countries*, *The Third World And Science-Technology Progress*, *Socialism and International Economic Relations*, *Economic Ties Between West and East*, *The World Socialist Economy*, *American Capitalism in the 1980s* and *World Economy: Trends, Shifts, Contradictions*.

Shmelyov's articles 'Advances and Debts' and 'New Worries', written in the perestroika period, received the greatest public attention. We could not read such articles during the time of stagnation. But why weren't these articles, along with many of his other writings, published earlier? Any why do many people object to them even now? The articles tell us the bitter, unembellished truth about the failures and disproportions of the Soviet economy during the days of Stalin and the time of stagnation. Shmelyov boldly and sharply criticized what he calls 'administrative Socialism', the Stalinist model of economic management, which is incapable of solving a single one of our current problems. He had particularly in mind the difficulties of the first two years of perestroika.

Only the truth, no matter how unpalatable it might be – that is what Shmelyov offers to his readers. And it is the truth that is needed in order to break up the old outdated dogmas, to advance economic development and, finally, to harness the economic potential of Socialism.

In his economic research and recommendations Shmelyov is not following directives from above; he gives the facts as he sees them. There is no nostalgia for bygone times, but a sincere desire for the revolutionary transitions for which he has been fighting in the forefront of perestroika.

Fighting the ghosts of the past

Tenghiz Yevgenievich Abuladze was born in 1924. He graduated from the Rustaveli Theatre School in Georgia and in 1954 started working as a movie director, producing a number of films and documentaries.

Abuladze is a master of subtle psychological portrayal, revealing his characters' inner world; he is also laconic and persuasive in his depiction of time itself. His films *Entreaty*, *The Tree of Desire* and *Repentance* have been most successful. The first two were interpreted as philosophical parables of good and evil, love and hate, and life and death. But even here one could see the concrete aim of denouncing the darker aspects of our past and present. The film *Repentance* is now seen as a true exposure of the crimes of those people who came to power, both in the State and in the Party, in the dark period of Stalinism. The film came as a warning to all of us that the past should never return. But the film was made at the very beginning of the 1980s. The people and groups in power then were convinced that it was harmful for the population to see such films, so it was 'kept on the shelf' for a long time. Then some studio personnel made a video tape of it and for a long time people watched it in private.

Today *Repentance* is known to the whole country. International recognition was not long in coming, and it received a number of prizes at several film festivals. The film is in the thick of the battle with the ghosts of the past, which are clutching at us still and still find some support in our society.

As to Tenghiz Abuladze, he is full of new ideas and his latest films are just as bold and uncompromising.

An unusual school

The school is not in a fashionable district and the children who go there are quite ordinary. But they are lucky, indeed. Shalva Amonashvili, psychologist and teacher, scientist, Corresponding Member of the Academy of Educational Science and Director of the Educational Research Institute of the Georgian Ministry of Education, works here. Shalva Amonashvili and his people from the Institute are out to bring about a radical revolution in the theory of educating and bringing up the younger generation.

It is impossible to give a detailed description of how they are doing it. The teachers of the junior classes have totally given up marking. So how do they evaluate the work of their pupils? In a very simple way. If somebody is good at something, they praise him; and if he does something wrong, they patiently explain his mistakes. And that is it.

At Amonashvili's school the children are uninhibited, inquisitive and inventive. His methods differ from the traditional ones in that they are totally devoid of pressure. Instead, he has been cultivating respect for the pupil: the teacher and the pupil cooperate and work together harmoniously. The gist of what Amonashvili has been doing is to make the child feel that lessons are not something compulsory, but something he himself would like to do of his own free will. Most of the classes cover the curriculum several months earlier than at ordinary schools, and the remaining time is used to review material, for discussions, going on excursions and working on the children's general intellectual and emotional development. Moreover, all children at the Amonashvili experimental school manage to cope with their work.

Amonashvili's experiment is becoming popular elsewhere, and the time will soon come when we will have many such teachers and many such schools.

Alexander N. Yakovlev

During the broadcasting of the 19th Party Conference, Soviet TV showed an unusual clip. During the break a Canadian journalist came up to Mikhail Gorbachev who was crossing the Kremlin yard and asked him a question. There were no interpreters nearby, so the interview seemed impracticable. Help came from Alexander Yakovlev who was walking at Gorbachev's side. Smiling, he started fluently translating from English into Russian and from Russian into English. Soviet audiences are not accustomed to such outcomes. Unconstrained, able to immediately respond to an unusual situation and, finally, having a perfect command of the foreign language, Yakovlev is exactly the statesman to be in charge of ideological issues at the time of perestroika. Alexander Yakovlev is a secretary of the CPSU Central Committee and a member of the Politburo. He comes from a village not far from Yaroslavl. During the Great Patriotic War he fought at the Volkhov front as a marine platoon leader. He was transferred to the reserve after he had been seriously wounded. But his civilian life has not been serene either. Yakovlev cannot be called a staffer, although he has worked on the Party staff for over twenty years. It would be inexact to call him a diplomat, though he has been Soviet Ambassador to Canada for ten years. He is not a scholar in the academic sense of the word, though he has been elected an associate member of the USSR Academy of Sciences and has headed the Institute of the World Economy and International Relations. He is all these things in one: a scholar, a high-ranking Party officer, a diplomat and a publicist. As for his command of the language, he learnt English during his post-graduate training at Columbia University, USA.

The Political Philosophy of Perestroika

ALEXANDER N. YAKOVLEV

The first three years of perestroika have been extremely spiritually intense. The wind of political and intellectual renewal has touched all aspects of life throughout the country. I am sure that future historians, when characterizing the present-day state of society, will write about the great dynamism and multicolouredness of the current processes, the daring thoughts in society at large and their far-reaching plans.

Within a historically short period of time we have covered an unprecedentedly long distance of self-examination. It is a difficult and in many instances painful path. It has been covered by society, the Party and – it would not be an overstatement to say – by every thinking individual, every responsible member of society. This process is not over yet. But we can put to perestroika's credit the unprecedentally large and intense work of the Party in the organizational and theoretical fields, quite a few concrete breakthroughs, and qualitative changes both in public consciousness and in the social activity of Soviet people.

The intense spiritual work of the Party and the people has been embodied in the decisions of the 27th CPSU Congress, the 19th All-Union CPSU Conference and the Plenums of the CPSU Central Committee. In terms of importance, lots of them have had no match for decades. It has been embodied in practical undertakings which – and there's no longer any doubt about this – will determine the destinies of our country and of Socialism for many years ahead. It involves democratiz-

33

ation and glasnost, economic and political reforms, and perestroika in the Party itself and in its work.

The analysis, the discussions and the research for solutions will, of course, go on. We shall have to re-examine certain things and correct others already deployed. It is inevitable; that's life. But the CPSU and the Soviet people already have an elaborated concept of perestroika, of revolutionary Socialist renewal . . . and, of course, it's all open for continuous development.

I

The 19th Party Conference has been the major political event of 1988.

It has summed up the results of perestroika for the first half of the twelfth five-year-period, has charted out our immediate objectives and has comprehensively considered the issues of continuous development of democracy in Soviet society.

What new features has it introduced into the theory and practice of perestroika? What determines its social scope and political importance?

First of all, the Party Conference has deepened the theoretical understanding of perestroika, and has politically substantiated the concept of comprehensive Socialist renewal. Thus, in some respects a decisive step forward has been made by the whole perestroika process. The resolutions of the Conference have extended and deepened the front of perestroika, and they have laid a solid democratic foundation for qualitatively new social processes of Socialist rejuvenation.

It would be wrong to assert that the concept of perestroika and the strategy for its implementation have taken shape all at once, 'in one go'. No doubt, when launching the restructuring drive, the Party and its leadership already had mature comprehensive ideas concerning not only what should be done in the economy, in the social sphere, and in the country's public life, but also the grounds for and the aims of these measures. These ideas underlay the fundamental decisions taken by the April 1985 Plenum of the CPSU Central Committee and to a large extent defined the preparation for the 27th CPSU Congress as well as for all post-congress work.

But it is just as true to say that, with growing democratization and glasnost, and with the in-depth comprehensive public analysis into every aspect of Soviet society's life and its ongoing processes, the concept of perestroika has developed and diversified. We developed a better understanding of the scale and nature of the problems we faced, their reasons and their interrelationships. We were more precise in formulating our objectives and in outlining the specific measures to be taken.

With what did the concept of perestroika begin? Strictly speaking, it began with the realization of the need for the renewal of the economic sphere in general. Not so much only the economy *per se* – though this is one of the top priority challenges – but the whole set of social, legal and other issues which in one way or another depend on and in their turn influence the economy.

It would be wrong to say that perestroika has revealed all the depths of society's economic life, and especially of its prospects. But perestroika has cast the light of glasnost on them. The very essence of the individual's and society's daily life should never be hidden from the public eye and never fall out of its sight.

Besides, the diagnosis of the problems with which this country entered the 1980s was to a certain extent self-evident long ago – even in the 1960s. It is sufficient to look through Party and state documents for the past two decades (and for some issues over an even longer period), and it will be clear that we have for many years spoken about the extensive development model, the unsatisfactory state of affairs in agriculture, producers' indifference to consumers' needs and demands, the economy's insufficient response to scientific-technical progress, its excessive formalization, and the dominance of red tape with the entailing lack of flexibility. Moreover, correct decisions were made to rectify the situation.

But they remained on paper. The situation did not measurably improve. Worse than that: by April 1985, when for the first time the Plenum of CPSU Central Committee developed and processed the idea of perestroika and its fundamental policies – by that time it had become perfectly clear that the country was in a state of long-lasting and potentially danger- ous stagnation. The stagnation was not limited only to the economy. It spread over to the social sphere and into public life. Serious signs of degradation which inevitably accompany stagnation surfaced everywhere – from the moral climate in society and its various cells to the state of affairs in numerous material sectors. This situation was correctly characterized by the Party as a pre-crisis one.

The following question arose: were the earlier decisions wrong in their premises or were they simply inadequately implemented? Or were there any deeper reasons and tend- encies which we did not take into account in these decisions or, which perhaps we did not even identify and properly understand? Experience showed that this situation had actu- ally resulted from all these and many other factors.

But the very fact of asking these questions marked a quali- tative change in political and public consciousness. This was the first step towards perestroika, its priority spiritual con- dition. Measurable intellectual and simply human courage was needed to challenge the inertia of thinking, the estab- lished clichés and the stereotypes. Furthermore, if these clichés and stereotypes were to be attentively and critically analysed by the public, much courage was needed to challenge those quite real interests and ambitions which disguised the concern for personal well-being and passiveness with argu- ments about a 'commitment to principles' or of an alleged 'threat' to the fortunes of Socialism. This is only natural: com- petition between the old and the new is the sole impetus of progress.

Firstly, it would be perfectly illogical to expect that someone is going to suddenly and whimsically change his convictions. History proves the opposite: even when they are completely at variance with reality, deep-seated convictions undergo changes with great difficulty.

Secondly, Socialism has enabled scores of nations inhabit- ing the former Tsarist empire to do away with underdevelop- ment, oppression and backwardness. It has rendered it possible to build a modern Soviet Socialist state which, economically, ranks second in the world and is characterized by advanced scientific output and level of cultural development. These are truly historical results.

But Socialism is not an icon or an idol to be worshipped in hope of some mythical favour. Socialism is freely created by a free people. It develops and progresses alongside that which it itself creates, society and a developed personality. It passes through various stages of its qualitative enhancement and progress, through well-known moments of 'negation of negation', and via periods of breakthroughs to new ideas and practices.

The first theoretical and practical result of perestroika is as follows: we have noticed in the socio-economic system of Soviet society a certain resisting force, referred to by the 29th CPSU Congress as the 'mechanism of deceleration'. This notion encompasses many things:

- we have recognized, *inter alia*, that there are conservative forces and interests in our society too;

- we have realized that we are lacking incentives in the economic and the social spheres, the incentives that would urge people, collectives and society to move forward and if necessary push them ahead;

- and we have come to understand the drawbacks of our economic planning and management, etc.

In the broadest political sense of the word the mechanism of deceleration is tantamount to everything that hinders and slows down normal progress in the economy and society. It is impossible to do away with it by simply removing a careless and incompetent worker or even a fairly considerable number of such workers and leaders. To meet this challenge we need large-scale social measures.

With this in mind the following steps were to be taken: the first thing to do was to introduce an elementary order and discipline everywhere and in everything. Regrettably it must be admitted that shoddyness and irresponsibility, breaches of discipline at the workplace and violations of contract terms

37

had become quite common in the stagnation period. And they were characteristic of all levels, from worker to Minister. This was to be expected: it was easier to live, and simpler and more convenient to manage this way. Besides, the established system of economic relationships as a whole did not punish in any way laziness, inertia and carelessness, just as it did not properly reward their positive opposites. To sum it up, only the introduction of proper order could – and later on did – yield measurable practical benefits of all sorts. It was an important precondition for changing over to perestroika, a victory of new ethics and modern psychology in practical management. And it was a necessary step; but the decisive contribution to the restructuring process was made by large-scale economic and politico-economic measures whose sum total makes the substance of a radical economic reform.

The economic measures outlined in the decisions of the 27th CPSU Congress (February 1986) have determined three stages in speeding up the development of Soviet economy and society as a whole. By acceleration we mean the qualitative substance of growth rather than the rates of growth *per se*. Acceleration was discussed in terms of production quality, of meeting real social requirements, of orienting the economy towards the end results, and of switch-over to a model of intensive development, etc. In the first stage, covering the current twelfth five-year period (1986–90), we planned to take all necessary organizational measures to convert the economy from predominantly administrative methods of management to economic ones, and to start modernizing the machine-building industry and its products. Relying on the progress made, we were to secure in the thirteenth five-year-period (1991–95) the accretion of quantitative and the improvement of qualitative economic indicators, and to exploit this success in the fourteenth five-year period (1996–2000). The measures and decisions taken by the 27th CPSU Congress made up the conception of accelerating Soviet society's socio-economic development.

The planned acceleration was to be carried through in a predominantly new way. Unlike what happened both in the relatively recent and more remote past, the Party pressed ahead with all-round development of Socialist democracy and glasnost.

Why do we somehow draw a distinction between these notions by using two different words, and at the same time wed them together by putting them always and everywhere next to each other? Are we not simply emphasizing different aspects of one and the same phenomenon? The answer is both yes and no.

The meaning of democracy and Socialist democracy is more or less clear. It stands for the broadest possible involvement of the population in managing society's life at all levels: from the worker collective and a team at the enterprise, right up to the country as a whole. Democracy is not limited to elections, though they are an integral and important part. Democracy means the people's participation in management through their legitimate representatives elected directly by the people in keeping with established procedures. This participation should be effected on a daily basis and as broadly as possible in the forms that are practicable and expedient for it. Its specific forms may, of course, be quite different depending on the concrete function, its sphere of activity and the aim.

But such democracy is impracticable without providing the population with complete information on a wide range of issues . . . and above all, information on the problems that people face in their everyday life. Meanwhile, numerous problems have stockpiled in this field. It is not only a matter, either of practical norms which, strictly speaking, were not always democratic enough, or of norms whose practical implementation sometimes deviated from the procedure provided in law.

The stagnation years turned out to be such due to a very peculiar and unnatural combination of inertness and irresponsibility on the part of some people, lack of expertise on the part of others, deliberate abuses here, connivance there, and comfortable indulgence elsewhere. Most people, of course, remained honest, decent and hard-working – otherwise perestroika simply could not have been launched. But increasingly, they were not the ones to set the fashion in public life. And since this situation lasted for years, many people had already started to regard it as a peculiar 'norm'. Quite widespread were the attempts to turn a blind eye to the pressing problems, fraud and self-delusion. Not only criticism but even usual factual information on the real state of affairs was increasingly viewed as objectionable, as a violation of established 'rules'. There appeared a large number of so-called 'zones beyond criticism'. They existed not only at the level of republics and regions, but also at lower levels: in worker collectives, in institutions and in organizations. This resulted in impairing society's progress rather than simply distorting its morals and ethics. There arose the situation when the common worker sometimes knew much more about international affairs or the work of the Politburo than about life in his own collective, district, village, or city.

Glasnost is called upon to change this situation. Glasnost is not limited to the right to discuss everything, to say things out loud, to be unafraid of anyone or anything. Glasnost is not confined to the right to voice one's opinion and stick to it. Glasnost is, first and foremost, the right to form an opinion, and to this effect it is necessary to know all that is happening, in all aspects and every detail. Glasnost is the right to independently assess the situation at all levels: from the enterprise up to the State. Besides, glasnost lays obligatory demands on the style of economic transactions and, above all, on the style of management.

Abroad, glasnost was interpreted as a new openness of Soviet society, a new image of the mass media and press. All this is true, but this is only one of its aspects. Glasnost, like democracy, should first of all exist at the local level. It should become a part of everyday life through the individual's first-hand social experience. The same phenomena at the national level simply reflect these profound processes. But the strength of any phenomenon lies in its roots. And in this respect, democratization and glasnost are no exception.

It all started exactly at the grass-roots level, 'from below'. Through workers' letters and statements, democratization and glasnost made a tangible contribution to the development of perestroika's theory and practice, and helped it gain momentum in the period between April 1985 and the 19th All-Union Party Conference held in June–July 1988.

Democratization and glasnost have promoted people's activity, have awakened the conscience and energy of the people. They have secured the workers' support for perestroika. Perestroika has truly become a nationwide drive. Currently, this has surfaced first of all in interested and heated discussions by the people of society's accumulated problems. Such discussions have been taking place at meetings, in the press, at improvised rallies, simply in the streets and even at home. Unconcerned, indifferent people, to say nothing of those who oppose the course towards reforms, will never behave like this.

It is sometimes asserted that perestroika is far from having reached everybody, that it is progressing slower than it could. Probably, there is something in this. But not much.

It is true that we have not yet irreversibly overcome social apathy. But it is impossible to deny the outburst of public interest and creativity. It has been especially manifest during the preparation for the Party Conference and at the Conference itself. This process goes on, it gains pace, which is only natural: every new step, every new stride, small as it may be, have recruited perestroika's new supporters and active champions.

It is true that perestroika has progressed at a slower pace than we would have liked. The Conference has also openly recognized this. But one must keep in mind the scope and the complexity of these unparalleled challenges. Excessive hastiness is no less detrimental here than sluggishness. And the fact that people think twice before they do something, that they assess variants and debate things, is normal and natural. Moreover, it is the best expression of support for perestroika which is viewed as practicable, necessary, important work rather than as just another campaign.

True, it is quite possible that not everyone will have enough resourcefulness and purposefulness. Some people may fail to overcome their deep-seated laziness, may shirk new demands and opportunities. Well, this may be so. But these are not the people who set the fashion. Life is improved and society is created by active, resourceful, hard-working people.

Interested, democratic, open and nationwide backing of perestroika has made the greatest contribution to hitting its top priority target: people have come to understand that large-scale changes in the economy will be practicable only if based on the radical fundamental economic reforms. They can be carried through only if such reforms are in perfect harmony with the processes of democratization and glasnost, going hand-in-hand with them and being interlaced with them by countless threads. The reforms will meet these challenges only if they strengthen and support democratization and glasnost, and vice versa. What, specifically, does this mean?

First of all, it means diversity of forms of property ownership in the economy and other fields. The basis of Socialist society remains immutable – public ownership of the implements and means of production, of products and objects of labour, as well as of natural resources. But if it belongs to the whole people it does not mean that it belongs 'to the State', or in other words – according to some – to no-one in particular. This actually opens up the possibilities for some relatively small categories of people to capitalize on this property at the expense of society's interests, and to do so quite 'legally' due to the established economic system. What other words but 'capitalizing on society' could we use when speaking about the planned manufacture of products no-one needs, or the allocation of funds for useless and even harmful projects and many other things, done to please the so-called 'departmental interests'?

Socialist property will truly belong to all the people, only when it is owned – in the fullest economic implications of that word – by a real legal personage – a worker collective. They will be its true master in practice, and they will shoulder the whole responsibility for it. But this function can be practicable only if there are several forms of property ownership. The Law on Co-operatives adopted at the end of 1987 equalized the rights of co-operative and public ownership. It will pave the way for the setting up of joint, municipal and other forms of property and, *inter alia*, on the basis of international co-operation, the initiation of joint commercial ventures.

Such ownership, the realization of the Socialist owner's rights, necessitates his indisputable autonomy. He should be enabled to determine the key lines of work on his own. He should enjoy the right to independently determine its specific economic parameters, to choose his suppliers and consumers. And he should bear full fiscal responsibility: financing his work, taking credits to provide for the process of production, living within his means on the money made, distributing it among the workers, social funds, capital restoration and re-investment.

This, in its turn, necessitates the reform of the established pricing system and mastering of fiscal–commodity relation-ships by industry as a whole. It brings about the need to set up a full-scale Socialist market. These are the issues on our agenda. In 1988, nearly 60 per cent of the total industrial output will be manufactured by the enterprises that have gone over to new economic conditions of work. By the beginning of 1989, the entire national economy will be switched over to them. Complete economic self-reliance and self-financing will become the universal norm. New forms of management have been taking shape: lease and contractual arrangements have been spreading not only in agriculture but also in industry. The question has arisen concerning the possibility of renting to worker collectives those modern enterprises which have tens of thousands of people on their payroll. We have set the task of transferring, by the end of the five-year period, to wholesale trading in means of production, i.e. to set up a Socialist market. And finally, we are planning to launch in the near future the reform of the financial system and price-formation.

We are at last to settle our outstanding debts. Today's press-ing problems of foodstuffs, housing, consumer goods and services, are to a great extent the result of our former neglect thereof, and of our life on credit.

Perestroika will really make headway only on paying these debts. But to this effect radical, cardinal and balanced measures are needed . . . measures that should drastically differ from the bureaucratic approaches used in the past.

We need a truly dramatic shift in favour of consumer goods production. There can be put one paradoxical answer to this problem: we must start a large-scale re-orientation of the economy towards the consumer and scientific-technical progress. We must launch, if you like it, the drive towards an advanced industrial society with its superquality production, information science, biotechnologies and with its really revolutionary channelling of person-power resources in favour of social infrastructure, first of all, in the social services sphere. Our national economy has got its chance due to the system of priorities developed by the 19th CPSU Conference: foodstuffs, housing, consumer goods, paid services, etc.

We can live up to this challenge – our economy, society, culture, and education have long since reached the requisite initial level. We must meet this challenge: slower rates and a worse quality of development largely stem from our failure to go straight over to a people-oriented economy, once we had defended the revolution, our independence and Socialism, and had guaranteed our security. Instead of a full-scale switch over to regarding people's needs as a top priority in deed rather than just in word, the Soviet economy oriented itself towards serving 'the needs' of bureaucratic and sectional structures.

But the experience of the first three perestroika years has proved the following: in many industrial sectors and planning the practice of economic reform, democratization and glasnost has had to rely on long outdated political conditions, mechanisms and institutions. The new wine does not always fit the old bottles, especially as these old forms were developed in their time specifically to maximize uniformity and to reduce to a minimum the independence of the subordinate enterprises.

The sources of resistance to perestroika are also more clear to us today than they were even a year or two ago. At that time emphasis was laid on subjective reasons. The force of inertia lay in psychology, habits, skills, or in the public mood . . . in the persisting social apathy . . . in the red tape of the bureaucrats' style of work . . . in the self-interests of those people who were forced by perestroika to live more honestly, to work harder and more thoroughly. All this is true, these factors have not disappeared, they persist and are in our way today too.

But we have come to see more clearly the resistance stemming from deeper and more serious reasons, from the reformed material itself: from social relationships, the economic and social infrastructure, and the political and legal organization of life. And one of the specific breakthroughs made by the decisions of the 19th Party Conference and the July 1988 Plenum of the Central Committee – and besides, its specifics are absolutely fundamental – has promoted us to *this* level of understanding, to *this* depth of work, and, to *these* criteria of responsibility.

Thus, the practice of perestroika and the entailing development of public consciousness have brought about the need to reform the Soviet political system, and have outlined the priority aims and objectives of these reforms. The decisions on its content were taken by the 19th Party Conference. The July 1988 Plenum of the CPSU Central Committee translated them into a concrete programme for work and specified the time-scales for carrying the reform through.

II

The 19th Party Conference has launched a consistent drive for the institution in the Soviet Union of rightful government. This is the course towards a radical reform of its political system through all-round democratization. This is the course towards a Socialist, self-governing society guided by law.

A people enjoying their full rights, an authoritative government and steadfast rights – these are the corner stones of a lawful, Socialist government.

What is the substance of the already launched political reform? First of all, it is to open up the broadest possibilities for democracy and people's Socialist self-government, at all society and State levels. It is to demarcate economic, political, ideological, cultural and other functions in society; to draw a clear distinction between the rights, the duties and the responsibilities of the Party, the soviets, the Government, and of public and economic bodies. The target of the reform is to put the whole life of Socialist society on a precise basis of lawfulness; to create a Socialist Government committed to the rule of law, and to determine the new mature correlation between powers central and local. The reforms must also measurably extend human rights, the rights of the collectives and society in counterbalance to the hypertrophied rights of the State which sometimes result in omnipotence and a tyranny of the individuals or groups in power.

Thus, we have set ourselves the task of developing, improving and efficiently using the whole system of two-way links in society: political, economic and other feedbacks. Special priority is given to political and economic feedbacks, and to the most democratic forms thereof.

A normal system of feedbacks can be compared to society's sense of belonging. It is here that our development was most severely damaged. Normal self-regulation of numerous processes which can and should be regulated at the grass-roots level was replaced by hundreds of thousands of instructions which continuously suggest to people that they are potential malefactors.

Perestroika started to remedy this situation. Special emphasis was laid on the political and economic reforms which were to develop a system of mutual feedbacks in the economy and society's political organization. But the objective of promoting feedbacks is valid everywhere – in every collective, every town and village, every region. It would be wrong to limit this problem to the centre alone. And the means of solving it can and must be diverse, depending on specific conditions.

We have actually pioneered and more than pioneered the work for the deliberate and purposeful creation and development of a political system which would be in harmony with the nature of a Socialist society, which would contribute to its all-round progress, and which would pay priority attention to overcoming people's alienation from government.

The political system that existed in the USSR for the last five decades and more was greatly affected by the then current factors of formation and development of Socialism in this country. Hence, both its merits and demerits, its inherent restrictions. This problem was thoroughly discussed by Mikhail Gorbachev in his report to the 19th All-Union Party Conference.

The major drawback of the system inherited by perestroika is this: it features many properties and structural characteristics which were introduced back at the beginning of the 1930s in order to create and consolidate the authoritarian régime, plus those which developed later under the impact of that régime. It is recognized that perestroika is actually a complete rejection of the Stalinist legacy in all spheres of life. But we cannot renounce this inheritance with the help of and by means of the very tools that created it and which later led to the period of stagnation.

The review of all accumulated experience, including that of perestroika, proves that the Soviet political system needs radical changes. The further progress of society and Socialism will directly depend on the extent to which we shall be able to use the initiative, enthusiasm and creative potential of every person and every work collective. This, in practice, will overcome people's alienation.

The experience of the reforms carried out in the mid-1950s and 1960s, and the analysis of the reasons accounting for the failure of many well-intended and necessary concrete decisions taken later on, prove that this is the only correct way of putting the question. We must act very resolutely but always think twice. This conclusion is also proved by the course of perestroika.

Today, more than thirty years after the 20th CPSU Congress, it is self-evident that it radically changed the Party and all our society. But this wholesome remedying process was not backed by development of Socialist democracy, and the consequences were regression, stagnation and the pre-crisis situation! Society was irradiated with amorality – in the economic, political and spiritual spheres. The dirt of dogmatic interpretations of Marxism persisted in ruining creative thought, trampling down the sprouts of fresh ideas. This was the price of reformism divorced from consistent revolutionary practice. And this is the price of defeat when the fear of hard practical work paralyses one's thought and consciousness.

It is always more difficult to climb up than it is to slide down.

The slip of the country towards crisis has been stopped by the efforts of the people and the Party. Now we witness the first measurable and promising results in the economy, the social sphere, population's incomes, in the moral-political atmosphere, of course, and in the social health of the people. Far-reaching economic reforms, and the radical and comprehensive democratization of society, are under way. People's thought, feelings, and initiative have been released. Apathy and alienation have been replaced by inspiration and activity. These are the actual results of the first three perestroika years.

Today's objective is to confirm and to multiply these results, to guarantee their build-up and enhancement. But the top priority aim is to make this progress irreversible. By irreversibility we do not mean the immutability of the recently or currently created new forms – they have been undergoing changes already in the course of perestroika; we mean guarantees against the return to all that has deformed, distorted and slowed down our advancement and society, the very ideas and ideals of Socialism.

The discussions before the Party Conference and at the Conference itself, and the practice of perestroika, clearly show that the profound reasons for deceleration have been spotted, more or less understood, but far from overcome. Until that is so, the destructive work continues. The mechanisms of renewal haven't yet started working properly. Perestroika has so far touched only the relatively easy-to-reach upper layer of problems. We must be well-prepared for facing the underlying problems and press for their speedy solution.

This situation is quite natural: it is impossible, in such a large, diverse and complex country as ours, to practically remake all that has been taking shape over decades within just a few months. We need logical and consistent work, thorough preparation of all its steps and stages. But we also need persistence in carrying it forward, when the time has come and conditions have matured. The next step to be currently undertaken is political reform.

The restructuring of the political system and a perestroika of the Party itself, both engendered by the practices of democratization and glasnost and by the new forms of economic management, have been put on the agenda by the course of development of perestroika policies. Yet these particular problems should be solved now to secure the continuing progress of perestroika. Only with this approach will it be possible to safeguard its development, deepening and irreversibility.

The key link in the reform of the Soviet political system lies in the restoring of the omnipotence of the soviets of people's deputies, at all levels. It should be secured by a change in the nature of their interrelationships with Party bodies, by the democratization of the electoral system, by a better interaction between legal and executive authorities, by broader rights and powers for the soviets in their own territories, and by strict restrictions of the executive staff's powers and actual functions.

It is a high priority to provide material and practical facilities for all their work rather than to simply extend the rights of the local soviets by law, and to put under their authority a wide range of republican, regional, city, or district problems. The organs of the Party are to delegate, whereas the soviets are to assume, numerous tasks. They are, for example, to provide for normal functioning of everything that serves the people in the territory under their authority. We must radically reform the system of interrelationships between the soviets and the enterprises located in their territory as well as with the Ministers and departments to which these enterprises are subordinated. A truly legislative, demanding and working soviet should replace the inactive, talking-shop soviets of today. Within the structure of the local government bodies, we should drastically build up the role of the elected deputies, i.e. of the real soviets and just as drastically step up the responsibility of the executive staff.

We are planning a large-scale legal reform which will go beyond the frame of enhancing the current legislation. It should aim at creating the entire structure of the new political system as a whole. To overcome people's alienation from government, to make it a true government of the people, and to involve millions of citizens in this process, we must, first and foremost, give full play to the processes of self-administration and self-government. Only then can citizens, representative bodies, collectives, and Party and mass organizations display that initiative which will yield maximum results.

In other words, we need a reasonable measure of decentralization at all levels, from national-State to the factory floor. We must re-examine in theory and practice the ways and means of optimum correlation between public and individual interests. Under the specific conditions of a multinational society and federal State system, we shall also have to reconsider the relationships between the rights and the duties of the Union and its constituent republics, as well as among the republics themselves.

Today, Party committees often assume State and economic functions. This is wrong in principle: everyone must do his own work and bear responsibility for it. The old approach gave birth to parasitism and a lack of responsibility, it became a drag on our move forward. And this old policy is simply incompatible with the new principles of economic management: no-one is entitled to dictate anything to the enterprises without bearing economic responsibility for it.

I am sure that the Party's prestige will only profit from denouncing such practices and by going over to political forms and methods of guidance. The Party at all levels will do exactly what it should, i.e. it will chart out and put into practice a political strategy for Socialism, working with the Communists in the soviets, State bodies, and worker collectives.

The key target is to do everything possible to involve – in deed not just in word – millions of workers in management. Two things are of top priority in this respect: guarantees of the people's rights and possibilities, and a strengthening of their political security on the one hand and on the other a consolidation and extension of the range of incentives that would urge them to use their rights, to full purpose.

All the efforts of the CPSU and Soviet society to step up

the individual's rights rely on the principles of Socialism, the requirements of society and its members. We are not at all just trying to please some external observer. The Soviet Union is ready for the broadest possible co-operation in these matters as we are fully aware that the internationalization of contemporary life will sooner or later require much greater internationalization of the rules and regulations in this field than exist at present.

Human rights are guaranteed by a combination of a broad democracry and the legality of the Soviet State's work. The revitalization of omnipotent soviets alongside the reforms of the legal system and other institutions of law and order (which both secure the regulation of State–citizen relationships within the law, and defend the political, economic, social and human rights of all members of society) will result in the establishment of a real Socialist rule of law. Its highest principle will be the unconditional equality of everyone before the law.

Therefore, we are facing the following task: to adjust, in the process of reforming the political system, both the mechanism of freely formulating and identifying the will and interests of all classes and social strata in Soviet society, and the mechanism of taking these interests into account in harmony with others in practical policies.

We should underscore the meaning of this. There are, today, practically no ready-made answers, no prescriptions as to how to do this in real life. We will have to learn by experience. But both practical and theoretical searches along these lines have already begun, and the first results are already there.

There should really be but one for all. Quite a few changes in the existing legislation, the legal and judicial system, are needed to update them to the new state in society's development. A set of new laws should be passed for those fields in which there never were any. We must do away with the established practice by which departmental norms could *de facto* cancel laws, so placing themselves above the law and sometimes even above the Constitution. All life and functioning of society should abide by the law and be regulated thereby. This is what we understand by a Socialist State committed to the rule of law.

As we sometimes lack norms, experience and traditions, and because the innovations are so striking and intense, some debaters start to, as it were, counterpose freedom to discipline and law to democracy. They reason in the following way: you cannot have it both ways, it is 'either-or', there is no third alternative. But with democratization and glasnost under way, society ever better understands that these are dialectically interconnected, rather than opposing categories; that true freedom can exist only under the protection of the law, and democracy without discipline will degenerate into anarchy; that all these good and necessary features of society and its members can develop only in the context of democracy and legality which are the sole source of the free human spirit; and that they are the only conditions that engender a conscientious discipline resulting from individual self-control and a respect for society and the law which, in their turn, respect the individual.

All the above-mentioned is generally true of the restructuring in the Party too: democratization of all its activities, changes in the forms of its work, and alterations of its concrete functions in the political system and society as a whole. But there is an important reservation: the Party should begin this enormous and crucial work with itself. This is what is actually going to happen in the Autumn of 1988, when the hustings and election campaigns start in the Party organizations.

The Party took the lead and managed to reveal the reasons for the previous deformation of Socialism. It fearlessly gave a critical assessment of the state of affairs in society and in itself, it put forward the programme for perestroika, rallied the masses around it, and pressed for the realization of perestroika's ideas in practice. Hence, the Party has proved to be a true political vanguard of society. At the same time it is imperative to fully revive the intra-Party democracy which was especially severely hit in the years, first of the cult of personality, and then of stagnation. We must go over from command-style and administrative methods of work to political ones, and we must carry through a whole range of other reforms.

Having launched perestroika, the CPSU deliberately made itself the object of public investigation. Only thus could we open all the locks for a truly in-depth analysis of the stockpiled problems, of all the strong and weak points of the economy and society. Only thus could we distinguish true strides from wishful thinking and mistakes. And only thus it is possible to resolve a high priority problem for the Party itself: to look into the mirror of unprejudiced public opinion and to examine those processes which were and are under way in the Party itself. Changes in the Party towards the revival of openness, discussions, criticism and self-criticism, collectivism and personal responsibility have already begun. This has been graphically proved by the Party Conference. The consolidation of these processes and tendencies is a guarantee of perestroika's irreversibility and success.

Among the achievements of the first perestroika years we can mention the following: due to their renewal, politics are once again a part of our life. Lenin said that politics begin when millions are actively involved. The administrative fiat of the 1930s etc. left to the millions merely executive functions. But perestroika gives a big hand to initiative. It recognizes and stimulates a pluralism of opinions and interests, and it looks for the ways and means of their optimum identification and account. It is all a political process.

The updating of the Soviet political system decided by the Party Conference is not limited to the structure of government bodies, to the differentiation of functions or the election procedure. We must all study politics . . . not just democracy, the culture of glasnost and discussions, but also politics as a peculiar field of human activity. We must take into account its regularities, its rules and its logic. Whereas perestroika is measured by its deeds, the efficiency of its political support is gauged by the realism of the aims and maturity of its actions of each Party organization.

The reform of the political system is oriented towards freedom and responsibility. This reform is neither a single act nor a once-and-for-all process. Society develops, the environment changes, and people do not remain immutable either. The system of Socialist self-government will evolve too. This, of course, is a long-term objective. It is impossible to achieve this only by reforming the 'corridors of power'. It is actually the problem of developing society's entire political culture. That is why the political reform aims, *inter alia*, at integrating a receptivity to innovations into the developed mechanisms and structures.

III

Socialism was born and developed on the very coal-face of theory and practice of civilization as a whole. Scientific Socialism as a theory is the result of insights during the entire pre-Socialist development of humanity, of all its accumulated experience. Socialism as a practice is both the science and the art of really taking into account all traditions and most recent trends, as well as economic, political, scientific and cultural phenomena, both at home and abroad.

Today, when Socialism is ready for most radical and comprehensive self-renewal, when new fundamentals of life are being laid down for decades ahead, we again turn to the theory and practice of world development, but this time reviewing both the Socialist and non-Socialist pages of history. We are turning to them in order to picture what the world will look like in the foreseeable future, what tasks it will set before us, which possibilities it will offer, to what criteria we shall have to aspire in different spheres of life, and what threats it can create.

The new political thinking answers many of these questions. But what is even more important is that it gives us an updated methodology for perceiving world developments on the eve of the twenty-first century, the methodology for participating in these developments and influencing them along ennobling and humanistic lines. In terms both of content and methods, new political thinking continues and develops the respective bases of scientific Socialism and Communist philosophy.

A new insight into Socialism's highest ideals and values is, above all, applicable to the specifics of today. The emancipation of the worker from the domination of private property must inevitably begin with his/her liberation from all types of exploitation and oppression. That is axiomatic. But this is only the first step towards turning civilization into a true kingdom of working people. From our own experience we know today how many more steps should be taken, how much is still to be done to really build a society of social justice.

We see that the movement towards this ideal will take much time. The idea of world revolution as something concentrated in time, just like similar ideas of easy and automatic sequences towards Socialism and Communism, proved to be utopian and groundless. The attempts to take a short historical cut – dictated, probably, with the best intentions – have cost nations too much.

Today it is self-evident: the transition to Socialism even in one country is a long historical process, with its regularities and stages. Thus, we are facing the task of finding optimum avenues and forms to continue this process, and the most adequate policies to this effect.

Nowadays the task of all tasks is to preclude the nuclear threat and to disarm for peace, confidence and cooperation, for the sake of humanity's survival and security. But historically, this is only the first most vital condition which will then enable people to resolve other problems on a just, democratic and rational footing: to give food to the starving; to protect the environment without which we cannot survive; to rationally use Earth's finite resources: to prepare and launch large-scale economic exploration of the world's oceans and of outer space, without which our children and grandchildren will not be able to live even if we can.

The interests of the human family are not an abstract category, theoretically developed by philosophers in their ivory towers. Today, when the whole planet would seem to have greatly shrunk in size, when the fate and history of humanity can end by pushing the button, when some 5,000 million people learn about any event within a few hours – today, human interests have been embodied in flesh and blood.

These are truly the interests of all humanity. Therefore,

they are also our interests, as we are part of humankind and a major contributor to humanity's social progress. These are the interests which unite people. Hence, they can overcome the forces of division, opposition, confrontation and war, which have already delayed civilization's progress for centuries. This is the coming together of the opposites: individuals' interests merge with the interests of all people; an abstract, philosophic category of history merges with everyday, earthly, practical substance.

Marxism is just such, the teaching which perceives the interests of all people in terms of history and the prospects of development of all humanity rather than just some countries or classes, some peoples or social groups. When they gave priority to the interests of the exploited and the oppressed; and when, in the social structure of their time, they identified the class-agent of the historic mission of liberating the individual and humankind, could we say that the founding fathers of scientific Socialism placed the interests of the oppressed in opposition to those of the rest of humankind? Certainly not.

They analysed and tried to comprehend the objective tendencies of social development. They tried to forecast where and on what stage this development would culminate in truly humane humans rather than simply *homo sapiens*. They aimed to find out what could and should be done to facilitate this development. They asked themselves the following question: what is to be done to change and transform the world in such a way that humankind will move towards social progress, humanism, light and freedom by the power of intellect, scientific prediction and creative work, rather than through catastrophes and crises, wars and violence, by excessively costly method of trial and error and experimentation on human beings.

The thesis on the primacy of human values is valid because it reveals an objective trend of development. It urges people to give up dogmatic ideas of the world, of their own country, of each national cell. It helps them realistically and sensibly to view the peaceful co-existence of countries with different political systems as history's *diktat* and the manifestation of internationalist tendencies in world development.

The individual's and humanity's emancipation from all types of exploitation and oppression, the struggle against the nuclear threat and for saving civilization and the active involvement of Socialism in the resolution of other global questions of common concern for all humankind – these are by no means differing, to say nothing of opposing, tasks. They complement each other. These are simply different facets, different components, different aspects of one and the same way – the way of freedom and progress of peoples.

IV

Today it is clear that Socialism should be developed by purposeful, balanced, consistent release of every potentiality for showing initiative and creativity, rather than by putting new administrative fetters on a rapidly growing society.

This presupposes a return to Lenin's ideals of Socialism, to its truly democratic and humanistic image, freed from all the deformations and distortions of the past. It also presupposes moving foward from the twentieth into the twenty-first century rather than backward to the phantasmagoric past.

A major line of the renaissance of Socialist ideals and the simultaneous invigoration of the stagnant social organism is a return to the individual human being. The person 'is the aim rather than the means', as Marx put it.

The goal of Socialism is the individual. A truly humane, free and democratic society that would live up to eternal dreams and aspirations of humankind (and these humanistic ideals have been fully imbibed in Socialism) is practicable only if the free, emancipated human has developed. Such a personality results from the sum total of conditions in which a person lives, works and relaxes. This is civilization's challenge for the future.

At the outset of Socialism, attempts were made to meet this challenge by influencing the human consciousness. Retrospectively it is evident that these attempts stemmed from the extreme poverty, and from the very difficult and complicated home and international conditions, in the world's first Socialist state, rather than from only the naîveté and idealism – in the best sense of these words – of the new society's pioneers.

Perestroika is gaining pace, it has been brought to life not only by the insight into the tasks facing our society, and not only (or rather not so much) by the above-mentioned economic and political imperatives. If we are to determine the source of its vitality which called it into being, we would by right refer to a moral feeling. Therein lies the reason why perestroika is so attractive throughout the world. Hence, this moral feeling is the source of perestroika's inner strength.

A Socialist system can safely rely only on the individual who enjoys to the full his inalienable natural rights . . . human rights both individual and collective . . . and the rights of ethic, regional and social groups . . . the rights, and responsibilities, not only to the State, but to society, to those with whom he lives and works and, finally, to himself.

This task actually boils down to restoring trust in each and every individual's common sense. They do not need any coercion to develop that Socialist society which their parents defended with their very lives and in whose affluence they and their children are vitally interested.

There was a moment when economic failures, unresolved and neglected social issues, the dominance of red tape, and wide-spread irresponsibility and impunity gave rise to the feeling of insult and offence among the healthy part of society . . . an insult to the ideals and the very idea of Socialism . . . and an insult to all those who are able and eager to work honestly and hard for due remuneration, but who were deprived of this chance. It was an offence to the achievements of the past, which then started to slip away . . . and an offence to the country which, having enormous and in many respects unique potential, started losing momentum. Ultimately it was an offence to Socialism which did not come easy to us, but which returned all efforts a hundredfold, and which itself seems today to be in need of protection from various parasites.

From the very outset all the problems of perestroika and the development of its concept were started and resolved in moral rather than purely pragmatic terms. Besides, we largely relied on innovatory approaches in settling them . . . though not on moralizing in a vacuum, or moralistic appeals to virtue. We have stated the problem of morality in our life, dialectically, in Marxist terms.

Ideologists of perestroika, its theorists and practitioners, do not relieve people of moral, and if necessary, Party and legal responsibility for their actions and/or for not taking an active civic stand whenever it is needed. But they have asked themselves another question: what prevents people from becoming better? Which established social conditions favour and engender immorality instead of backing and consolidating morality? And how does this happen?

Therefore, perestroika put forward the demand for a moral rather than simply an efficient economy. We do not need economic progress and achievements at any price. No matter how profitable in fiscal terms might be the results obtained at the expense of moral damage and outraged morality, they eventually and inevitably weaken and degrade society rather than enrich or strengthen it even financially. Remuneration according to work for concrete work and concrete results, and the organization of the economy and its functioning, should in every component rely on the laws of morality and conscientiousness. Honest work should be remunerated; its opposite – punished in this or that way.

We realized the moral content of such economic notions as economic self-reliance, self-sufficiency, lease and contractual arrangements, the Socialist market and many others. Thus, economic self-reliance and the market are forms of evaluating an individual's and/or a collective's performance and their usefulness for society, rather than simply definite aspects of the economy. Hence, they are practical moral criteria in everyday life; things produced only to 'achieve gross output targets' 'to fulfil the plan', or 'to keep the bosses happy' cannot be moral.

Similarly, economic self-reliance, cost-efficiency, lease and contract arrangements provide the conditions for showing the individual's and the collective's self-sufficiency, initiative, enterprise and resourcefulness. Therefore, they are the conditions for inculcating these traits which are so valuable and helpful both for society and the human being. They result in the ideology of the Socialist proprietor – a major solution to the problems of mismanagement and a wasteful economy – and the no less important development of a sense of responsibility and self-discipline.

We simply ought to see these humane aspects of the economic and political reforms and perestroika *in toto*. Because real humanism starts here, not somewhere else. One cannot be the caretaker of one's country if one is not a true caretaker at the workplace and in life. These fundamental principles of humanism must serve the interest of society and the individual and it's our job to identify and develop their creative aspects.

The creativeness of the ideology of the Socialist proprietor is manifest in that it deliberately and purposefully emphasizes a cornerstone of Marxist teaching: the relationships of ownership are the core of philosophy, the kernel of social consciousness. Socialist society cannot and should not be free from relationships of property ownership. We know from history that two extremes are possible here. Private property divides people and society, contrasting them one against the other. But 'nobody's' property is no less destructive, though its destructive force hits, as it were, from the opposite direction.

Individual and public interests should be united in life in general (through people's world outlooks and consciousness) rather than only in the practice of settling specific managerial problems. But this target can be met only if that Socialist property owned by the whole people is simultaneously, in some part or form, the property of the collective and individual producers. Only given this condition will the producer, while defending his own interests, advocate at the same time the interests of society, the order of society, and the norms of society. He is *in favour of* all this, not *indifferent* to, let alone *against* it.

In other words, the ideology of the Socialist proprietor is creative because it disproves the dogmatic thesis on the inevitable and unconditional subordination of the individual's interests to those of the State; and smashes the argument that the individual's interest is always self-interest. This latter argument translated into practical policies is to blame for the 'ideology' of the alienation of individual and mass self-consciousness from everything relating to the State.

And, finally, this Socialist proprietor ideology, keynoted by greater collectivism and democracy, builds up in consciousness and in practice the significance of the phenomenon of a 'people's economy'. This notion has till now been used in this country to characterize the national economic complex as a whole, and sometimes even as a propaganda cliché. But we urgently need a people's economy as a means of meeting society's requirements, as a socio-oriented economy. Besides, it must be developed as a factor of public consciousness. For example, a zealous environmentalism is practicable only within the framework of this notion. A more precise, more concrete ideology of self-government relying on the first-hand experience of perestroika can in the long-run be developed only along these lines.

We could go on with the list of examples. But I would like to emphasize the most important conclusion: we have revived, as if found anew, the theoretically well-known but in practice long forgotten Leninist ideas that people can be educated only through first-hand social experience and in no other way. Eventually a person is educated only by life and his social existence, and he will be educated anyway, whether he or the ruling party realize it or not, whether they take it into account or fail to do so. He is educated properly if healthy processes get the upper hand in life; and improperly, if the difficulties which any society is facing are not overcome or, worse still, ignored and slurred over, or if society's words are at variance with its deeds. It is impossible to develop a person of integrity if there is a gap between the word proclaimed and the deed performed, especially if they are mutual opposites. The Church has for two millennia taught Christian morality; but it is the conditions of a person's life rather than the Church which are to blame for the fact that real people have always been far from angelic. We have assessed the importance of democratization and glasnost policies along the same lines. Their moral, educatory functions cannot be over-estimated. People can get first-hand experience of participation in social affairs only in a democratic society, in the atmosphere of glasnost. Only given these conditions can they enjoy self-expression, take delight in their work and pleasure in their achievements. Only in such a society can they test their strength against evil, can they learn to appreciate true collectivism and strive to achieve it.

To sum it up, only in a free democratic society can there be the best conditions for people's spiritual development and the practical application of its results.

No matter which of the above-mentioned issues we consider, it is quite easy to distinguish its moral content. This moral content inevitably flows from any state of objective conditions and yet, in its turn, bears influences upon them. It shapes the morrow, so as to engender those of the day after tomorrow! Such are the dialectics of the process.

Much of the negativity that still persists in society and in people themselves essentially takes root in the phenomenon of alienation. People are alienated from the results of their work, which they themselves created. They are alienated from real power, from other people. The historical roots of alienation are of two kinds. One line goes back to the division of labour in modern industrial society, and Socialism cannot alter it. The division of labour will stay with us for many years ahead. But alienation also takes root in social organization of public life. And Socialism can and should reconsider the legacy it has inherited in this respect.

The struggle against alienation in all its forms and manifestations is the moral pivot of perestroika. However, emphasis in this campaign is laid more on 'for', rather than 'against'. . . for a resourceful, conscious person of integrity, for a just and conscientious citizen, for a hard-working person, for a good family-man, for a devoted son of his nation, for a patriot of a Socialist motherland.

It is perestroika's distinctive feature that all its policies rely on a solid basis of the dialectics of life and consciousness, objective conditions and people's subjective traits. Perestroika is not limited to a sum total of political and economic reforms. It is spelt out as a set of interacting and complementary changes, a dialectical unity and an integrity of transformations which are always person-oriented whether we discuss food production or the most complicated avenues of shaping the individual's consciousness.

Moral aspects of the practices of Socialist renewal are both the beginning and the end of the perestroika concept which has spread over the whole superstructure of society since the Party Conference.

Socialism is a humane society of truly free and equal people. It can be built only provided every deed, every action and every undertaking are checked by the highest moral criteria.

V

Such interpretation is a sign of the strength and maturity of the Party, of people and of society. Intellectual timidity and spiritual stagnation should be replaced by the epoch of a truly creative, developing Marxism-Leninism, erected on the stable foundation of experience. This is also one of perestroika's aims and objectives.

For an in-depth elaboration of topical theoretical and practical problems of perestroika it is imperative to restore the undistorted concept of the teachings on scientific Socialism developed by the classics of Marxism-Leninism. Marx and Engels, of course, regarded it as the certain qualitative condition for the new social formation rather than only as a theoretical alternative to utopian Socialism.

Theoretical and political revival of the ideas of scientific Socialism will render it possible:

● to lay greater emphasis on the scientific approach for Socialist construction;

● to re-establish in practice the scientific principles of managing public affairs and society's development;

● to equip the Party with powerful means for introducing technocracy while safeguarding guarantees against voluntarism;

● to build up the prestige of knowledge and science, general and professional culture of the working people and to start a sort of 'Renaissance' of the people's spirituality;

- to actually promote the Party's target of a theoretical break-through in the academic community, and

- to press for theoretically competent decision-making at all levels.

Looking back at our own experience and the experience of world Socialism, we are entitled today to draw at least three conclusions.

First – the general orientations and aims of our Socialist movement, its ideals and principles, have been chosen rightly; basic key trends in humanity's historical development have been predicted and perceived correctly. Historically, the Socialist choice has been justified; it is in line with the interests of the people and it secures social progress.

Second – the road to the outlined targets turned out in practice to be much more difficult, and the practicalities of Socialism much more complicated and manifold, than it had been once believed. The distance between the desire and the reality is much longer in all respects and shortens only slowly.

Third – the building of Socialist society successively undergoes a number of changes from one qualitative condition to another. Perestroika itself is such a transitory state. In the process of change, we badly need reliable prognostic orientations, and those can be prompted to us only by the creative development of Marxism-Leninism.

We are surprised to find today much that has been thought out and stated by Marx, Engels and Lenin; it is there for everyone to read in the published collected works, but it has fallen out of our memory and practice or has been unrecognizably distorted in them.

Let us take but two examples – cooperation and the market.

Evaluating the potentialities of cooperation one should ask the following question: what do we expect from it? It is rather easy to define our short-term expectations and hopes of cooperation – they are mostly in the field of agriculture, light industry, construction, services and trade, especially in the domain which presupposes direct ties between the producer and the consumer or, as economists sometimes term them, servicing the process of consumption. These spheres are of key importance for people's well-being and here we must frankly admit that large-scale, State-owned industry has turned out to be inefficient.

One of the stable stereotypes of the past is the attitude towards cooperatives and cooperative ownership. Too often, theoretical thought has approached this issue from the standard point of view, neglecting the problems raised by current realities. Today we have a greater insight into the cooperative movement's contradictions and potentialities, and we are more aware of its ups and downs, due to the large experience accumulated by the cooperatives under both capitalism and Socialism.

The advocates of the revolutionary conception of social transformation paid priority attention to the cooperatives as a form of collectivization of production. K. Marx, the founder of scientific Socialism, wrote about 'The cooperative factories of labourers themselves', which 'show how a new mode of production naturally grows out of an old one, when the development of the material forces of production and of the corresponding forms of social production have reached a particular stage.'[1] At the same time Marxists rejected the socio-political utopia of the so-called cooperative Socialism whose supporters believed that capitalism would be peacefully transformed into Socialism due to a growth of cooperation.

Lenin's position in this matter should be analysed in terms of this historical reality. Levelling sharp criticism at the ideas of 'cooperative Socialism', he at the same time regarded cooperation as the high road to Socialism in the conditions of post-revolutionary Russia. In his article 'On Cooperation' Lenin wrote: 'At present we have to realize that the cooperative system is the social system we must now give more than ordinary assistance, and we must actually give that assistance.'[2] He called Socialism the system of 'civilized co-operatives'.

Cooperation has today taken its due place. But in this particular case Lenin's approach to the analysis of the specific

[1] Karl Marx, *Capital*, Vol. 3, p. 440, Moscow, 1971.
[2] V. I. Lenin, *Collected Works*, Vol. 33, p. 469, Progress Publishers, Moscow, 1966.

situation is of interest. He was never afraid to renounce his point of view if it started contradicting reality.

The other issue: on a Socialist market. In the heat of scholastic debate we have forgotten its main feature: the market is historically formed as an objective economic and social reality. It is not only a natural mechanism of identifying the existing requirements; it is also, as Lenin put it, the most democratic mechanism of 'social accounting', i.e. society's rather than the bureaucrat's recognition of the price and quality of the commodity, as well as of the demand for it.

Of course, in conditions of private property and social antagonism, the market is, inevitably, pregnant with crises, wrecks and numerous adverse implications for the working people. However, it is the capitalist use of the market rather than the market *per se* which is to blame.

Let us put the question in the following way: have we other reliable means of identifying *all* the countless requirements which actually exist in society? From the largest to the smallest ones? Are we able to take into account their extremely mobile dynamics? And even if we somehow identify these requirements without the market, shall we be in a position to manage to meet them from a single centre? Up till now, all such attempts have ended in failure. And what is most important, should it be done this way? Do the real interests and needs of Socialism, the people and the Party ask for such enormous efforts of centralization?

Today we know – and this I emphasize – we *know* from experience the answers to all these questions. And they are very simple answers. It is not that it is simply technically impracticable to practise such totalitarian bureaucracy, but that human flaws in the command method cannot be compensated for by even the most sophisticated computers. Such approaches should be rejected in principle, from moral considerations, in the economy and the social sphere, in the work of soviets and in culture but, above all, in Party work.

But then – only the market, only self-regulation? One should keep in mind that the market is not only a managerial solution which is optimum for a wide range of problems. It is also the field for displaying and using individual and collective initiative, resourcefulness, responsibility and self-realization about which we talk so much. What's more, it is the measure of the social usefulness of work, the regulator of thriftiness, the incentive for building up efficiency and for scientific-technical progress. It is actually, at present, the only known reliable anti-waste mechanism.

Is it feasible to back up fiscal–commodity relationships and economic self-reliance and at the same time deprive the market of the right to exist? Where, then, would these relationships materialize?

As for contrasting the market to the planned economy, there has long been no free, absolutely elemental and unregulated market even under capitalism. Economic relations have been regulated both within individual countries and at the inter-State level. Large and mammoth corporations along with the State have long been using various forms of programming. And generally speaking, the market has become more civilized in keeping with its society: its coordinates are multiple and mobile.

But where is then the demarcation line between what we reject as undoubtedly capitalist and what we nevertheless borrow from capitalism, with or without any changes?

It is evident that such a demarcation line exists but it is determined neither by the *forms* of society's life nor by the implements and means of its activity. Be it Socialist or capitalist, the market does not depend on the movement of commodities, capital, or even labour; it depends on the social content of the resulting processes. The demarcation line is determined by the individual's status in society: whether society regards humanity as its ultimate goal or as a source of profit. It is determined by whether society's words and deeds are in keeping with the ideals of humanism, equality and social justice; by the social substance and content of all the processes of society's life and development.

The monopolies of property ownership and power are far from tantamount to Socialism. They existed back in ancient Egypt. Normal and healthy exchange of work equivalents is practicable only in the market. Only due to the market is it feasible to translate into practice the basic principle of Socialism 'From each according to his ability, to each according to his work.' A market-free Socialism is still a utopia; in order to justify itself it denies, alongside the market, Socialism itself.

It is clear that perestroika will go on engendering new questions which will require theoretical study. It goes without saying that some of them can be answered by social science only on the basis of an in-depth analysis and insight into life processes. Such analysis must rely on Lenin's tradition of creative Marxism and fearlessly break the fetters on the living and continuously developing social organism.

Hegel, by the way, built his spiral on three-dimensional Euclidean postulates and could not know that in the fourth dimension, historical time can flow in both directions. Marx and Engels had no idea that Time is a distortion of Space whereas Lenin perceived that Time is the speed of information transfer and that matter in any form is the shell of information.

And there is nothing unusual in that. The substance of dialectics is developed. Science proceeds from fact, from reality, rather than from a pre-established principle or ideal.

Socialist society is badly in need of normal, intense, growing exchange of information: scientific-technical, economic, commercial and social. Information in all its forms, including computer-based commodities (the rough equivalent of science-intensive products), has become the number one commodity in the world market, whereas manufacturing the means of information science is the locomotive of the world economy. Such exchange is feasible only in conditions of democracy and glasnost. This is true of everything. Any type of information autarky or incompleteness of information will result in both society and the individual marking time. This is true irrespective of whether it concerns the achievements of the world of art, unrelated to the masses for many years, or the shortage of information on internal processes in society, or excessively closed departmental information.

Democratization and glasnost are cultural and economic categories rather than merely socio-political ones. To hold these processes down in order to please personal ambitions, departmental comfort and sectional interests is to doom society and people to deceleration.

The political philosophy of perestroika has covered a historically short distance which was nevertheless very meaningful in terms of content. What conclusions can be drawn from the experience of the evolution of our views on perestroika, its reasons and objectives?

First – we seem to be learning anew the ABC of Marxism. We are learning it from our first-hand social experience. We comprehend its basic truths through practice rather than dogma. We are all studying and we are all equal in this unique political and ideological study: Party and non-Party members, rank-and-file workers and the leadership, young people only entering life and veterans. We are learning the ABC which we have all known in theory. But in practice we have long put up with a neglect thereof, resulting from the pressure of meaningless dogmata.

Marxism is a good, necessary, useful school. It is a must for everyone.

Second, in-depth self-knowledge is a truly nation-wide and Party-wide process. This has been once again proved by the Party Conference, the preparation for it, and the discussion of its results which still goes on in worker collectives.

Third, with the penetration of perestroika into new layers, people have come to more fully understand the complex reasons which necessitated it. And whereas at first priority was given to the most pressing and eye catching objectives in the social and economic spheres and society's moral condition (all this was much spoken of in every detail), we are now disclosing more profound causal relationships, the reasons for the reasons. We are comprehending perestroika as an objective stage in the development of Socialist life-style rather than a sum total of concrete social tasks.

The concept of perestroika should not only be viewed as a theoretical achievement and entity, a comprehensive system of practical targets and orientations. It has a methodical value too. The ideology of renewal revives the heart of Marxism. It is scientific Socialism in practice impelled by the yearning for human benefit due to a cognition of the world and society . . . A cognition in which facts of life are of higher priority than any slogans . . . a cognition which, in its turn, is promoted by social progress and earlier acquired knowledge.

The Party Conference and the July 1988 Plenum of the CPSU Central Committee have opened up a new leaf in perestroika policy . . . a leaf never before turned over in Socialist society. They launched a reform of the superstructure which would give Socialism a new start, ready for the twenty-first century. They drew up the list of reforms and set the time for them. They shifted emphasis on to practical work, on to translating designs into practical deeds. The major result of the Conference and the Plenum is that from all points of view the Party events turned into capital investments into the future and for the future, in terms of the substance and in the content of their decisions; in terms of the comprehensiveness and creativeness of the thus developed concept; in terms of their style of work and the impact on society; in terms of the range of raised problems many of which were stated for the first time; in terms of their influence on people's consciousness, on their social, political and scientific thought; in terms of the potentialities opened up before the country and Socialism by the implementation of the decisions and the realization of perestroika policy. The most difficult tasks lie ahead. The time has come for action.

Abel G. Aganbegyan

Abel Aganbegyan is Academic Secretary of the Department of Economics of the USSR Academy of Sciences. A distinguished figure in the memorable group of 'young Academicians' which was formed in Novosibirsk (the centre of the Siberian Branch of the USSR Academy of Sciences) at the time of the region's scientific upsurge, he became head of the Siberian Institute of Economics and Industrial Production Organization. If perestroika is a 'revolution from above', it is also to some extent a 'revolution from Siberia' – since many fresh economic ideas connected with scientific-technical acceleration, self-financing, profit-making and khozraschot,[1] etc., were developed and discussed in the Novosibirsk academic community on the initiative of Abel Aganbegyan – who, like many other champions of perestroika, worked his way up from opposition to general recognition by all social strata and by the country's leadership.

[1] Khozraschot – comprehensive cost-accounting.

Economic Reforms

ABEL G. AGANBEGYAN

Economic reforms have laid the foundations for the comprehensive restructuring of society. The April 1985 plenary meeting of the CPSU Central Committee put forward a new economic strategy for the country's economic development – the strategy of perestroika. The substance of this new strategy is to speed up national socio-economic progress. Acceleration, however, is not limited to higher rates of economic growth, though this is also an important target. We have set ourselves the objective of doubling our gross national income by the year 2000. It means going over to a new quality of growth. On the one hand, there will be a greater social orientation of economic development; and on the other, our economy will be based on the road of intensification, facilitated by the breakthrough of the technological revolution. To trigger off the speed-up we must, above all, carry through a radical reform in the sphere of management. The old administrative system must be dismantled and replaced by a fundamentally new and comprehensive system for managing the overall economy; the latter will rely on economic methods of investment planning, proper accounting procedures for all financial transactions, market development and stronger incentives for more productive work, as well as the country's fuller integration in the world economy.

The new strategy for national economic development will require reconceptualization in all spheres of our country's diversified economic life. It will necessitate the search for new approaches for qualitative changes to the economic base.

The 27th CPSU Congress and the subsequent plenary ses-

73

sions of the Central Committee have worked out the following:

• A strong social policy oriented towards priority development of the entire social sphere, from agriculture to the house-building and high consumer-based industries. Such a policy must be consistent with the principles of social justice.

• A scientific-technical policy providing for social planning commensurate with the world technological revolution.

• A new investment policy aimed at large-scale progressive shifts in the structure of the national economy resulting from:
    (a) deeper redistribution of raw materials;
    (b) priority boosting of the engineering industry;
    (c) massive investment in the chemical sector of the economy;
    (d) the development of information technology and other hi-tec branches of industry;
    (e) resource-saving measures;
    (f) a drastic increase in the share of the gross national product relating to consumer goods production and services.

• A new agrarian policy designed, first, to spread intensive technologies, to redistribute investments in favour of storage facilities and to assist comprehensive processing of agricultural raw materials; and, secondly, to grant broad autonomy to the collective and State farms, and to implement a change-over to family and collective leasing and contractual arrangements on a large scale.

• An active foreign trade policy oriented towards boosting foreign trade, increasing the efficiency of export and import arrangements and granting the organizations and enterprises the right to establish direct access to the world market and to start joint ventures, as well as going over to a freely convertible rouble.

• A new financial and banking policy within the framework of comprehensive reform in management spearheaded by building up the role of fiscal-commodity relationships in economic development as well as expanding and deepening the Socialist market, including that of commodities and services, securities and currency.

All these policies have been pursued in the context of pluralism in the development of forms of property. Alongside various forms of public or State property, cooperation and self-employment have considerably gained in scope in all spheres and sectors of the economy. The June 1987 plenary meeting of the CPSU Central Committee laid the foundations of the new economic policy. It approved the concept of the new economic and management system and the programme for passing over from administrative to economic methods of management. The recently enacted law on State enterprises envisages the conversion of the main production centres to the principles of complete fiscal autonomy (khozraschot), self-financing and self-administration. To this end the Party and the Government are to draw up and pass a series of decrees on restructuring in all sectors of the management system – including planning and pricing, finance and banking, material-technical supply and trade and the organizational pattern of branch and regional management, as well as reforming the working practices of the various organs of labour, statistical and scientific-technical bodies, and so on.

All the changes in the economy that are being carried out in keeping with the adopted decisions of the Party are being greatly influenced by the process of democratization currently taking place throughout society. Economically, democratization manifested itself in drawing broad sections of workers into management; this necessitated drastic extension of the rights granted to work collectives in all sectors of the economy and their transfer to self-government.

Why do we need such far-reaching and comprehensive economic reforms? In the first place, to overcome the stagnation and pre-crisis phenomena inherited by this country as a result of negative development tendencies at the start of the 1980s. However, these are, so to speak, surface reasons. More profound ones stem from the pressing need to put an end to the deep-seated deformations in the development of the

Soviet economy and in the administrative command and fiat methods of management that burgeoned during Stalin's cult of personality and were aggravated during the recent fifteen to twenty years of stagnation.

What is the substance of these economic reforms? What would we like to do away with, and where are we heading? First of all, we would like to do away with the shortages in the economy and the resulting situation in which the producer dominates the consumer. We would like to go over to a deficit-free economy in which the production of commodities and services is directly guided by social requirements and is oriented to consumer demand. Such a switch-over is closely geared to large-scale economic restructuring. The economy must undergo a radical transformation in order to meet social requirements. In this way, we shall build up a truly efficient economy, because in a Socialist society efficient production is equivalent to satisfying social demands. This approach lays emphasis on quality rather than quantity, since articles of higher quality more closely meet social requirements.

The prioritization of social requirements should be in favour of everything that is directly aimed at improving people's well-being in the broadest sense of the word – at securing higher living standards and providing conditions for freer and greater all-round development of human society as a whole. In this context, we must do away with the priority of production targets and abolish a system of management designed, above all, to meet production targets. Under the new conditions, social aims and objectives must come to the fore: the economy should be devoted to the people, so that the person is the measure of all things. Perestroika is being carried through in the people's interests, towards a better life. It therefore follows that we must go over to a socio-oriented economy, with the social sphere highly developed and modern consumer goods and service industries.

The satisfaction of people's spiritual requirements must be an even higher priority. People's jobs should be made easier, more attractive and more creative. In a Socialist society, economic advance must ensure guarantees for all human rights – including the right to work, to rest and leisure, and to housing and social security. Our economy should enjoy full employment, highly developed health protection, public education and social insurance. In other words, we must pass over to an economy servicing the people's interests in a renewed Socialist society.

But for the economy to meet such great social challenges it must be put on the road of general intensive development rather than development based on the priority growth of particular industries. The main source of our economic development should be higher efficiency and better quality, due to new machinery and technology, rather than the accretion of resources. Hence, we must go over from a wasteful to a thrifty and highly efficient economy – an economy of maximum labour productivity and of competitive high-quality production. To build such an economy we have to reject the evolutionary approaches to scientific-technical progress that have been typical of the USSR for the past fifteen to twenty years. We must press for speedy, revolutionary changes in techniques and technology; switch over to the manufacture of a new generation of machinery and to large-scale application of fundamentally new technologies; and move on to the economy of the scientific-technical revolution, the economy of technological breakthrough, the economy of renewal.

We must also do away with autarkic tendencies in our economic development. Today we are paying priority attention to improving our foreign economic relations, planning for their growth outstripping home market production. Thus, the Soviet Union will play a more important role in the world economy and its economic cooperation with other countries will gather momentum. In terms of economic ties with Socialist states, we have been working for an integrated Socialist economy; internationally, we are moving towards ever greater openness of economic relations.

The economy of administrative command and fiat methods of management is to be replaced by an economy with predominantly economic methods of management, a market economy, an economy with developed financial and credit relations. From wage-levelling and neglected material incentives, we are working towards an economic system oriented to

77

take due account of economic interests based on economic self-reliance and material encouragement.

In carrying forward these policies, we have to do away with the centralization of the economic system and develop diversified forms of property ownership. We are moving towards an economy with advanced cooperative and extensive self-employed sectors. The monopoly of some industries and branches will increasingly be replaced by Socialist-style economic competitiveness and competition.

We are going over from an authoritarian to a democratic economy – an economy governed by the people, with the substantial involvement of the masses in economic management. The work collectives have enjoyed ever broader rights and greater influence in this country, resulting in increased social activity on the part of every worker. Economic self-development and self-government are gradually taking shape. In short, the transition to a rejuvenated system of Socialism is under way. This will be a qualitatively new, transformed system fully and comprehensively giving play to all the advantages that the Socialist system offers. It will be a modern economy, profiting from the best aspects of economic development in other countries – an economy of social and scientific-technical progress and, simultaneously, an economy of Socialism whose potential has been released to the utmost. The challenge is to restore Lenin's understanding of the Socialist economic system, adapting it to the modern conditions of a developed society.

This economy will, of course, be part and parcel of a rejuvenated Socialist society: it will co-exist in harmony with the new political, legal and ideological systems, and will be backed and secured by them. The establishment of a qualitatively new economic system will demand time, enormous efforts and major structural changes. We are creating a real economic revolution.

Today we are in the initial stage of the process of perestroika. Three years have passed since the historical April 1985 plenary meeting of the CPSU Central Committee. What progress has been made in restructuring the Soviet economy during these three years?

First, a comprehensive programme for economic reform was drawn up. To develop it we undertook a number of experiments, including large-scale economic ones, designed to work out certain features of the new management system. The first pilot reforms were directed at granting the enterprises broader rights. Then, in 1986 and especially in 1987, came the second 'wave' of experimentation with an eye to mastering the system of economic self-reliance at the enterprise level. At the same time, we conducted large-scale experiments in developing leasing and contractual arrangements for worker-collectives and families, and we studied the possibility of converting research institutes to economic self-reliance, and so on. Much time was taken by the elaboration and nationwide discussion of the three main bills on economic reform: the Law on State Enterprises, the Law on Cooperatives and the Law on Self-Employment. Much work was also needed to restructure the top management institutions, including the State Planning Committee, the Ministry of Finance, banks, branch ministries and departments etc. Now the preparatory work is practically over. A new stage in the restructuring drive has begun – the large-scale application of the new economic methods of management. The first day of January 1988 saw the enactment of the law on State enterprises, which underpinned the economic reforms with a new management basis. In the first three years of this five-year period the comprehensive economic reform relied mostly on the old administrative methods of management. This has, of course, curbed the potential of perestroika. From now on, however, the transformations will be ever more extensively carried forward with the help of new economic methods.

What did we manage to achieve in the economy over the past three years? And where did we fail? What are our immediate and long-term targets? These questions were answered by the 19th CPSU Party Conference, which I was honoured to attend. The Conference self-critically assessed our achievements and noted the progress made – but it paid particular attention to untapped reserves and potential, reviewing our errors and analysing faults committed in carrying through the policy of perestroika. A brief estimate of the work done shows that basically we have overcome the pre-crisis state of affairs and the stagnation that crippled our economy. We have stepped back from the edge of the economic abyss to which we had been brought by the years of stagnation, but we have failed to bring about a radical reform and the positive trends are not as yet irreversible. We did much less than we could have done in these three years.

However, this conclusion does not disarm us, we do not lose heart. On the contrary, with concentrated energy and resources, we are starting an offensive to do away with the negative tendencies completely and to make perestroika irreversible. This is the target set by the decisions of the 19th Party Conference.

Now let us discuss each part of the perestroika policy specifically. We can single out three major objectives. Our first concern is to build up social orientation in the development of the national economy drastically, to shift the emphasis on to the challenge of improving living standards. Secondly, there is the intensification of the national economy by the dramatic speed-up of scientific and technological progress. And, thirdly, we are intent on carrying through a radical reform in management. This third objective is of the utmost importance today, because the system of management predetermines advances both in the social sphere and in the switch-over to intensive development of the national economy.

Let us start with the first area, since it provides a key to the goals of managerial reform. First of all, we must admit that, although the Soviet Union is one of the most powerful and advanced states in the world, living standards and the level at which people's requirements are satisfied are out of proportion to our industrial might, to our scientific and technological advancement, and to the population's educational standards. Our people deserve a much better life than they have now.

The lag in the social sphere grew little by little. At first it stemmed from the forced channelling of funds (for a number of reasons) in favour of heavy industry, stronger defence and the restoration of the war-ruined economy etc. But later on it resulted, above all, from the negative tendencies in economic development that surfaced during the past fifteen years.

I am referring to the sharp fall in the rate of economic growth at the end of the tenth five-year plan. At that time, at the beginning of the 1980s, stagnation and pre-crisis trends were manifest in the economy. This had an especially detrimental effect on the social sphere, because the previous leadership tried to slow down the aggravation of the economic situation by channelling large resources from the social sphere into industry and agriculture. The social sphere received its funds on the so-called 'left-over' principle (i.e. from money left over from industry, agriculture and defence). Comparing the mid-1980s with the years 1960–5, in terms of various social criteria, the country had definitely regressed.

Let us take some more concrete examples. Housing is today the most pressing social problem. By the beginning of the 1960s the USSR was building 2 million flats a year. Taking all sources into account, 100–110 million square metres of housing were annually opened for tenancy. In quantitive terms of housing-construction rate per thousand inhabitants, the Soviet Union was then second to none. This seemed only natural, since we lagged behind all other industrialized nations in housing facilities. In 1960, 23 per cent of all capital investment was earmarked for house-building.

But what happened then? The Soviet Union turned out to be among the few countries in the world in which the rate of housing-construction per thousand inhabitants decreased. In 1985 we built 2 million flats, the same number as twenty-five years before. But the population had measurably grown in those twenty-five years, hence the reduction in the per capita rate of house-building. This resulted in very slow improvement of the housing situation. Some 15 per cent of Soviet families are entering the last quarter of the twentieth century without a flat or house of their own; and half of the available housing, especially in rural areas, has few of the essential amenities.

But housing has always been a basic human need. That is why it is socially so important today to overcome stagnation in housing construction. It is not an easy thing to do, due to underdeveloped house-building facilities. People have simply reconciled themselves to the fact that a large part of investment funds went into industrial construction, while house-building programmes remained on the waiting list. It was essential to improve the situation and to mobilize our resources; and, generally speaking, we have succeeded in doing so. In 1986, for the first time in many years, we made headway with housing construction: 2,000 flats, or 118·2 million square metres, were opened for tenancy – a measurable increase compared with the previous period. Last year saw a rise in housing construction, too: 2,300 well-appointed new flats, with a total floorage of 129 million square metres, were commissioned in 1987. Needless to say, this progress did not just come about of itself: the share of capital investment for house-building went up, and up to 10 per cent of industrial capital investment was channelled into house-building and communal construction projects etc.

The dramatic rise in the housing construction rate has not been easy for us, as we simultaneously made a 1·7-fold increase in the rate of school-building. This increase was necessary since all children will soon go to school one year earlier (at the age of 6) and we are also about to do away with the afternoon session which still exists in some schools. To fully meet in the near future the population's requirements in nursery schools and kindergartens, we are stepping up construction by a factor of 1·5–2·0; and the rates of construction and start-up for hospitals and polyclinics (out-patient departments) have already gone up by 50 per cent. But we have very limited building facilities to provide for this increase in the number of construction projects. That is why we have to resort on a large scale to the so-called 'self-sufficient method of construction' whereby an enterprise builds flats for its workers using its own funds, materials, technical facilities and workforce. We have also encouraged the building of condominiums and individual cottages, as well as the so-called 'dwelling complexes for young families', which are built with the active participation of the future tenants. In other words, we have taken every opportunity for the speedy solution of the housing problem.

By the beginning of the 1990s we shall be commissioning 3 million new flats per year (i.e. we are to increase the volume of house-building by 150 per cent) and at the same time aiming to improve quality, gradually going over to the construction of more comfortable flats.

All in all, in keeping with the decisions of the 27th CPSU Congress, by the year 2000 the population is to get at least 40 million separate flats and cottages, representing more than 2,000 million square metres of well-appointed housing. This is half of the present-day national housing stock. According to the estimates, if we meet this challenge we shall be able to provide every Soviet family with separate accommodation by the end of the 1990s.

Another social issue of great concern is the food problem. Compared with other developed nations, we have a low rate of meat consumption – 62kg per capita a year, as against 75–80kg or even 85kg. But this is not our only weak point. The estimates show that the Soviet Union takes second place to most countries in the consumption of milk and dairy products, the variety and quality of which are quite poor.

The Soviet Union is also considerably behind other countries in terms of the consumption of temperate and sub-tropical vegetables, especially vegetables out of season. Our population consumes only 33 per cent of the medically recommended fruit consumption norm. This has an especially detrimental effect on children's health. In short, we must radically improve the quality of our diet as well.

But this is not the end of it either. Imported feeding-stuffs account for 25 per cent of our national meat production. In the previous five-year period, we annually bought millions of tons of grain fodder. This is more than is sold to the State by such Soviet republics as the Ukraine and Kazakhstan taken together.

Hence, it is not enough simply to improve consumption. We must do away with large food imports as soon as possible, namely, by the beginning of 1990.

In this respect, too, we face a worse situation than at the

beginning of the 1960s. At that time the Soviet Union exported rather than imported agricultural products and the population's requirements were better met in terms of per capita income. This is especially true of the end of the 1960s when, due to the measures taken by the March 1965 plenary meeting of the CPSU Central Committee, our agricultural output increased during the eighth five-year plan by 21 per cent. But what happened then? During the ninth five-year plan it went up by only 13 per cent; in the tenth by 9 per cent; and in the eleventh by 6 per cent, as against a 4 per cent population growth. In other words, we made no headway in the eleventh five-year plan at all and our per capita agricultural production has not gone up in real per capita terms since 1978.

According to the twelfth five-year plan, we are to raise the rates of agricultural development 2·5 times, and to build up agricultural output by 14·4 per cent. We have taken tangible steps to meet this challenge: we have changed the investment policy in agriculture, giving priority to intensive techologies and their large-scale application; we have radically changed the methods of management on the farms; and we have introduced contractual and leasing arrangements for individual families and worker-collectives. Furthermore, we have channelled large resources in favour of better processing, storing and transportation of farm products.

The year 1986–7 marked a clearly discernible turning point in agricultural development. Agricultural output went up by 9 per cent. As against the average annual figures for the eleventh five-year plan, grain production rose from 180 to 210 million tons, meat production from 16·2 to 18·6 million tons, and that of milk from 94·6 to 103·4 million tons.

Unfortunately, we could not sell all the accrued farm products to the population as we had to halve food imports, and a considerable part of the increment was used to compensate for reduced imports.

If we compare the development of agriculture in the perestroika years with agricultural development during the stagnation period, we can claim tangible progress. However, we should instead compare it with the social requirements and the set targets. From this point of view it is clear that the food problem is far from resolved; accordingly, we are to build up efforts drastically in order to make a real breakthrough in the next two to three years. The July 1988 plenary meeting of the CPSU Central Committee set the task of measurably outstripping the planned targets for 1990 in terms of the production of foodstuffs; and specifically provided for the building up of State purchases of cattle and poultry by a factor of 2·5, and those of milk by 4·3 million tons. To this end we have allocated a large capital investment to the provision of storage facilities for all farm products; we are taking new steps towards the development of agro-industrial firms and the large-scale use of contractual and lease forms of labour organization; and we intend to improve social conditions in the villages.

We are also extremely concerned about the health care system. The 'left-over' principle of earmarking funds for the population's well-being resulted in a continuous reduction in the share of national income allocated to medical services. Today it is below 4 per cent, as against the 8 to 12 per cent allocated to medical services by other countries. This accounts for the very poor state of our hospitals and polyclinics. They are underequipped, lack modern facilities and do not have sufficient pharmaceutical supplies. In addition, doctors' and nurses' salaries are too low.

The health of the population has also deteriorated as a result of large-scale liquor sales. To build up budgetary income, the production and sales of vodka have increased two-fold over the past twenty years, and those of wine four-fold. Higher alcohol consumption has also affected health indicators, especially those of the male population. This is the reason for the fact that the world's largest discrepancy between the average life expectancy of men and women is in this country. According to the 1984–5 data, life expectancy for men was ten years lower than for women. This is one of the lowest levels of life expectancy indicators.

As a result of deteriorated health services and higher levels of hard drinking, average life expectancy went down during the past twenty years and both the crude death rate and the infant mortality rate went up in absolute terms.

In contrast, at the beginning of the 1960s our health indicators were quite impressive. You may remember that the death rate in the Soviet Union was then the lowest in the world (6·7 per thousand) and average life expectancy (70 years) was at that time only equalled in Japan, which is today the world champion in terms of life expectancy.

But since then all countries have made significant headway. As a result, twenty years later, the USSR lags behind other developed nations. In 1985 our death rate was 10·6 per thousand; life expectancy at birth 68 years; and infant mortality 26 per thousand.

This eventually turned health care improvement into a pressing social problem. After the April 1985 plenary meeting of the CPSU Central Committee a number of urgent measures were taken to remedy the situation as quickly as possible. We immediately launched a campaign against hard drinking and alcoholism. Economists, sociologists and medical officers believe that the halving of liquor sales in the past two years has brought about (despite larger production of bootleg liquor, revealed by increased sugar consumption) a 37 per cent drop in the death rate among working-age males as a result of injuries, poisoning and accidents. According to the experts, this drop was immediately apparent in all health indicators. The crude death rate went down from 10·6 to 9·7 per thousand and average life expectancy went up.

It is worth noting that during this period doctors' and nurses' salaries were increased by 30 per cent and the budget of medical services went up by some 5,400 million roubles (or 25 per cent) as compared with the five-year-plan targets.

As for other social development issues, we must first of all mention the comprehensive programme for the build-up in production of consumer goods and everyday services. The previous five-year plan marked a 25 per cent rise in the volume of paid services to the population. It is planned to step up the volume by 50 per cent during the current five-year period; in the first six months of 1988 it rose by 17 per cent; and we took additional measures towards outstripping the high targets of the five-year plan by 15 to 20 per cent. Nevertheless, the next five-year period must see a 60 per cent increase in the volume of paid services.

The situation in the consumer goods production is more complicated. Light industry has been working ineffectively. In 1986 its output increased by only 1·4 per cent and in the present year by only 2 per cent. There are serious reasons for this: light-industry equipment has not been modernized for decades and the depreciation period for about 40 per cent of the equipment is overdue. However, although large-scale updating of equipment is needed, the domestic production of equipment for light industry is insufficient.

We have taken some measures to resolve this problem, but it is difficult to change the situation in a couple of years. It will take time to meet this challenge, especially as we are witnessing an obvious underestimation of the consumer goods sphere. Although it accounts for 37 per cent of the entire national accumulation, it receives only 8 per cent of capital investment. It is true, however, that the priorities have been changed and all that has to do with people's standard of living has come to the fore.

The measures taken in the recent years made it possible in 1988 to drastically speed up progress in light industry and in the sector of consumer goods in general. The first six months of 1988 saw a rise of approximately 5 per cent in their output. The July 1988 plenary meeting of the CPSU Central Committee took additional decisions designed to overfulfil the plan of consumer goods output by 24,000 million roubles in 1989–90.

Nevertheless, we must continuously boost efforts in this field – not only concerning quantity but, above all, the quality of the produce. The point is that the Soviet Union manufactures many consumer goods in large quantities while the population's requirements are not met as the result of their poor quality – so we have to import them.

The heightening of the quality of consumer goods is today a top problem. We have done a lot along these lines: we have reduced the price of low quality goods and introduced incentive bonus payments for novelties. Unfortunately, the latter are badly controlled and, in my view, result in inflated prices. Moreover, the measures taken are insufficient.

When goods are in short supply, the consumer is deprived of the chance to choose. In such a situation the quality of consumer goods is not regulated simply by the customers' refusal to buy them. Accordingly, we have been forced to resort to administrative methods of control. This is done, *inter alia*, through a system of State quality inspection designed to protect the consumer against the defective products that have become typical of the consumer goods industry.

Tangible efforts are therefore needed to meet the demands of the population more fully, since there is a dangerous gap between these demands and material supplies.

Public education, above all schools, is in serious need of help, too. In keeping with the targets of the forthcoming school reforms, we are allocating an additional 11,000 million roubles to their development. Teachers' wages, in particular, have been raised by 40 per cent, and the material and technical facilities of schools somewhat improved. But we have not yet witnessed a transition to the new quality of schooling or the unity of instruction with productive labour. No fundamentally new and interesting textbooks have been published. Clearly, measurably greater efforts are needed to carry forward and develop these school reforms.

Recent years have seen the aggravation of still one more social problem. I am referring to the financial situation of 58 million pensioners in this country. Thirty years ago, in 1956, we passed a pension law which decreed what was at that time the lowest retirement age anywhere in the world. Since then the cost of living has risen and requirements have grown, but the size of many people's pensions has remained practically the same. In terms of pension size relative to wages, this country has now started to lag behind other nations.

In keeping with the directives of the CPSU Central Committee, a new pension bill is therefore currently being developed. Having been considered by the central organs of the Party, this draft, like all other important documents relating to the standard of living, will be put up for nationwide discussion. The bill will, of course, envisage a considerable increase in pensions, including minimum and maximum pension size, which are at present rather low in this country.

Generally speaking, positive changes have been gaining pace in all branches of the social sphere and the economy is becoming more socio-oriented. However, the changes are very slow and effort-consuming. The personnel's thinking and psychology and the historically established planning system are aimed at priority commissioning of industrial capacities. They still enjoy overriding attention as compared with social projects.

We all see and feel to what extent our spiritual life has changed for the better. Magazines and newspapers, films, television and radio programmes have become increasingly interesting and informative. However, many Soviet families fail to notice any tangible improvements in their everyday life, although their standards of living are slowly changing for the better. As a result of shortages and serious underproduction of foodstuffs and consumer goods, there has developed a certain 'threshold sensitivity'. People fail to notice a 4 per cent increase in meat production if there is still not enough meat on sale.

The June 1987 plenary meeting of the CPSU Central Committee set the task of taking sufficient measures to enable every Soviet family to feel tangible improvements within two or three years in the supply of foodstuffs and consumer goods, in the development of everyday services, in health care, in schooling and in housing.

At the same time, it is obvious that it is impossible to consume more than is produced and the solution of social problems ultimately depends on the efficiency of our work. One of perestroika's top priorities is therefore to enhance efficacy and to put the Soviet economy on the road of intensification. It is essential that our future socio-economic development will take place against a background of reduced growth in the consumption of resources.

What are the reasons for this? A restricted labour force can be accounted for by the demographic implications of World War II. Before the war the size of the working-age population generally went up by 8 to 12 million people every five years, but in the twelfth five-year period the growth amounted to only 4 million. In the thirteenth and fourteenth five-year periods the growth will be somewhat greater, but average population growth in the working-age bracket will on the whole be 8 million people less by the year 2000 than in the previous fifteen years.

A smaller accretion in the workforce will be compensated for by an additional rise in labour productivity and efficiency of production. Their growth will be doubled, both to make up for the reduced increment of resources and to secure the acceleration of the economy. As early as the twelfth five-year period we are to step up the growth rates of labour productivity by 50 per cent and, during the 1990s, by a further 50 per cent. All in all, by the year 2000 the efficiency of labour in the country is to go up 2·3–2·5 times, while the total production output is to double.

In addition, we are to release a part of the workforce employed in material production and channel manpower into the badly needed service sector and health care services, currently so lacking in personnel. We shall also have to measurably increase the number of schoolteachers in order to reduce the pupil/teacher ratio, and to start schooling at the age of 6. We need to build up the number of kindergarten teachers, as well. A larger housing stock will require additional personnel for communal utilities and housing administration, and their work must be greatly improved too.

Today the Soviet Union ranks first in the world in terms of both fuel and raw material output, and in the yield of many basic materials. It annually mines and produces over 5,000 million tons of fuel and primary material resources, excavates 15,000 million cubic metres of soil and deforests 2 million hectares due to the felling of trees.

Such an enormous scale of work – or, to be more exact, interference with nature – has, of course, entailed depletion of the best deposits and areas. We are forced to mine deeper underground, and to shift our fuel and raw material bases ever further northward and eastward. This requires a high level of investment. In addition, the rate of growth in the mining industry has decreased and our fuel and raw material output has gone down. Whereas under the ninth five-year plan the output of these resources was stepped up by 25 per cent, the previous five years saw an approximate increase of only 8 per cent.

Clearly, it is time to go over to resource conservation, since it is much cheaper to conserve a ton of fuel than to produce it. That is why in the twelfth five-year period we are planning to meet 75 per cent of our requirements in fuel and raw materials by conservation and reduced consumption.

The correlation between capital investment and the output of primary products is undergoing a change. Slower rates of economic growth and smaller increases in the level of national income have reduced the increment of capital investment. Whereas in the ninth five-year period it amounted to 42 per cent, in the tenth five-year period it only amounted to 28 per cent and in the eleventh to 17 per cent. This reduction was followed by a corresponding fall in the accretion of primary products. In the twelfth five-year period they only went up by 30 per cent, as against 37 per cent in the eleventh five-year period; and in the previous years the rate of growth had been still higher. We shall therefore have to learn to use basic primary products and capital investment better and more efficiently, as we badly need them for carrying forward both the social programme and the large-scale programme of modernization.

Where can we get these primary products from? There is, in fact, only one source – accelerated production and increased efficiency. In the past two years we have managed to raise labour productivity in all sectors of the economy. From 1979 to 1985 labour productivity in industry grew at a rate of between 2 and 3 per cent; but 1986 saw a 4·5 per cent growth and in 1987, despite a loss of momentum in January and February which witnessed no rise in labour efficiency in industry at all, the annual increase totalled approximately 4·1 per cent.

The past years saw a very tense situation with regard to the average return on capital investment: each year it fell by about 3 per cent which was extremely detrimental to the economy. The first year to witness a slow-down in this process was 1986, when the return on capital decreased by only 1·3 per cent. The target of the thirteenth five-year plan in this area is to stabilize the rate of return on capital investment, and the aim of the fourteenth one is to secure its rise.

As you see, some positive changes are on hand here too, though a radical improvement is still a long way off and we have not yet provided a solid basis for it. To meet this challenge we need a programme of technical modernization, which we are just launching; and a new system of management, to which we are transferring. In the meantime, the speed-up will result from short-term factors: better management, stronger discipline, more order and responsibility, additional incentives, etc.

In short, the application of scientific and technological break-throughs depends, above all, on technical updating. In 1985, only slightly more than 3 per cent of the civil engineering industry was renovated, which was unpardonably little. But major progress has now been made here too, and 1987 saw a 9 per cent modernization of the mechanical engineering industry.

The current target is annually to update 13 per cent of its output by 1990. This means that 13 per cent of the machinery and equipment will be taken out of production and replaced by new equipment or machines. On the whole, according to the data for 1985, about 70 per cent of the machinery and equipment currently manufactured does not meet present-day requirements. Their production therefore has to be phased out. According to our estimates, it will take us only seven years to carry through this large-scale and fundamental overhaul.

But it is not enough simply to replace outdated machinery. The new equipment must be 150 to 200 per cent more efficient and reliable, and 12 to 18 per cent less metal-intensive than its predecessors. This is the task set by the 27th CPSU Congress. Only if this condition is met shall we be able to build up efficiency; the old in the guise of the new will not enable us to make any additional profit.

It is impossible to develop new modern equipment using outdated technical facilities. Hence, mechanical engineering in itself needs up-to-date technical facilities. This is the target of the programme for accelerated modernization of this industry which we have already launched. Whereas in the previous five-year period the re-equipment rate in operating enterprises amounted to only 1·8 per cent in the current five-year period the target we are to achieve is an annual updating of 8 to 9 per cent. For that we need, first and foremost, the equipment itself. Where can we get it? Large funds have been earmarked for the machine-tool industry, and manufacture of equipment at the enterprises of the engineering ministries is to go up four-fold. In addition, at the expense of reduced imports of foodstuffs and metals, we have been importing new equipment, mostly from Socialist but also from capitalist countries.

In order to maximize output of new products, we shall have to employ the up-to-date equipment in two, or in some exceptional cases, even three shifts. A high level of capital investment will be needed for that, too.

In the previous five-year period capital investment in the engineering industry increased by 24 per cent, whereas in the current period it was due to accelerate by 80 per cent and has actually gone up even faster. Unfortunately, however, the programme for the redesign of existing machinery and the start-up of new machine-building capacities has fallen short of the targets.

Viewed as a whole, the engineering industry has been witnessing a most complicated period in its development. Re-equipment and a change of product are already under way, but the output at many enterprises has gone down, contract obligations have frequently been violated, accessory manufacturers have let the engineering plants down, and so on. We shall have to overcome all that in order to radically overhaul the engineering industry. Our strategy is aimed at starting mass production of up-to-date machinery at the modernized enterprises, and on this basis to launch a large-scale overhaul in all the branches of the economy. These are so to speak two wings of perestroika – the social wing, on the one hand, and the scientific-technical, on the other. We shall be able to make headway only with their comprehensive and harmonious development.

The third perestroika area has to do with the radical reform of management: 1 July 1987 saw the enactment of the Law on Self-Employment; 1 January 1988, the Law on State Enterprises; 1 July 1988, the Law on Cooperatives. Beginning with 1988, 60 per cent of the entire industrial output will be produced at enterprises that have gone over to self-financing. Thus, the preparatory stage of the radical management reform is basically over; it will be followed by the most difficult and responsible stage – the putting into practice of the new economic legislation and reforms.

We have set ourselves the task of converting the entire national economy to new economic and managerial terms within three years (1988, 1989 and 1990), and will thus enter the next (thirteenth) five-year period, which begins in 1991, with a comprehensive new economic system.

The conversion of industrial enterprises to the basis of economic self-reliance and self-financing started the period of transition to the new management system. It boils down to going over to an economic system of management, with a developed market, full monetary value, a credit-finance system and material incentives for good work. To this end, the law envisages broad operational autonomy for the State enterprises in this new system of management. The enterprise is not liable for the State's debts and the State, in its turn, is not liable for the enterprise's accounts. The enterprise is run on the principles of full self-accounting, self-financing and self-administration. In the transitional period, and especially in 1988, the enterprises will enjoy limited operational autonomy – since the transition takes place in the middle of the current five-year plan, and the targets thereof were set for the old management system and have not been adjusted to the conditions of self-financing. These targets have not simply been put on paper. They have been translated into budget allocations under the old financing system for development and overhaul, etc. – and with an eye to these allocations, construction projects have been launched and equipment has been manufactured. We are therefore forced to take this into account to some extent, when setting economic norms and State orders.

In addition, there is another restriction: the enterprises have been going over to economic self-reliance and cost-effectiveness under the old pricing system, which does not secure the harmony of interests of society and the enterprise. It is impossible to be guided by these prices in placing orders and in production, as many products necessary for society are unprofitable at present-day prices. Conversely, a whole group of outdated products which should be taken out of production are still profitable. As you may know the period, 1989–90 is to witness a reform of prices and pricing mechanisms – and this will be an extremely important component in the reform of management.

Under the old pricing system, we cannot replace centralized material and technical supply methods merely by introducing wholesale trading on a large scale; hence, the transitional period will feature a predominantly centralized (and limited) distribution of resources among the enterprises. The State has therefore been forced to plan a higher share of State orders in production – thus retaining, through State orders, direct administrative pressure on the output and range of the most important products. In most branches of industry, instead of setting economic norms for each product for all the enterprises in a particular industry, we have resorted to the practice of setting individual norms for each enterprise in accordance with the individual targets of the twelfth five-year plan. The enterprises go over to the new economic terms under the guidance of the existing institutions – the State Planning Committee, the Ministry of Finance and the State Committee for Material and Technical Supply, as well as other central bodies and branch ministries. However, the functions and structure of these institutions were reformed and the number of staff radically reduced (on average by 40 per cent) some months after the development of the national plan for 1988.

All this has had serious implications for the economic and management system introduced to the enterprises in 1988. In some branches, State orders have encompassed 90 to 100 per cent of their industrial output and have been set by the ministries to which the enterprises are subordinated. In other words, the old content of imposed indicators has sprung to the surface in the new form of State orders, and the setting of State orders has actually been very much like the previous practice of obligatory production quotas handed down from above. The ministries have also been entitled to set the norms for contributions to the State budget and ministerial funds deducted from profits and to distribute the profit left among the funds. Only the Ministry of Chemical Engineering was resourceful enough to draw up a special scale and develop a uniform technique of carrying this procedure through, whereas the other ministries simply set individual norms for each enterprise, relying primarily on the targets of the twelfth five-year period. As a result, efficient enterprises found that a large part of their profit was being deducted – and so turned out to be in a worse situation than the loss-making ones, which capitalized on this advantage. In fact, the latter were exempted from payment for resources and were assigned a low rate of deduction to the State budget, and so on. In other words, the old adverse practice of channelling funds from the efficient in favour of the inefficient enterprises was retained. If we also take into account the fact that the norms for formulating wage bills were not quite properly set, as they did not encourage the conservation of resources – once again putting efficient enterprises in a worse position than inefficient ones – it will be clear that such economic terms did not bring about cardinal improvements in work efficiency and/or quality of product. Such administrative practices were denounced by the 19th CPSU Conference, and measures have been taken to hold down State orders for 1989 to approximately 60 per cent. Moreover, we are planning to drastically restrict the rights of the ministries in setting State orders and, taking due account of the lessons of 1988, are setting different economic norms for those industries going over to the new economic conditions as from 1 January 1989. At an ever wider range of enterprises, the wage bill will be geared to the economic indicators of the finished product, thus stimulating the conservation of resources.

These and many other measures have promoted the consistent practical implementation of the Law on State Enterprises. But only the thirteenth five-year period will see truly consistent and comprehensive observance of the law. The conception of the plan for this five-year period is being drawn up now. It will be the first five-year plan to be developed on the basis of the new economic system. This means that, even at the early stage of plan elaboration, uniform economic norms for the enterprises and economic agencies are being recalculated, taking into account the new prices, and will therefore be fixed in harmony with the plan's targets. The Law on State Enterprises envisages two models of economic self-reliance. In keeping with the first model, the wage bill will be set according to the prescribed norms and economic performance. In addition, a part of the profit will be channelled into the material incentives fund. In the second variant, the norm for the pay packet will not be set at all. This fund will be formed depending on the enterprise's performance, products sold and stock in hand. The second form of self-financing essentially boils down to converting the enterprises or economic agencies into worker-collectives. This variant is, of course, pregnant with more powerful incentives for heightening efficiency and achieving better results. However, in the initial stages of economic reform the vast majority of enterprises have preferred the first model of economic self-reliance and thus have had weaker incentives for self-development. At the same time, a number of enterprises and even some industries have started mastering the second variant of economic self-management, though only on a pilot basis. Many production associations of the Ministry of Geology, for instance, have been sticking to the second model of fiscal self-sufficiency since the beginning of 1988. As a result of a year's work, they have pushed up their labour productivity by 26 per cent, while their average wages have increased by 12 per cent. In terms of all indicators, this branch has considerably overfulfilled the plan.

This country is featuring a powerful drive towards the use of leasing arrangements by workers' collectives and families. According to the terms of the lease, capital goods used in production are assigned to the tenants who then pay the rent for them. Their earnings are directly geared to the results of their work. The pay packet is distributed among the co-workers on a democratic basis, either at a membership meeting or at a session of the elected board. These measures will contribute to a wider use of the second model of economic self-reliance in the future.

Right now we are living through the crucial period during which the development of the new price system is under way. Its objective is to draw much closer together the level of home prices and their correlation with world market prices. To meet this target, we are to raise the wholesale prices of fuel and raw materials drastically, as well as the State retail prices of bread, meat and dairy products. To prevent the eroding of living standards as a result of price reform, all the money saved by the State due to granting smaller subsidies will be channelled to the population in the form of additional incomes. It is also planned to alter the system of price fixing: the share of centralized pricing will go down, while the share of free and contract pricing goes up.

We plan as early as the twelfth five-year period to complete the main transition from a centralized system of material and technical supply to a multi-channel wholesale system of trade. Besides the new prices, this conversion will be facilitated by the reform of the financial and banking systems, which will render it possible to stop the issue of surplus purchase-bonds in the monetary system.

Lately, much attention has been paid to banking reform. A new banking system has been set up in this country. It is made up of five specialized banks: the industrial and construction bank, the agricultural bank, the housing, social and communal bank, the savings bank, and the bank of foreign trade. All these banks have already formed their own branches. Under the new system, the State Bank of the USSR remains the national money supply centre and becomes a 'Bank of all Banks'. It will no longer be involved in the direct crediting of clients. The cooperatives now also have the right to set up cooperative banks. The reform is already gaining momentum and the banks are preparing to go over to economic self-sufficiency and self-financing. In our view, the near future will see commercialization of the specialized banks. Each enterprise and organization will eventually be in a position to choose a bank to service it, and the banks will start competing for clients. Under conditions of self-financing, the banks will be more particular about granting credits and will increase their assets due to the profit made. In other words, they will go over to self-development.

An important role in radical management reform is being played by reassigning functions to the structural and higher management bodies. The administrative system required an inflated 'apparatus', whereas the economic system does not need one. This accounts for the ongoing radical reorganiz-ation of ministries, departments and local government bodies; their functions are changing, surplus branches of management are being eliminated and managerial staff reduced. Practically everywhere we have liquidated the mid-dle-level management bodies – the main departments which stood between the ministries and their enterprises. An attempt was made to simply rename this management cell the State Production Association instead of doing away with it but, luckily, the supporters of perestroika spotted this attempt in time and it ended in failure. Branch ministries should be reformed so that they become the headquarters of economic planning and scientific-technical advance for their industries. They must stop supervising the enterprises' everyday activi-ties. These functions are to be assumed by the production associations. Taking into account the change-over to econ-omic methods of management, the structure of the State Plan-ning Committee, the State Committee for Material and Technical Supply and the Ministry of Finances is being reor-ganized and their staff is being reduced, as in the ministries, by 30 to 40 per cent. The reduction of managerial staffs at the republic level will be even larger: they are to be halved. The importance of local government bodies is increasing, but the new economic system of management does not need the inflated 'apparatus' of the past, so the number of their staff will be reduced too.

At the same time, the country is witnessing a voluntary drive on the part of the enterprises towards joining various econ-omic concerns and associations. This is also true of the cooperatives. Leningrad, for example, hosts the first concern covering the power plant and electric machine industries. These enterprises are no longer subordinate to any ministries. And this process will most probably gain momentum. Under the new economic conditions resourceful managers are guided by the recently proclaimed principle that 'everything that is not forbidden is allowed'. For instance, some State enterprises started on their own initiative to issue shares and bonds, and to distribute them among their own personnel and those of other enterprises. The decision is currently being taken to press ahead with this innovation in order to set up a market for financial securities in this country. The cooperatives are very resourceful. According to the data for July 1988, there are about 39,000 cooperatives in the Soviet Union – but this, in my view, is just the beginning. The cooperatives have penetrated every branch of the economy: production, construction, transport, research, marketing and servicing and, of course, agriculture. The idea is to create a powerful cooperative sector in the economy that will participate actively in the market. The Law on Cooperatives grants them extensive rights in terms of production activities. They are free to choose which goods to produce and which services to provide; they are run on a democratic basis; they issue shares, join together to form associations, found their own banks, and so on.

We should frankly mention that at the time of the nationwide discussion of the Law on Cooperatives, the Ministry of Finance drew up a draft decree on the taxation of the cooperatives without informing the public. It envisaged progressive taxation of the cooperative's personal incomes, with the progression being very steep and actually prohibitive. The decree was passed by the Presidium of the Supreme Soviet – also without any discussion or consultation with experts or with the cooperatives themselves. On its publication, the cooperatives were backed up by the general public, who came out against the decree. There were numerous appeals to the Supreme Soviet Session to abrogate the decree and the public scored a victory. The Session of the Supreme Soviet, while considering the Law on Cooperatives, did not ratify the decree and the system of taxation is now being developed anew, taking due account of the public's and the cooperatives' opinions.

The restructuring of foreign trade relations and of economic mechanisms for their regulation is an important part of the radical reform of management. However, we are not going to deal with this issue in detail here, as there is a separate chapter devoted to it.

This brief review of perestroika shows that the ongoing restructuring of the economy is comprehensive and varied. In some areas we have made more progress and have achieved good preliminary results (for example, in house-building), whereas in others we are still seriously lagging behind (for instance, in the conservation of resources or conversion to economic methods of management). If we look back and unbiasedly assess the past three years, we shall see how much our thinking has changed and how much headway we have made in our work and, especially, in our plans. To evaluate the progress made, one must keep in mind that in the pre-perestroika stagnation period there could not be a worse stigma for an economist than to accuse him of being an advocate of 'market Socialism'. The very word 'market' was practically forbidden, and such notions as shares or convertibility were simply unthought of in the context of our society. The notion of self-government was also almost abusive and leasing arrangements were considered almost tantamount to a return to the old days – whereas today these are actual deeds, not just rumours. We have gone a long way in these three years. We have made extensive changes and, thanks to new and higher criteria, we are now assessing the work done more exactingly and critically. Yet this new assessment, made from the heights of today's understanding, shows that we have done little; that the policy of perestroika has gained pace slowly; that many Soviet people have not yet felt the fruits of perestroika and have not actively participated in the process of reconstruction. What are the reasons for this? I think we can single out three groups of factors that account for the failure over the past three years to bring about a truly radical restructuring of the national economy and make it irreversible.

First of all, we have underestimated the depth of the abyss of stagnation out of which we are now climbing and have underestimated the forces of inertia that took root in the old economic pattern and old ways of thinking. For an advancing economy they are like fetters.

I think that we have also greatly underestimated the implications of financial imbalances inherited from the past. In the first two years of perestroika we did not make strenuous enough efforts to eliminate these disproportions and relied largely on traditional methods in attempting to do so. Unfortunately, our attempts ended in failure. Then, in my view, we made a bad mistake when we raised the price of hard liquor for the second time. The anti-drink campaign started well when we published the relevant decision on 17 May 1986. All strata of society joined in the campaign; during its first year the consumption of hard drinks went down by at least 61 per cent and, judging by the reported reduction of per capita sugar consumption by 2–3kg a year, the sale of bootleg liquor also went down. We then raised the price of liquor for the second time, and simultaneously drastically reduced the number of shops selling alcohol. In many areas, sales were kept down by administrative methods. These ill-advised measures were taken in complete isolation, without any serious discussion. They resulted in a drastic increase in illicit distilling and in a 4–5kg rise in the annual per capita sugar consumption, though the rise was rather spasmodic. The purchases of hard liquor in State shops saw an additional 30 per cent fall, but they were compensated for by excessive bootleg production. The State lost its monopoly on the production of wines and spirits, and must have lost some 8,000–10,000 million roubles a year in revenue. This has aggravated the already large deficit of the internal budget and the imbalance of the population's finances, in that their income exceeds their current expenditure. This process was also affected by the consequences of the fall in the prices of oil and other fuels and raw materials, which account for the predominant part of Soviet exports. The exports in money terms fell by 9 per cent in 1986 and by 2 per cent in 1987, so entailing a reduction in imports. Imported consumer goods were most severely hit by this reduction, resulting in further aggravation of those financial imbalances.

This problem seemed to be recognized and the June 1987 plenary meeting of the CPSU Central Committee passed a resolution calling for the drawing up of a special programme for balancing our finances. But a year has passed and this programme has neither been drawn up nor approved. But we need cardinal and, frankly speaking, extraordinary measures to this effect. These financial imbalances – partly the result of various enterprises' financial situations and partly the result of shortages in consumer goods and services – are among perestroika's major retarding factors. To do away with them quickly would in effect open up broad vistas for economic methods and material incentives – which are the source of our accelerated advance. The recent July 1988 plenary meeting of the CPSU Central Committee developed a system of measures towards fulfilling and exceeding the planned targets of the current five-year period for the production of farm products, consumer goods and paid services; taken together, these should improve the financial situation.

In a word, rectifying the deformations in the economy which had taken shape during the long years of Stalin's rule and the period of stagnation turned out to be more difficult and painful than we at first believed.

Secondly, we underestimated the strength and sophistication of the forces of resistance opposing the main direction of economic restructuring – namely, the reform of management. They failed to interfere with the development of the concept of a new economic system relying on economic methods, but they manged to squeeze through compromise or halfway decisions in the formulation of various laws and articles or clauses, the language of which turned out to be insufficiently precise. This is true, for example, of the articles on State orders and economic norms in the Law on State Enterprises and of many of the articles in the Law on Unearned Incomes. It is these last-mentioned articles that obstruct self-employment and the cooperatives. Profiting by them, the forces of inertia managed, at least in the plan for 1987, to include in the new form of State orders and economic norms the substance of the old administrative system so that obligatory production quotas were still allocated from above by omnipotent ministries. For the time being they have managed to paralyse the system of self-government in the enterprises, which in many cases retain only the external appearances of the system. Nevertheless, glasnost rendered it possible to unmask the forces opposing perestroika and to reveal their mistakes, which were politically assessed by the 19th Party Conference.

The situation is being remedied now. The victories won by the progressive public last year in the campaign against the plans for reversing the flow of northern rivers and this year in the campaign against the taxation of the cooperatives give rise to confidence in further victories. A great achievement of late is the Law on Cooperatives, which already has few halfway or ambiguous terms and is better tuned to perestroika.

Who resists perestroika? Of course, some part of the managerial personnel – and above all those who, due to perestroika, are deprived of the right to give instructions to subordinate enterprises and are consequently stripped of their privileges. Another group is made up of those managers who are lagging behind; they are afraid of being independent, and of the worker-collective's greater participation in management. They side with those managerial staff who oppose innovations. And, finally, not everyone is happy about the direct dependence of income on results that has been brought about by the policies of perestroika. In the past, much of the population grew accustomed to wage-levelling, whereby they pocketed unearned wages for bad work. State quality inspection, for example, revealed large-scale manufacture of rejects, for which manufacturers regularly got paid. Today they have to replace rejects without any additional payment, and so are impelled to improve the quality of their work. And, of course, there are people, few as they are, who do not like what is happening. Perestroika is being desperately resisted by drunkards (against whom we have been campaigning), by the so-called 'carriers' (people who steal things at work and carry them home), by those who plunder public property, by profiteers and bribe-takers, by those who capitalize on their posts, and by other antisocial elements who have their own reasons to oppose it. Perestroika has cut the ground from under their feet, and they are ready to do anything to survive.

Thirdly, the measures taken towards the change-over to new economic conditions were not radical enough to quickly push back the forces of inertia and deceleration or to do away with the administrative fiat of the 'apparatus'. It took us too long to draw up the new conception of management, and we were too timid in our first steps towards its implementation.

The 19th Party Conference doubled or even trebled the strength of perestroika's supporters. Perestroika policy in the economy has been supplemented by the decisions to carry through political and legal reforms. The conference's resolutions, *inter alia*, on glasnost and fighting red tape are helping us to remove the obstructions on the road to perestroika. In this context, the July 1988 plenary meeting of the CPSU Central Committee, held soon after the conference, was of great importance: it took specific steps to translate its decisions into practical policies and to set out the terms for carrying this work through.

There is no alternative to perestroika for our society. As Mikhail Gorbachev has put it, 'we have nowhere to retreat to'. And we are optimistic, because we are looking and going forward, ever more vigorously liberating ourselves from the fetters of the past.

Vladimir N. Kudryavtsev

A distinguished Soviet scholar in the domain of constitutional law, Vladimir Kudryavtsev has been the Director of the Institute of State and Law for fifteen years. He is the author of many books on the socialist legal state, sociology and law, theory of criminal law and criminology, published both in the USSR and abroad. His publications include: *Reasons for the Infringement of the Law* (1976); *Law and Behaviour* (1978); *Social Divergencies: Introduction to General Theory* (1984, Editor-in-Chief); *A Course in Soviet Criminology* (1985); *Law, Action and Responsibility* (1986); and *Principles of Soviet Criminal Law* (1988). Vladimir Kudryavtsev is a member of the Presidium of the USSR Academy of Sciences, a foreign fellow of the Academies of Sciences in a number of countries and Vice-President of the Association of Soviet Lawyers. He also contributes to the work of a number of other Soviet public organizations. Kudryavtsev is currently Vice-President of the International Association of Legal Sciences, the International Society of Criminology and the International Society for Social Defence, as well as being a member of the Board of the International Criminal Law Commission and other international organizations.

Towards a Socialist Rule-of-Law State

VLADIMIR N. KUDRYAVTSEV

The restructuring process taking place in this country is impossible without revival of the major values of Socialism – without revealing its humanistic, moral nature, which makes for the free all-round development of man. Such intransient values are democracy, law and legality.

Democracy, freedom and law are closely interlinked notions. In the words of Karl Marx: 'Freedom is so much the essence of man that even its opponents implement it while combating its reality. No man combats freedom; at most he combats the freedom of others. Hence every kind of freedom has always existed, only at one time as a special privilege, at another as a universal right.'[1]

I

The primary principles of law that gradually became one of the elements of general human culture are rooted in antiquity. Today they seem elementary truths the importance of which is obvious. But each of these principles was worked out in a complex and durable struggle, and epitomized the political, philosophical and moral outcome of acute conflicts and social contradictions.

For instance, the Digest of the Roman emperor Justinian (sixth century AD), which is one of the most thoroughly elaborated sources of law, formulated such principles as judicial

---

[1] Karl Marx and Frederick Engels, *Collected Works*, Volume 1, p. 155, Progress Publishers, Moscow, 1975.

objectivity (one cannot be judge in one's own case), the burden of proof (evidence is when a person is asserting rather than denying something) and the requirement of completeness of evidence (one eyewitness is not enough). These precepts, which are now accepted as irrefutable truths, were closely interwoven with anti-democratic ideas about the inequality of persons of different estates before the law and the admissibility of corporal and cruel punishments, etc.

The humanistic ideas of equality before the law, just treatment of offenders and the prevention of crime originated and began developing first in a slave-owning society and later in feudal society.

The Greek philosopher Democritus (fourth century BC) wrote: 'A man who educates by persuasion and reasoning will be better than a man who resorts to law and coercion.' Developing the same ideas nearly 1,500 years later, the Islamic humanist philosopher Al-Farabi (9th–10th centuries AD) stressed the importance of the principle of personal responsibility and a fair attitude to people. In the sixteenth century, proclaiming the value of human life, Thomas More came out against the cruel punishments of the Middle Ages: 'God prohibited killing anybody, but we so easily kill for a stolen penny,' he wrote in his *Utopia*.

The ideas of legality were developed in detail by the progressive representatives of political thought of the new age, who counterposed the rule of law to feudal arbitrariness (Charles Montesquieu, John Locke). In Russia Alexander Radishchev, Alexander Herzen, Nikolai Chernyshevsky and other revolutionary democrats deeply criticized the unlawful actions of Tsarism.

The philosophical foundations of a rule-of-law State were formulated by Immanuel Kant, who regarded the State as 'an association of many people subordinated to laws'. The principle of the rule of law in social relations was further developed in works by Russian jurists of the liberal trend – N. M. Korkunov, B. A. Kistyakovsky, S. A. Kotlyarevsky, P. I. Novgorodtsev, G. F. Shershenevich and others.

The value of the idea of a rule-of-law State consists in asserting the sovereignty of the people as a source of power, in guaranteeing their freedom and in subjugating the State to society. This idea was clearly formulated by Karl Marx: 'Freedom consists in turning the State from an organ standing above a society into the organ fully subjugated to that society; in our time too, greater or lesser freedom of State forms is determined by the measure in which they limit the freedom of the State.'[1]

Unlike liberal trends, Marxism-Leninism has never over-estimated the role of bourgeois democracy and legality, and, at the same time, has noted the positive opportunities afforded by them for the struggle of the working people for social emancipation. These are universal suffrage, the repu-blican-democratic structure of the State and the responsibility of officials to the people, etc. Frederick Engels wrote: 'It is certain for us that relations between those who rule and those who are ruled should be based on the law.'[2]

Socialism creates economic, social and political conditions under which the shaping of a rule-of-law State is inseparably linked with the democratization of all social life and with the realization of the true sovereignty of the people. Of course, the practical opportunities for shaping a socialist rule-of-law State, its specific features in each country and its stages and prospects are not determined unambiguously. They very much depend on the concrete historical situation.

In Russia this process was slow and hard. After the 1917 Revolution, a new, Socialist legal system based on the prin-ciples of equality and social justice began to take shape. One of the first juridical documents, 'The Guidelines for the Criminal Law of the Russian Soviet Federative Socialist Repu-blic' (1919), pointed out: 'The armed people have dealt and are dealing with their oppressors without special rules, with-out codes. However, the experience of struggle inculcates general measures in them, leads to a system, gives birth to a new law.'

The transition to the NEP (New Economic Policy) paved

[1] Karl Marx and Frederick Engels, *Collected Works*, Russian edition, Volume 19, p. 26.
[2] Karl Marx and Frederick Engels, *Collected Works*, Russian edition, Volume 41, p. 125.

the way for the assertion of the idea of legality. At that time Lenin formulated an important principle: 'The closer we approach conditions of unshakeable and lasting power and the more trade develops, the more imperative it is to put forward the firm slogan of greater revolutionary legality.'[1]

The consolidation of legality under the historical conditions in which the world's first Socialist State found itself was a complex matter. It was necessary to overcome the legal nihilism generated by the masses' hatred for and mistrust of Tsarist laws and laws in general, and to reject methods of 'War Communism' and adherence to acts guided by 'revolutionary expediency'. Knowledge of jurisprudence among most of the Party functionaries, executives and managers was inadequate. The theory of law rapidly 'withering away', being an attribute only of bourgeois society, was widespread.

Nevertheless, in Lenin's lifetime the legal foundations of the young State were consistently shaped. In the early 1920s the first codes of laws were adopted, and extraordinary bodies were demolished or transformed. The role of the People's Commissariat of Justice and of the courts and legal profession increased. The sphere of State coercion was narrowed. The Procurator's Office was instituted, its main function being to supervise the legality of the activity of State management bodies. The search for effective legal forms in regulating political, social and economic processes began. The development of Socialism entered a normal channel.

In the late 1920s quite a different situation began to take shape, which for complex social and historical reasons grossly ran counter to Lenin's ideas of social development. However, one should not ignore the fact that by that time the Soviet political system had not formulated political and legal mechanisms which would ensure the rule of law in social relations, or bar management by injunction. As a result, command-style methods for running the country gradually predominated, and the absence of legal protection for society became one of the major causes of a tragic chapter in our history.

Assessing the lessons of the past, we should ask why all

[1] V. I. Lenin, *Collected Works*, Volume 33, p. 176, Progress Publishers, Moscow, 1966.

this was possible? Can the social system fully depend on the psychological qualities of the leader? And should it have reliable methods of protection against abuses of power, arbitrariness and wilfulness on the part of officials and power bodies? Other questions arise, too. Did Soviet society have an alternative? And was it feasible to build Socialism without unprecedented loss of human life, the extent of which has not been fully revealed even now?

The authoritarian methods of leadership introduced by Stalin were inevitably linked with a limitation of democracy and with gross violations of citizens' rights. Under these conditions, law was regarded not as an expression of a measure of freedom for the personality and society but as a command, a ban, a restriction. Any idea of protecting the rights and liberties of citizens and the honour and dignity of the personality was eradicated from the official theory of law and legal practice of that time. The major democratic values formed by progressive juridical thought for many centuries – independence of judges, presumption of innocence, contestation of the judicial process and considerations of humanity – were consigned to oblivion.

Disregard for elementary legal principles and gross violation of them led to enormous political, social and moral losses in our society. Law is indivisibly linked with ethics. It is destined to assert the ideas of human freedom and dignity, to promote the attainment of social justice. Lawlessness robs Socialism of morality, of its basic principles and values, inevitably leading to a deformation of the Socialist system. Of course, it would be naïve to attribute all deformations of the social system to deviations from legal principles or inadequacy of legal mechanisms. We should take into account the low political education of the masses and the boundless trust that was transformed into blind faith in the leader. However, if society had been highly civilized in legal matters – if the inviolability of the individual, freedom of opinion and protection of human honour and dignity had been guaranteed, if restrictions of democracy had been outlawed, deformation of the social system would have been prevented or at least minimized.

113

Having unmasked the arbitrariness and lawlessness of the period of the cult of the personality, the 20th and 22nd Congresses of the Communist Party mapped out a system of measures aimed at restoring the Leninist principles of Socialist legality. In the late 1950s and early 1960s a large-scale rehabilitation of those who had been innocently convicted was carried out and the bodies of extrajudicial repression ('special courts', etc.) were disbanded; the simplified procedure for hearing cases of crime against the State was repealed, and the State security bodies and the bodies of the Ministry of the Internal Affairs were cleansed of criminal elements and taken under the control of the Party and higher State bodies.

However, wider measures for strengthening legality, for protecting citizens' rights and freedoms, were not translated into action. This was primarily because the authoritarian approach to civil society, which had formed over many years, had not yet been overcome. The political structures and institutions remained the same, and the democratization of social life was minimal. Methods of management by injunction continued to be pursued, although in a somewhat transmuted form.

The growth of negative phenomena in the economy, the development of departmentalism and bureaucracy and the absence of reliable legal guarantees for citizens' rights adversely affected the legal regulation of social relations. In particular, this found reflection in an unsubstantiated growth of departmental legislation and in the violation of the principles of legality and social justice.

In the 1985–8 period essential changes took place in the sphere of the State guidance of society. The publication of the code of laws of the USSR and the codes of laws of the constituent republics was completed. The plan for the preparation and discussion of projected legislation for the five-year period was drawn up. On its base, a number of the laws of the USSR and decrees of the Soviet government were prepared and adopted. The aim was to restructure economic management and to introduce board democratization of society and of the political system. The Law on State Enterprises (Amalgamations) of 1987, the Law on Cooperatives in the USSR (1988) and the Law on Individual Labour Activity (1986) are among these acts. They have considerably expanded citizens' rights in the economic sphere, have given appropriate guarantees of independence for the economic activity of work collectives and individual citizens in industry, agriculture, education, the health service and culture. These laws are based on the principle 'Everything is permissible unless prohibited by law'.

The Workers' Councils have been granted extensive rights, and managers at all levels are now being elected. This democratic order of recruitment of leading cadres is one of the major elements in the Socialist self-government of the people and in citizens' rights to take part in running the State and society.

The main line of the development of the USSR's political system is its all-round and full democratization. The main objective is to draw the widest sections of the population into decision-making in the sphere of State matters. Democratization of the legal system presupposes legal status for the individual, stronger guarantees of citizens' constitutional rights and liberties, and expanded and strengthened mechanisms for protecting the rights and interests of different social groups and strata.

II

Carrying out consistent democratization of all spheres of our life and developing the Socialist self-government of the people, we should focus our efforts on the revival of respect for the law and on the firm establishment of the principles of legality. Without this, the moral purification and humanization of our society is impossible. Nor can there be normal functioning of the political system, or its transformation on the basis of developing government by the people. The 19th Party Conference held in June and July 1988 has set the task of completing the formation of a Socialist rule-of-law State.

The creation of a Socialist rule-of-law State presupposes that societal life will be delivered from undue regimentation by State bodies. If the people are really to exercise power, the

State must be subjugated to society, must become the exponent of its interests, and must adhere in its legal activity to the will of the whole people expressed democratically. In this connection, it should be stressed that the development of principles of self-government is a *sine qua non* condition for limiting 'the freedom of the State'[1] and for strengthening the influence of the popular masses on its activity.

The introduction of the principles of a rule-of-law State is now regarded as a major condition without which it is impossible to deliver society from everything which is associated with the consequences of the personality cult, management by injunction, red tape, the alienation of the working people from power and deviations from the Leninist standards of Party and State life. Such deliverance calls for the radical reappraisal of the widespread concepts of the 'primacy' of the State over law and for the rejection of the old stereotypes which have piled up in this field over several decades.

Relapses into such an approach are far from being overcome. That is why the idea of a rule-of-law State is not limited to certain practical measures and principles. This is a major ideological and moral milestone in the reorientation of popular awareness and in the assertion of a decisive role for the people in the State and society.

A rule-of-law State requires consistent implementation of basic principles. The first of them is the supremacy of the law and its rule in all spheres of social life. This is an inalienable feature of Socialist civilization, a manifestation of the real power of the people and democratism.

In a rule-of-law State, a Law adopted by the supreme power body with the strict observance of all constitutional procedures cannot be repealed, changed or suspended by departmental legislation – including governmental decrees or decisions of Party bodies, no matter how high and authoritative those departments and organizations may be. If there is a discrepancy between departmental orders or Party decisions and the law, the law prevails. It is only under such conditions that true supremacy of the law can be ensured.

[1] Karl Marx and Frederick Engels, *Complete Works*, Russian edition, Volume 19, p. 20.

In this context, the problem of the quality of laws and their correspondence to the interests of society and the person arises. Our economy, social and spiritual spheres have been greatly damaged by insufficiently considered, scientifically unsubstantiated legal acts which have cramped the initiative of organizations and citizens, implanting bans and restrictions.

The 19th CPSU Party Conference put on the agenda the implementation of large-scale legal reform in order to secure the supremacy of the statute of the law in all spheres of society's life and to strengthen the mechanisms for maintaining Socialist law and order on a basis of developing government by the people. We have to introduce essential changes through legislation on Socialist property, planning, financial and economic relations, taxation and environmental protection as well as other issues, including the norms regulating labour, housing and pensions.

Administrative legislation also needs revision. We should put up legal and moral barriers to departmentalism and parochialism, to unscrupulousness, abuse of office and attempts to deceive society and the State.

An enhanced quality of law is directly linked with improvement of activity by the Supreme Soviet of the USSR. Great work is under way to reorganize the system of Soviets, including the country's highest representative body. It is intended to democratize their activity, remove the pressure of the executive apparatus and separate the functions of Party and State bodies.

The idea of the rule of law in social life as an inalienable sign of a rule-of-law State should not give rise to faith in the omnipotence of the law or a sense of juridical euphoria. In social consciousness there is a widespread opinion that, in order to solve an acute problem, it is enough to issue a law providing for severe sanctions. The role of law in society's life is great, but law cannot be a panacea for all evils. The process of implementing law includes a complex system of economic, political, ideological, socio-psychological and moral factors. Social processes can be influenced only by putting into operation a complex system of measures in which law is an important component, but not the only one.

The State and all its bodies must be governed by law. This is the second major legal and ethical-political principle characterizing a rule-of-law State. The State, having issued a law, cannot violate it. This principle opposes all forms of arbitrariness and self-will and the mentality that anything goes.

For a long time a disdainful attitude to law shaped among workers in the State apparatus. The principle that law is obligatory to all, irrespective of rank, position or services to the State, was violated. The certainty of not being punished untied bureaucrats' hands, leading to abuse of power and even to crime.

Regrettably, violations of the law are not an infrequent phenomenon in our society. To a considerable extent this is due to the atmosphere of complacency, mutual amnesty and readiness to pardon everything which appeared in some spheres of our life that lay beyond the zone of criticism, and which lessened requirements for observance of the law. This weakening of principle led to a double standard in assessing the behaviour of ordinary citizens and officials. There were cases of direct interference by local leaders in the activity of the militia, inquiry bodies, the Procurator's Office and courts aimed at freeing persons guilty of violation of the law from criminal responsibility. Such phenomena create a negative moral and psychological atmosphere and undermine the law's prestige.

Many officials lack tact and respect in their contacts with visitors – and are reluctant to offer help despite the fact that the caller's requests correspond to the law. In the course of the restructuring process citizens draw attention to the necessity of waging a resolute struggle against red tape and paperchasing and of introducing honesty, decency and a conscientious and solicitous attitude to people in our life.

The increased flow of complaints to State and Party bodies is caused by bureaucratism and a soulless attitude to people. This results not only from certain negative phenomena in the working of the State apparatus but also from the inadequate organization for considering complaints. Since early 1988, a new order has been introduced: each man whose rights, in his opinion, are violated can appeal to court against the illegal actions of an official. However, this opportunity is still rarely used by the population.

It would be naïve to explain disregard for the law only by the fact that officials have inadequate knowledge of the law. The phenomenon is more serious than that – an invulnerability syndrome has taken shape among public servants, disregard for the law and legal nihilism have become endemic. It is much more difficult to overcome these phenomena than to eliminate the ignorance of jurisprudence.

However, this must be done. The tasks faced by society in the perestroika period can not be solved without a revival of the prestige of the law in public consciousness, without knowledge of jurisprudence by officials, without an end to professional deformation of consciousness. This can be achieved only by means of glasnost, which presupposes open and authentic information about all important political, social and economic events and processes and about the activity of State and economic bodies and public organizations. This has also been pointed out in the resolutions of the Party Conference.

The principle that the State is bound by the law is not only an internal matter: this principle is important in the international sphere, too. A Socialist rule-of-law State is bound by international commitments, strictly observes them and cannot in any way deviate from the generally accepted standards and principles of international law. International law must be inviolable. This is an important feature of the new political thinking, a principled line in Soviet foreign policy.

The inviolability of the freedom of the individual – of man's rights and interests, honour and dignity, and their protection and guarantees – should be regarded as the third principle of a rule-of-law State. Law personifies the norm of freedom. Karl Marx has noted that legally recognized freedom exists in the State as law: 'Laws are rather the positive, clear, universal norms in which freedom has acquired an impersonal, theoretical existence independent of the arbitrariness of the indivi-

119

dual. A statute-book is a people's Bible of freedom.[1] Guaranteeing the freedom of the individual through law is a major function of a rule-of-law State.

The Constitution of the USSR proclaims a wide range of Soviet citizens' rights and liberties – economic, political, social, cultural and personal – and contains a detailed list of guarantees for them. We justly take pride in the successes of Socialist society in ensuring and protecting human rights, and have ratified international covenants on human rights. But we should not close our eyes to the defects in a legal system which ought really to eliminate and prevent all violations in this sphere.

The democratization of social life and the formation of a rule-of-law State both presuppose a broad range of legal measures aimed at expanding citizens' rights and liberties. They include:

1 Further expansion of glasnost, ensurance of the openness of legal and other State bodies and enhancement of the role of the mass media.

2 Democratization of the electoral system and clear demarcation of the functions of the Party and State bodies.

3 Expansion of the rights of public organizations, creative unions and citizens' creative self-expression associations.

4 Fuller realization of constitutional provisions aimed at ensuring citizens' social, economic and information equality, and at expanding the opportunities for the entire population – especially in places lying far from central regions and in the various republics – to enjoy all socio-economic and socio-cultural rights on an equal footing. Also, further strengthening of the guarantees of political and civil rights and freedoms, and creation of reliable juridical mechanisms for their protection.

5 Expansion of the competence and enhancement of the

[1] Karl Marx and Frederick Engels, *Collected Works*, Volume 1, p. 162, Progress Publishers, Moscow, 1975.

role of courts in protecting the rights of citizens, in ensuring their true independence.

Administrative command-style management methods are giving way to methods based on economic interest, self-government of work collectives and broad participation of all citizens in the democratic processes under way in this country. At present an all-round reform of criminal legislation is being prepared, the gist of which is a narrowing of the sphere for using measures of punishment and a general humanization of criminal law. This will be followed by similar reforms of criminal-procedural and penitentiary legislation.

Since the beginning of 1988, the procedure for Soviet citizens making trips to other countries has been greatly simplified. It will be democratized further. The resolution of the 19th Party Conference concerning legal reform has stressed that 'it is necessary to devote the utmost attention to the legal protection of the individual, to consolidate the guarantees of the political, economic and social rights and freedoms of Soviet citizens.'

Soviet jurists are widely studying and applying the experience of protection and ensurance of human rights in other countries. International cooperation in this field is especially important now that relations between countries with different political systems are improving and the role of universal human interests and humanitarian values is growing. Indeed, the entire international community and the United Nations Organization have an important role to play in protecting and guaranteeing respect for human rights and in promoting exchanges of useful experience in this sphere.

Restructuring is destined to destroy the system of relations between the State apparatus and Soviet citizens whereby the latter act as applicants even when the satisfaction of their indisputable rights and legitimate interests is intended. Such a system has been shaped over many years. Today, too, it causes numerous complaints by citizens to higher Party and State bodies and to the mass media. Respect for the rights and dignity of the individual should be an immutable law for all State bodies, officials and economic and public organizations.

Mutual responsibility on the part of the State and the individual is the fourth principle of a rule-of-law State. It expresses the moral principles in relations between the State, as the bearer of political power, and a citizen as a participant in the realization of this power. Establishing in a legislative form the freedom of society and the individual, the State itself is not free from restrictions in its own decisions and actions. The state, via law, must assume commitments of an internal and foreign-political character and must ensure justice in its relations with citizens, public organizations, other states and the entire world community. The State determines legal measures regarding the responsibility of its officials for actions taken by them on behalf of the State and its bodies.

A rule-of-law State is inconceivable without clear and concrete juridical measures ensuring the responsibility by its officials for failure to execute their obligations to the people. A specific person or group of people stands behind every case which is not fulfilled, and it is impossible without real responsibility by them to count on greater efficiency in the activity of ministries, departments and Party bodies. In other words, a rule-of-law State must rely on a smoothly functioning system of juridical responsibility.

In this connection the elucidation of the causes of the insufficiently high efficiency of some normative legal acts is of special importance. It is common knowledge, for instance, that laws geared towards the implementation of environmental measures concerning nature protection have not yet justified initial hopes. This is not only due to low standards in people's environmental education and illegal actions by officials who violate the norms of rational use of natural resources and environmental protection established by legislation; it is also due to the imperfection of some normative acts which do not determine clearly the measures of responsibility for violation of the law and sometimes do not even contain specific sanctions. Unfortunately, the pollution of rivers and lakes with sewage, an increase in the maximum permissible norms of emissions and the irrational use of natural resources are still widespread phenomena. Nature protection laws are also violated because the direct interests of enterprises, linked with the fulfilment of plans, often contradict the need to bear expenditure on environmental protection which does not give economic profit to the enterprises, although useful to society at large. However, a special agency dealing with ecological monitoring and environmental protection has recently been set up, and it is to be hoped that the laws governing this sphere of life will be observed more consistently.

Finally, the fifth principle is that a rule-of-law State must have effective forms of control and inspection over the execution of laws and other normative juridical acts.

Today our country has different forms of control: courts, arbitration, procuratorial supervision, and public organizations that inspect representative and managerial bodies. However, despite numerous forms of State inspection the priority in the consciousness and behaviour of citizens belongs not to them but to political and public channels. Indeed, most complaints and proposals are sent to Party bodies and to the editorial boards of newspapers or to radio and television. This shows that State control mechanisms are not efficient.

The principal role in resolving conflicts of interest that emerge in different spheres of life should be played by courts. The replacement of an independent collective 'court of equals' by any managerial structure leads to a bureaucratic distortion of State activity and to violations of civil rights. Meanwhile, the supremacy of the court in the system of juridical bodies is far from secured. Consequently a large-scale reform of the court system is currently being carried out, which aims at radically improving the work of all juridical bodies.

Immediate measures to be taken constitute a reinforcement of the democratic principles of judicial proceedings – including contestation, equality of the parties, openness, and presumption of innocence – and proposals to increase the number of lay judges when courts hear important cases are being discussed. Of special topicality is a boost for the prestige and functions of the legal profession. Defence lawyers will be involved in pre-trial investigations from the moment of arrest or announcement of charges. In addition, increased prestige of the courts is needed, as well as legislative, political and moral conditions ensuring the independence of judges and their subordination to the law alone, so that there is absolutely no interference by Party or State bodies in the functioning of the courts. All these are vital attributes of a rule-of-law State.

Under Article 121 of the Soviet Constitution, the Presidium of the Supreme Soviet of the USSR monitors observance of the Constitution. Regrettably, this aspect of the Presidium's activity has not been developed far enough. Now a Committee for Constitutional Supervision will be established which will determine whether or not normative juridical acts are in conformity with the Constitution of the USSR, which is the country's fundamental law.

The Procurator's Office should work along new lines. In keeping with Leninist views, it should ensure effective supervision of the uniform application of laws; firmly safeguard the rights and interests of Soviet citizens; and see to State and public discipline. Judges, procurators and investigators should be free from any pressure or interference with their activities. They must be subordinate to the law and to the law alone. It is also high time to reorganize the investigative apparatus, to ensure its independence and strictly supervise its activities.

III

The shaping of a rule-of-law State is one of the major aspects of the democratization of the Soviet political system – an inalienable guarantee for its normal development which prevents any possibility of its deformation and any deviation from the principles of Socialism. The idea of a Socialist rule-of-law State is generated by the new political thinking which carefully preserves the democratic values of mankind and imparts new meaning to them. The Soviet Union fully realizes the importance of this idea – the implementation of which is designed to ensure the legal foundations of perestroika, to make it irreversible and to instil confidence in the freedom of the individual and his or her legal protection.

Many declarations and resolutions of the UN General Assembly, UNESCO and other international organizations recognize that the major objective of our time is to preserve peace, since without peace there can be no economic, social and cultural progress for the human race. The law and its institutions are one of the means for meeting the truly historic challenge now facing all nations. The comprehensive system of international security proposed by the Soviet Union also bears a legal aspect – since implementation of this programme is only possible through the attainment of accords and through the conclusion of mutually acceptable agreements between states.

Law is an element in human culture and one of the instruments for its protection. The consolidation of the legal foundations of international relations and the popularization of democratic legal ideas is an imperative of our time. Its implementation promotes the development of people's political and legal standards, and is therefore a major contribution to their spiritual development.

Garry K. Kasparov

The youngest world chess champion in history, Garry
Kasparov won the thirteenth world championship in an
unprecedentedly long 'two-serial' match with Anatoly Karpov in 1985. He has several chess 'Oscars' to his credit.
Being the disciple of Mikhail Botvinnik, the first Soviet
world chess champion, Kasparov has followed Botvinnik's
example in actively popularizing the art of chess among
teenagers and young people, and is at the head of the young
chess-players movement guided by the Central Committee
of the Young Communist League. Kasparov comes from
Baku, the capital of Soviet Azerbaijan. His quick southern
temperament, energy, sharp judgements and chess genius
have won him the heartfelt support of millions of chess
fans.

Your Move, Perestroika!

GARRY K. KASPAROV

I sometimes seem to think in chess moves – not at the chess-board, during a match, but in everyday life. Simple pawn moves like shots, the ornate jumps of the knight, the infinite manoeuvres of the queen . . . The form is no less important than the content, and sometimes the form becomes the content for me. This is how I arrived at a dialogue. A dialogue with myself. Questions and answers. I ask myself a question, then give myself an answer.

How much does contemporary sport need perestroika? Or is perestroika something for the sphere of economic and production relations alone?

To answer that question, one must appreciate the role of sport in our life. Let us imagine ourselves a hundred years ago: the word 'sport' meant very little for the people of the previous century. Some kind of activity, perhaps, not so very popular, not giving any prestige . . . Sport was much more popular two thousand years ago in Greece. It had some kind of value there, it was a means of self-expression for the nation, the city, or the community.

In the twentieth century the situation is different. Even though the Olympic movement has been restored to life, the Greek ideals in their pure form have not been revived. How-ever, the idea itself has been accepted by twentieth-century society and it has been transferred to a plane that has made it closer to the people. Sport has become the very entertain-ment so much needed by the masses; the criteria are simple and acceptable for the average man. Painting and music are quite popular passions – but look how steadily sport is leaving

129

such things behind. And this is, I believe, because it is so simple, so accessible to everybody.

The electronic age, an age of high velocity, demands the maximum simplicity of which human perception is capable. Sport has won a vast audience, which is very understandable – people tired of everyday cares want to know who is the best today. The best in everything – in football, in athletics, in swimming. Gradually the sphere of professional sport has broadened, and thanks to sport the prestige of television has risen sharply. Television needed a boost and sport gave a hand. Because anything can be sold through sports. Or, at least, a great deal.

And another plus is the important factor of advertising. There are so many goods produced, and the production output is so great – which means the major sphere of economic competition, of economic influence, moves into the information sphere. You must sell information about your products in the most accessible form. How can you do it? Advertising and sports are inseparable, because sports are perceived through the subconscious. When a person is under stress, he is in no position to decide whether he wants to buy a product or not. But when he is relaxed and watching the advertisements, say while a football game is on the TV screen, his choice is easier and quicker.

Advertising is money, and sport started automatically to attract immense financial injections. In America this happened earlier, but in Europe it took place in the 1960s and 1970s, when sport was being given a professional outline, when new powerful professional clubs started to take shape. The USA has a number of purely American sports – baseball, American football and boxing, for example, which in international terms attract only a local audience. Even if we forget about the difference between America and Europe, sport remains one of the easiest ways of influencing the mind of the man in the street, because it is universal. Nothing happens on television or in advertising without sport. It involves millions of people vicariously. And what is also important for the nation, sport helps people relax. You can go to a swimming pool, to a tennis court; you can enjoy yourself while watching your sporting idols. You discover what to do with your spare time; you grow healthy. Such care for health is not far removed from the parallel of the ancient Greeks, who took pride in the health of their own bodies. I am now speaking about mass sports, of what mass sports provide for the vast majority of people. Not only an imitation of the process, not only a substitute or emotion, but a matter of physical fitness, as well. Because people like to feel healthy, which means sport becomes a necessity. The age which has forced people into the ocean of emotions also pushes them into sport.

In any Western country, the system of social welfare includes a network of student, communal and other structures providing for health. So, amateur sports are constantly monitored and, although they are not free of charge, the prices are so low that they allow all strata of the population to go in for sport under very good conditions. Professional and amateur sports (*a*) are quite separate and (*b*) have different sources of finance. Money can pass from the professional sports into the amateur sports, as one would expect, but there can be no reverse process.

You have given quite a full picture of how sport has been developing in the West. But how do things stand in the Soviet Union?

Seventy years ago, our social institutions started to be reconstructed. Russia was an undeveloped country and many things did not reach a high level. The same held true for sport. In the 1930s a new sports system was initiated. The people were eager to invest their energy. They built stadiums together, went in for track and field athletics, and performed the necessary exercises to earn a badge declaring them to be 'Ready for work and national defence' (GTO). The same kind of commendable impulse made the people enthusiastically participate in building the incredible Magnitka and Dnieproges. Yet, ironically the system which was formed then and which was oriented for that historical period, later moved with little change into the beginning of the 1950s and the middle of the 1960s. This is where we can see the contradictions of that time. The 1930s laid the foundations of mass sport. The system worked quite well but the period after the war demanded some reappraisal of our values, if not a restructuring of the system. The emergence of Soviet sport on the international scene provoked a strong political temptation. Politicians demanded a separate cohort that would become famous, would receive prizes and take first places.

From the 1950s, when we moved into the international sports scene, mass sport gave way to leaders and champions. But the sports basis remained unaltered because the money in sport remained the same. At first some degree of proportion was observed. The mass sports were still alive, still retaining the traditions of the 1930s when the Spartak team included all the Starostin brothers, and mass sport was still receiving donations. We were the first state where a government invested in sport. We did not go professional, but we started building up a caste of leaders. And nobody thought of what was to become of the record-breakers and champions after their success. And a sporting career is so brief!

Prominent Soviet sportsmen in the 1960s had an unfortunate fate. Take Alimetov, the hockey player, or Chislenko, the footballer, for example – or the life of Voronin, a prominent halfback, which ended in tragedy. Somehow, all of it is a burden on our conscience. But at that period the situation did not seem to worry anybody, things were looking up. And then the late 1960s produced the first signs of crisis. Standards of living were improving, people's expectations were increasing and the new athletes did not like to run barefoot along the track. They needed comfortable facilities, decent equipment and proper conditions. But nothing was done in this respect.

Moreover, mass sport yielded more and more money to professional sport. If instead of 100,000 swimming pools the country can build only a hundred, this means all hundred must be at the disposal of the national first team. This is the kind of process which started then and went on year in, year out. The money that the trade unions were supposed to spend on mass sport automatically went to those sports clubs and sports schools which were training national teams. All club or school coaches have their norms, but what should the results be according to those norms? They are judged by the number of athletes with a rating, and the number of instructors trained. Nobody worries about the number of children taking part in sport. Ratings and titles are what matters. The coach's status depends on it. And this is not even a case of quantity without quality as in industry, because in sport quality matters. Eventually, everything in sport is subordinate to one idea – winning medals.

You can invent plenty of people with GTO badges, as Sergei Pavlov, the former Chairman of the Sports Committee, did. You can list as badge-carriers all those people who take part in cross-country races once in a blue moon. The number of people going in for sport will not increase as a result. Little by little, mass sports money starts working only for pseudo-professional sports.

Ah, this is something new. How do pseudo-professional sports differ from professional sports?

Pseudo-professional sports differ from Western sports in that our sports cannot support themselves, because the athletes have no status. And don't forget that we are fighting for medals, and medals always have the same weight. The medals we have been trying to win in Olympic football, and have failed to get in thirty years, have the same weight as the medals we receive in freestyle and classical wrestling, in which nobody is interested. Reports say we are great because we have the largest number of medals. But look at the prominent sports – the situation is becoming more and more serious. We have the upper hand in secondary sports, but they flourish at the expense of the leading sports. In other words, several types of professional sport shore up the others. And how do we spend the money received from tennis, football, hockey, cycling and basketball? It goes to archery, shooting, the pentathlon, classical wrestling . . . Because these sports also need money for training people. And the reports only take account of medals. And it all sounds highly successful. Yet in reality, our gross output, which for many years has been the major index for the officials from the State Sports Committee, is disastrous. It is ruinous for Soviet mass sports.

So, you insist that mass sports are falling into decay because the money goes to professionals?

I spoke about this at a trade-union congress eighteen months ago. Do we know the whole truth about the mass sports? Why, for instance, is no Soviet citizen in a position to take his child to a swimming pool or sports complex? Nor will he be able to do so in the near future, not until we break the mechanism allowing officials to take money away from the mass sports. That was why I defended professional sports then. By admitting the status of professional sports, we shall forever block the chances of pumping money from the mass sports into professional sports.

But won't it influence other sports negatively?

Yes, some sports will suffer and we shall get a smaller number of medals at the Olympic Games. So what? We must choose what is more important for us. An extra fifty medals at the Olympics or the health of the whole nation, of the community of nations? There are different answers to this question, and our answer will differ from the answer of the State Sports Committee officials, because they have different values. But there is no other way. There are not so many professional sports in the world. Football, hockey, basketball, tennis, chess, cycling, motor racing and motorcycling, baseball, boxing, and one or two others. Track and field athletics and swimming are semi-professional. They produce a lot of money – not for the sportsmen themselves, but for the Federation.

The other sports constitute a great problem. Let them develop the way they like, but not at the expense of the Soviet mass sports and of the major sports. Because we are lagging behind in these major sports. Take tennis, for instance. The sport is neglected, is not developing, though the tennis players earn millions. Why so? The money goes (*a*) to officials and (*b*) into other sports.

But isn't it somehow controlled? Cannot sportsmen themselves influence it?

134

Perestroika has touched upon these spheres a little. Sports are profitable enough, and in the last few years the leadership of the Sports Committee have reported their results on one more point – currency income. Do we earn much? A trifle. Could we earn more? Of course. We must open the road to the West, as I stressed in a speech three years ago. But how? Our athletes have no real status. None at all. What is one athlete under our conditions? Hard to say. Why is the official apparatus afraid to allow sportsmen to turn professional? Because they would not be dependent. A professional sportsman has his price. If a football player named Protasov 'costs' two million dollars and somebody else 'costs' a hundred thousand, you will include Protasov in your combined team. And what about the Sports Committee? How will the sports officials, who often do not understand anything about sport, go on ruling? Because today they decide who is going to coach the national team and who will play in it. Today they hush up any kind of mutiny very easily: you are not allowed to go abroad, you are not selected for the national team – and that is the end of it. If they admit the rights of a player, if they admit that every player has a price, if they allow us to appear for Western clubs without their services as mediators, how are they going to rule? Everybody will see that they are good for nothing. The people will understand: nobody needs the Sports Committee and its huge sluggish cogs. So they will have to agree to building up federations, to treat the Chess Union, the Tennis Union and the Football Union as independent federations. The Committee would remain, but only as a small ideological institution exercising a purely general influence. But the Committee and its officials (supported by some authorities from the top) do not want to give up power, because a lot of people feed off sports. I am deliberately making a point of this – sport has been supporting them until now . . .

And not only the officials?

Of course not. Look how ironic the situation is. Professionalism and commercialism were always the worst enemies of Soviet sport. And then, all of a sudden, the second word disappeared. It is nowhere to be seen. Professionalism is here all right, but not commercialism – it is as if it had never existed.

And how do you account for that?

Our Sports Committee has started making a business out of sport. They have the product in their hands, so they obtain the monopoly right for sales. If, say, Renat Dasayev, our famous goalkeeper, is to be sold for a sum three times lower than his real price – and I can give you several examples of contracts being seriously understated – a certain difference in money may arrive in the Committee in some other way . . . And what about all those advertising arrangements whereby Soviet athletes are sold wholesale? How can a group of leading athletes be sold wholesale? What kind of man, if he can put two and two together, would sell athletes or players wholesale when they might be sold one by one, making a hundred times more? But in such a case it is the State that would make a hundred times more – whereas if you sell sportsmen wholesale, the person or organization that signs the contract makes the profit. So there is a situation whereby vast amounts of money pass through the hands of mediators self-appointed for the post. And isn't it true that sport has reflected many of the negative aspects of our economy? If the Sports Committee opens up the road to the West for our athletes, its officials will lose power. Again many Western sportsmen in the West live off advertising, but this source of currency income has not yet been exploited in this country.

How is it possible to improve the lives of players and to make them more independent?

Let them have official professional status; introduce a proper system of taxes for them; and, in the major professional sports, build up federations that can professionally train and develop their own sport. Why should tennis have to support the pentathlon? I simply can't understand such thinking. If tennis is the more popular sport, then it ought to be developed. Everything has to pay its own way and sport, too, must turn to self-financing. Then again, we need clear State laws to prevent money from trickling out of trade-union funds into team funds. Let it be done even at the expense of disbanding some of the country's football teams, all those second and tenth leagues. Let the best combined teams suffer – there is no other choice until we break this parasitic structure which is preoccupied with working only for gross output, for medals.

How can we give Soviet sport closer contacts with the West?

Western sport is a huge social and political power today. Take the clubs, for instance. In America there are basketball clubs and in Spain football clubs with millions of fans. These are real financial empires, which are increasingly active and are constantly gaining impetus, involving more and more people. Of course, there are all sorts of people among them – fanatics, hooligans, semi-fascists, etc. . . . But for the most part they are just ordinary people thirsting not for blood but for pleasure. If we are allowed direct contact, we shall have friendly relations as well as money. And let the taxes take their due.

Not that I think a player should have to pay taxes according to the highest tax category existing in the Soviet Union. I shall deviate a little here, but the problem deserves it. As far as I know, the USSR is the only country in the world that differentiates people according to what they do to make money and not according to how much they earn.

The Soviet tax system provides for different taxes for different occupations, and not for different incomes. But how does this correlate with a constitution which promises equal rights to all of us? We are not against high incomes, but we are against high incomes being earned by a certain stratum of the population only. We may have a composer who is a millionaire, because composers pay 13 per cent tax on their income. But we can't allow an inventor to become a millionaire, because he has to pay taxes according to other regulations. In other words, our workers, composers, inventors and sports people pay taxes according to different rules. And what about the division of Soviet people working abroad into four categories? Why do we differ in categories and not in the benefits we bring the country?

Even today there is a very strange rule operating for those who work abroad: you cannot leave yourself a single penny out of what you earn. You hand all the money over to the State, and then the State pays you as much as it thinks necessary. Thus, although I earn a million Swiss francs and hand them over to the State, the State takes my million and then pays me so many thousand. If my memory serves me correctly, in the last five years I have handed about two million Swiss francs to the State. This is a larger currency income than that of many big industrial plants. There is one more important detail. If I have to pay income tax of one million US dollars, I must know what I am to get back. Our tax system is not concerned with advantages for the population. It makes no difference whether the taxpayer is good or bad, so long as he is paying taxes to be used to support some organizational apparatus – for example, he may pay for the maintenance of privileged medical clinics to which he has no access. In other words, our tax system has a purely feudal character.

So far you have defended sport and sportsmen in general, but what about your own sporting career?

When my matches with Karpov began, I did not realize that it was in fact the beginning of a duel with a powerful and well-organized mafia. I mean the Sports Committee (FIDE) which held sway over the chess world. It was only natural that they should come down upon me with all their might, because I constituted a serious threat to their existence. It wasn't so bad at the very beginning. At first they were simply defending their own contender against a stranger. But later on, when it finally became clear that there were no chances of merely substituting a Kasparov syndicate for a Karpov syndicate – that I was not going to play their game – that was when they started using ideology as a weapon. They used an approved lexicon of abuse: Kasparov is anti-Soviet, he is undermining our ideology, he is Western-oriented, we do not need such things, we must defend our ideals . . . Traditional wording of the Nina Andreeva type, I would call it.[1] It was not a new method, though. It had been tried with Korchnoi. It was during the match with Korchnoi that Karpov was lauded to the skies and acquired the influence which was later to bring Campomanes to power. Campomanes gave Karpov a hand in the campaign against Korchnoi. His 'services' were not forgotten later by the officials. In 1982 he was 'helped' into the FIDE presidency and has been backed ever since.

You are so persistent in what you say about there being a mafia. But you have your own group of supporters – and they, like you, dislike the opposite side. Isn't your own team a mafia, too?

I gathered a group of people with the same views – among them players and coaches – as far back as when Karpov was still champion. To join me, to 'march under my banner', required courage besides being professional. And courage my assistants did have. We were united by the idea of the world championship, and for some it also meant a chance to acquire a standing in life. Everybody was fighting for his own principles. But when the goal was attained, and I was wreathed with laurels, there was some confusion. I had to go on fighting, but some of my people couldn't understand this. Why did I have to do it? I had attained everything I wanted, and we could now get our share of fame and money and relax. However, I couldn't relax.

Was that because you don't like a quiet life? Because you like fighting?

Waging a war for the sake of waging a war is not an end in itself for me. But fighting against things that are socially wrong is a part of me. Part of my nature. This is a difficult point. I think you will agree that it is not possible for everybody to understand why such a young world champion, who has all the chances of leading a nice quiet life, is intent on rising up against many things and many people.

[1] Nina Andreeva was the author of a letter to a Soviet newspaper that started a heated discussion in the press and later became known as the manifesto of anti-perestroika forces.

But aren't you jeopardizing your own career?

Some of the people around me were living through a moral crisis. And that moment was used by my enemies to attempt to break the Kasparov team. First they got at Vladimirov, one of my coaches. Then the same happened to Dadashev, my psychologist. The enemy was not squeamish about which means to try. I had to face truly dirty methods of warfare. My opponents violated the moral code and demonstrated their power, trying to prove that it was their power which was the truth.

After Karpov and Baturinsky attacked me in the press, one of my pupils from the Botvinnik-Kasparov chess school asked me: 'Why don't you write a letter to the press telling the people the truth? Why don't you smear them with dirt?' I told him that we couldn't use such methods. We could not allow ourselves to employ dirty tricks to defend a just cause. Every new match brings new tasks. I was opening a new front and began to realize that the war would inevitably make me choose a definite position in life.

Now the fourth match is over, has life stood still?

No, there is a war going on in chess and in sport. The very foundations have been shaken. Too many people were pressurized into backing Karpov. The precedent is too dangerous. If I am successful in my fight, many people will join it.

Is your fight a good example of perestroika in action?

Karpov received extremely powerful support before the fourth match, but I got backed by the progressive forces which had stood up for me before – and they stood up for me honestly, in an open manner. When the film *Champion Thirteen* about me was not allowed on the screen, Alexander Yakovlev ordered the film to be sent to a festival – to let the public decide for themselves whether it was worth seeing or not.

Aren't you laying it on a bit thick? You are the champion, after all.

My title affords me protection against immediate reprisals,

but brings no other privilege. We want to build not a parallel mafia but new public associations with a proper democratic basis. The war with FIDE is a vicious one. After the 1986 Chess Olympiad, I understood that it was necessary to fight against the conditions that had engendered the mafia; against the rules and regulations that had allowed such an organization to appear. That is why I initiated an association of grandmasters – in effect a kind of independent trade union of free grandmasters. Today it has become independent and powerful thanks to the malpractices of FIDE and other organizations.

What, briefly, are its principles?

They have varied. At first it was an organization built up specially for the World Cup, but then we realized that it ought not be an elite organization. It is based on democratic principles and at present has minimum working personnel. However, a much larger organization is now being built up, which is going to include professionals. It will require a powerful commercial structure in order to promote chess and have contacts with television. The association is to control the top of the chess profession. It will continue paying money to FIDE to use for chess development, but the rules must be changed and new people must be brought in.

For the time being these plans are a kind of one man ideology, aren't they?

A single person is only a part of an objective process. In general the direction is clear. In the same way, you might say that perestroika pivots around Gorbachev alone – but that would not be quite correct, perestroika had definite preconditions. For my own part, I happened to come along at the right time. Had it not been for the Fischer tragedy, I don't know what might have become of me. What happened to Fischer prevented FIDE from outlawing a second world champion. I have been lucky enough to see my personal destiny interwoven with public interests.

And what about your immediate plans?

I am going to organize a chess enterprise to publish a chess magazine, the best in the world, with the best polygraphic basis, that will be distributed worldwide. This is to be a joint venture and it will be economically independent of the Sports Committee. It will be supported by Pergamon Press, one of the world's largest publishing concerns.

What is the main idea of the magazine?

To give the chess movement a new banner and to address the movement to everybody. We shall open the first professional teaching department for mass chess, because here in the Soviet Union we have accumulated a vast number of teaching programmes at all levels.

Is it going to open up a new frontier?

Yes, we must look for new people, teach them to use new methods. We are as yet few. But time is on our side.

What are your chances of success?

As I have said, sport offers many more opportunities for entering the world community. We associate too closely with Western consciousness. If we really want perestroika to be a success, we are going to have to actively cooperate with the whole world – and if we want to break patterns and overcome obstacles, then it would be downright criminal not to take the chances sport offers.

Ivan D. Ivanov

Ivan D. Ivanov is one of the 'wizards' involved in restructuring USSR foreign economic relations. Since perestroika got under way, he has been promoted from the scientific ranks to the post of Deputy Chairman of the Soviet State Foreign Economic Commission – the section of the USSR Council of Ministers in charge of foreign trade. As his background includes research, business and United Nations experience, he has been able to play a major part in designing Soviet legislation on foreign investment. He has been a frequent visitor at international conferences, and is chief Soviet negotiator with the EEC. Ivanov's pet research topics are the transfer of technology, trade policy, export promotion. For many years he served as a UN expert on transnational corporations, and he is on speaking terms with the top international business circles. He has written several books and booklets on R & D management, and transnational and international competition, and he has over a hundred scientific studies to his name.

Perestroika and Foreign Economic Relations

IVAN D. IVANOV

Foreign economic relations, being part of the Soviet economy, are also undergoing radical changes. Their role in the development of the national economy is to be increased to make the country by the beginning of the twenty-first century not only a great industrial nation but a great trading power as well. Restructuring in this sphere is based on the same principles as the general economic reform: it covers the whole range of foreign trade, from central planning agencies right down to the commercial activities of individual enterprises. The foreign economic policy of the USSR will receive a new impetus, its ways and methods being modified to meet the requirements of the contemporary world.

A new approach to foreign economic relations

In the post-war period the Soviet Union has entered the world market on a large scale, and its national economy is now considerably involved in the international division of labour. The turnover of foreign trade has grown faster than national income, and by the mid-1980s the export element already accounted for 6 per cent of the GDP. Now imports provide for 20 per cent of the increment in installed machines and equipment, and up to 15 per cent of consumer goods in retail trade.

But the mid-1980s also marked the time when stagnation phenomena had accumulated. They impeded the growth of foreign economic relations and held in check the integration of the country into the world trade system.

The former centralized directive-laden system of planning regulated contacts with the outside world rigidly, and in the development of the country the inertia of reticence and non-sensitivity to outside influences was kept intact. This resulted in plans being dominated by the principle of 'residual' allocation of goods for export purposes. Exports have become oriented towards energy and raw materials, which does not carry prospects along the lines of expanded demand and is also vulnerable to market fluctuations. Due to these reasons alone, the country received 20,000 million dollars less in export earnings in 1985–8 than was expected. Imports are basically tailored to tackling immediate problems and the consumer goods element has soared unjustifiably, to the detriment of an investment component.

At the micro-level of the economy, enterprises were screened from the foreign market. Compulsory mediation by the organizations of the Foreign Trade Ministry and the isolation of domestic prices from world prices deprived producers of any real impetus to expand economic operations abroad or develop the skills necessary for competing in international markets. As a result, the export potential of manufacturing industries became under-utilized, external economic ties were characterized mostly by an ordinary commodity exchange and a new industrial form of cooperation did not gain ground.

In addition to the radical structural changes in world trade and economy, all this was aggravated by the comparatively weak position of our country in the world market and by the inability of foreign economic relations to make the required input into the plans to modernize and accelerate the development of the national economy mapped out by the leaders of the country.

In this context, restructuring is aimed at establishing a new model for Soviet foreign economic relations – industrial, technological and competitive. It would link Soviet and world science, and turn foreign economic relations into an important, independent factor in the growth and intensification of the country's economy, reserving the nation a worthy place in the international division of labour.

Introducing new thinking into the management of the Soviet economy, the model proceeds from the premise that, in the modern interdependent world, our economy is a part of the world economy and therefore should develop and be managed as such. It is also understood that attainment of world standards in major technological and economic indices is only possible when the national economy of the country interacts with and competes in the world market.

Finally, plans are being made to use foreign economic relations as a catalyst for domestic economic reform, primarily for promoting money-and-commodity relations and competitiveness in the domestic market.

The model calls for intercomplementation of the Soviet economy with other economies, above all with those of Socialist countries, and for continuous use of foreign economic capabilities and alternatives to resolve the problems of the national economy. In the future, imports will be viewed not only as a means of satisfying domestic demand, but also as a competitive substitute for inefficient home production. Exports will be regarded as an independent channel for expanding the sales of products and, most important of all, as an undistorted indication of their cost, technological level and consumer properties.

This basis would enable the USSR by the year 2000 to increase its turnover of foreign economic activities by 2·4 to 2·5 times as against 1985 (thus doubling national income over the same period), while the proportion of income contributed by exports is planned to reach 9 per cent. Soviet exports are to grow at an overriding rate to enable the country to increase its share in world exports from 4 to 6 per cent.

Of course, a number of complicated tasks will have to be tackled in this process. It is planned to have all regions of the country actively involved in the world market, with traditional exchange of commodities being replaced and supplemented by cooperation in science and production. In particular, the renewed mechanism of Socialist economic integration within CMEA member states and the mechanism of economic and technical assistance to foreign countries will be oriented to serve these purposes. A start was made in the use of all well-established forms of international business cooperation (leasing, engineering, operation with securities, consortium financing, etc.). Foreign capital investments in the USSR as joint ventures are allowed. Soviet investments in foreign infra-structure that support the foreign economic activities of the USSR (warehouses, support centres, service networks, banks, transport companies, etc.) will be expanded. At present some 120 firms are involved, and in the future the number will grow not only through new commodity-handling companies but also through new manufacturing enterprises.

Central to the problem is the task of determining the most rational foreign economic specializations for the country in industrialization of its exports and rationalization of its imports.

Considering the prospects of development for the Soviet and world economy and bearing in mind the likely development of science and technology and the place the USSR occupies in the contemporary world, it was decided that the country should specialize primarily in the export of manufactured industrial products – in particular machines, equipment and chemicals – and a wide range of services. So far as the export of raw materials is concerned, the object is to sell mostly processed replenishable materials, which naturally puts timber in the foreground; and the volume of energy carriers exported will be stabilized, with the share of gas and coal growing at the expense of oil.

In addition to power engineering and metallurgy, the USSR will render economic and technical assistance to foreign countries in the field of machine-building, agri-business and infrastructure components.

As to imports, it will concentrate on investment products and technologies, needed above all for modernizing the machine-building industry, and on non-replenishable raw materials. There will also be a wide range of exchange in chemicals and consumer goods. The national investment policy will shift from new construction projects to modernization and renovation, which will reduce the construction of turnkey projects. Industrial and investment collaboration in different forms, as well as technology transfer, will gradually open up the Soviet market. Measures are envisaged to replace imports, above all in such fields as foodstuffs, rolling stock, basic chemicals and standard equipment.

It is planned by the year 2000 to increase the share of manufactured products in Soviet exports to 65 per cent, with the share of machines and equipment increasing to 40 per cent, as against 30 and 20 per cent respectively in 1985. The share of raw materials and fuel is to go down to 25 per cent, while the proportion of machine and technical products in imports is to go up to 55 per cent as against 40 per cent in 1985. As a result, the Soviet Union will enter the twenty-first century with a progressive structure of sales turnover and will enjoy a stable position in the world market. Soviet economists estimate that the realization of the new model of foreign economic relations will by the year 2000 yield an additional increment of national income of the order of one-tenth of the total increase, and will save 130,000–140,000 million roubles in capital investments and about 15 million people in terms of labour resources.

Naturally, the country will take measures to preserve its technical and economic invulnerability against unfriendly outside actions. But overall, foreign economic relations will play a role in the formation of an intensive open-type economy in the USSR.

The organizational basis of restructuring

Such an important and far-reaching process requires a principally new organizational and legal basis. For the most part this has already been set up, though in the future much will have to be done to improve it.

The key element is a radical change in the forms by which the State monopoly on foreign economic activity exercises its workings. The forms are being modified along the lines of democratic centralism to replace the rigid centralization of the Ministry of Foreign Trade, which used to be involved in up to 90 per cent of all transactions. The All-Union bodies are now left with only general, strategic management of foreign economic relations, while operational management of commercial activities is being largely decentralized and given to individual branches of the economy and enterprises. This makes it possible to concentrate the previously divorced functions of production and trade in the same hands. If cost-accounting (on the profit-and-loss principle), self-financing and self-repayment (including that in foreign currencies) are consistently realized, foreign economic activity becomes an integral part of the general economic performance of Soviet enterprises, and the enterprises themselves will get a real impetus to turn into organizations which operate internationally.

These functional changes are to transform the process of planning foreign economic activities. Instead of aggregating current decisions, we will start with long-term forecasting for the Soviet economy as a whole and the role played in the economy by foreign economic activities, encompassing a twenty-year period and taking into account the prospects for world trade and economic development. All this will form the basis for a strategy for Soviet foreign economic relations over the next fifteen years, with a detailed study made on the perspective for the next five years. Combined with the main directions of economic and social development of the country taken as a whole, the strategy will be specified in separate five-year plans of development for foreign economic activities. This procedure is to be introduced when the thirteenth five-year plan begins in 1991.

The first 'Strategy of Soviet Foreign Economic Relations' was approved in the summer of 1988, and its top-priority part contains the 'Programme for Developing the Export Base of the USSR' for 1991–5. This programme lays the foundations for the specialization and industrialization of Soviet exports. The strategy also envisages measures to rationalize imports and to balance the country's international accounts. Development programmes for foreign economic relations have been included as special chapters in the five-year plans of all ministries, departments, Union Republics, enterprises, amalgamations and organizations – but, in contrast to past practice, they do not look like detailed lists of volume indices. Instead, summary currency (balance of payments) plans have become central to the new planning. Thereby, various industries, Union Republics and enterprises receive targets shaped as general value indices and independently determine their commodity values. Moreover, the plan is envisaged as a dialogue between planning and operating organizations.

This allows for a more flexible reaction to fluctuations in foreign markets as well as for real provisions for planning export priorities. Contrary to the previous 'residual' approach, fulfilment of export orders is to have priority in the production programmes of enterprises. The foreign commitments of the country in this sphere are to be supported by obligatory State orders distributed within industries. Finally, in the future, with the development of wholesale trade, enterprises will have a free choice as to whether they sell production in the domestic or foreign market.

Under the new economic conditions, the foreign economic ties of the country are to be managed at Government level as a unified complex. The State Foreign Economy Commission built up in 1986 as a standing organ of the Council of Ministers is the supreme organ of such management. It guides and coordinates the work of all ministries and departments participating in foreign economic activities, takes part in working out the strategy and the plans for such activities, works out drafts for relevant legislation, and keeps an eye on how these plans and this legislation is effected.

The newly born USSR Ministry for Foreign Economic Relations directly represents the interests of the country in the foreign market. Unlike the previous Ministry of Foreign Trade, it is largely free of operational commercial functions. Instead of the eighty or more foreign-trade associations that worked for the old ministry, the new one retains only twenty-five associations, which carry on trade in fuel, food and other primary commodities.

Instead, the new Ministry is concentrating on the analysis, planning, organization and political functions of trade. It is working out drafts for foreign trade plans, regulating export and import operations, improving its own economic mechanism, and shaping the foreign trade policy of the country and its system of operating controls. The Ministry renders technical and economic assistance to foreign countries, supervising the construction of projects in which foreign companies are participating. It is also responsible for supplying the foreign economy complex with commercial information and for the training of personnel.

Democratization of social and economic life in the Soviet Union has considerably increased the authority and widened the functions of the USSR Chamber of Industry and Commerce. Embracing nearly 5,000 enterprises and having a vast network of representative groups, it now stands out as a 'collective voice' for Soviet business. The Chamber has the right of legislative initiative, it keeps up contacts with foreign enterprise amalgamations and renders all kinds of services to Soviet and foreign clients, giving them consultations and advising them on patents, exhibitions, advertising and arbitration. Since January 1988, an association of exporters, the council of directors of joint ventures, and associations for business and cooperation with a number of foreign countries and regions have been working at the Chamber.

At the same time, the epicentre of the reform of foreign economic relations may be found at the level of enterprises. A stable course has been pursued for their contacts with foreign markets and for working out a mechanism for making them economically interested in such contacts.

By 1 August 1988 fifty-five Soviet ministries and departments and over ninety enterprises and industrial associations had received the right to conduct direct operations in foreign trade. The same right was granted to the Council of Ministries of all Union Republics, to the city management of Moscow and Leningrad, and (by 1 July 1988) to the largest cooperatives. These Ministries and Councils of Ministers have organized their own foreign trade amalgamations; and industrial enterprises, consortiums, cooperatives and city management bodies have organized foreign trade entities of their own. The criterion for allowing an industrial enterprise into the foreign market (the decision is taken by the State Commission for Foreign Trade) is the ability of an enterprise to produce commodities that will stand competition and evidence of some experience of exporting.

Thus, amalgamations for foreign trade such as Avtoexport, Traktoroexport, Soyuzkhimexport, Stankoimport and others were handed over by the Ministry of Foreign Trade to the relevant industrial ministries. Within the various ministries, foreign trade activities differ and are determined by the specific features of different industries. For example, the USSR Ministry for the construction materials industry has centralized the trade of its export production in the branch amalgamation Stroimaterialintorg, the reason for this being the industry's uniformity of production. On the other hand, the USSR Ministry for the automobile industry permits direct access to the foreign market for its plants in Togliatti, Gorky, Moscow, Zaporozhye, Minsk and Naberezhniye Chelni, whereas the rest of its plants (in Lvov, Kremenchug, Lipetsk, Kutaisi, Ulyanovsk and other parts of the USSR) trade through the Avtoexport amalgamation. The same Ministry deals with the market situation, prices, and legal problems within the industry.

In the course of the reform many Soviet (joint) companies abroad have acquired new masters. Thus, alongside the foreign trade association Soyuzkhimexport, the USSR Ministry for Chemical Industry has taken over the technical department of the association in Hungary, the German Democratic Republic, Poland, the Czechoslovak Socialist Republic and Romania, as well as the shares in the joint-stock companies Sogo (France), Sobren (Federal Republic of Germany), Socimes (Italy), Sober (Sweden) and Interprom (Austria). A number of positions in the trade missions of the USSR in foreign countries has been reserved for representives of industries.

In 1987 these 'novices' provided for 20 per cent of the general trade turnover of the USSR and over 40 per cent of the export of machines and equipment. The drop in turnover which had been expected was stopped, and the share of machines and equipment in the country's export total grew. At the same time, the experience of industries directly participating in foreign trade varies. While a number of enterprises

(Avtovaz, Atlant, the Minsk refrigerator plant, the First Moscow watch plant, the eye microsurgery complex and others) have been quick to utilize their new rights, others (Avtozil and Moskvich, for example) have been slow and passive in foreign markets. The reason is their lack of experience, initiative, information and personnel, poor knowledge of foreign markets, and setbacks in international competition.

The economic status of those enterprises which conduct their trade through mediators has changed considerably. Their relations with foreign trade associations have been transformed from administrative orders to a system of relations on a contractual basis, and they have received the right to choose partners and contract terms. In addition, direct access to foreign markets has opened up for them through the new forms of production cooperation. In particular, they can establish direct production ties with partners from the Socialist countries, participate in frontier trade and coastal trade, and found joint ventures with foreign partners in the USSR and abroad. The organizations of the various Union Republics and large universal shops are allowed to conduct exchange of consumer goods with analogous organizations in other Socialist countries, too.

By 1 June 1988 Soviet enterprises and organizations, collective farms included, established more than a thousand direct ties and built up 137 joint ventures, amalgamations and organizations of various kinds (eighty-nine of them with partners from the Socialist countries and forty-eight with partners from capitalist states). The turnover of frontier and coastal trade in 1987 was over 200 million roubles and it became an important factor for technical and social development in many frontier regions (including the Far East, Estonia, West Byelorussia and Lithuania), the total turnover being a little less than 25 million roubles.

Soviet science has been noteworthy for its active participation in these operations. Eight interindustrial scientific and technological complexes and the Novosibirsk Akademischesky Gorodok campus received direct access to the foreign market. Over a hundred Soviet research centres lead programmes for scientific and technological development of the countries that are members of CMEA and coordinate practical R & D within their Complex Programme in some ninety directions. They also supervise and coordinate over 3,000 research themes for the organizations of the CMEA members.

With the passing of time, the number of ministries, departments, enterprises and amalgamations having direct access to the foreign market will grow. In this connection, the reform's future largely depends on reliable adjustment of a new economic mechanism for foreign economic activity.

The new economic mechanism: progress and problems

In continuity with the general economic restructuring, the management of economic ties has consistently been pointed toward better performance. Besides control planning data, the most major innovations are normatives for currency assignments, differentiated currency rates, and a workable rate of rouble exchange and credit percentage. Taken together, they provide for proper conditions allowing enterprises to increase their business activity and increase their responsibility for commercial results.

Earlier, before the reform, all currency received from exports went to the budget. The general situation was not influenced by small occasional currency bonuses granted to some enterprises, the bonuses being hard to use because of bureaucratic procedures. The new economic mechanism has introduced a substantial stimulus in this sphere. Now the enterprises are to receive some share of the currency receipts agreed upon earlier, with the right to use it freely. The norms for such currency assignments vary from 2 to 95 per cent and grow proportionally, depending on the degree to which the goods have been processed. In order to mobilize local resources for export, the Union Republics, Moscow and Leningrad are assigned a stable figure of 70 per cent hard currency to finance their exports, and enterprises and local bodies of government in frontier and coastal trade receive 100 per cent.

According to the 1987 totals, the industries had thus

received over one million dollars in hard currency and 2·5 million convertible roubles. Enterprises may spend this money on technical readjustment, and convertible roubles may also be used for the social needs of working collectives. This innovation profits both industry and the State, as it removes pressure from the centralized currency budget. Initially, it is only being used to finance new construction projects and to provide the country with raw materials, food and consumer goods. In the future, however, the norms for currency assignments are to be raised, as a step on the way to full enterprise currency self-financing.

Similarly, initially the differences in home and world prices did not allow an enterprise to introduce real and stable khozraschot (full cost-accounting) and export operations. Under the new conditions this is to be achieved through the application of differentiated currency rates 'linking' these prices. Ratios are to be calculated through the division of the first by the second, with later corrections in different currency zones, then used for transforming the contract prices into purchase prices, the difference being paid for by the State budget.

In general, industry gains from such a system. But it criticizes these ratios for being too multiple, too complicated and rather relative. Therefore, the radical second stage of the reform in the sphere of foreign economy and in the process of price reform in the USSR is to bring domestic prices for some groups of commodities close to world prices, thus providing a basis for a new economically founded rate for the rouble rate in relation to foreign currencies. Import price corrections necessary to regulate competition in the domestic market will be provided for by the introduction of a new customs ratio.

Such a new rouble rate, by reliably registering our foreign trade performance, is a step on the road to a convertible rouble. The degree of convertibility may be evaluated after the country has built a major basis for competitive industrial exports that is powerful enough to back up the stability of the new rate and provide stability for the country's balance of payments.

The stimulation of Socialist enterprise by economic reform has had the effect of making the credit system more active. Among other things, the USSR Foreign Economy Bank has started giving credits to industrial enterprises in order to develop their foreign economic activity and, above all, to enhance the basis for exports. By mid-1988 enterprises had received about a hundred such credits, with the relevant industrial ministers acting as guarantors for the enterprises. The USSR Foreign Economy Bank plays the role of a mediator for enterprises exchanging mutual currency credits where the enterprises have free currency stock. This is done with the aim of integrating the means for solving joint problems regarding investments abroad, etc. Channels for receiving credits in the foreign money markets have been widening. As well as attracting bank credits, the Foreign Trade Bank has begun to issue bond loans in the foreign money market. A right to conduct operations with securities abroad has also been granted to Soviet industrial enterprises, and preparations are being made for the internal sale of free currency to those enterprises which may need it.

The USSR Promstroibank (the bank for construction materials) and the USSR Agroprombank (the bank for agribusiness) are getting ready for participation in this sphere of foreign trade.

The financing organs are constantly monitoring the country's foreign accounts. This is done with the purpose of limiting the volume of foreign debts, regulating them within reasonable limits, and providing for punctual foreign payments abroad. In future, the Soviet Union is going to continue to maintain its status as a first-rate business partner and its reputation for punctual repayment of loans.

At the same time, the USSR has been taking measures to recoup the money loaned to the developing countries. These loans are usually given almost totally on favourable terms (as a form of assistance for development) for specific projects. The loans are generally repayable in commodities rather than in hard currency that is in short supply. For this reason the USSR's credit relations with these countries do not provoke extreme situations. However, the global debt crisis has indirect consequences, resulting in payment delays and lack of commodities to cover payments.

The Soviet Union is therefore now concentrating its credits in the sphere of export-oriented projects, those constructed on a compensatory basis being among them. It has also been enlarging the list of commodities acceptable as payments, and writing off some part of the debts as a way of investing in countries in need. The idea of using some proportion of the debts in the foreign secondary market of liabilities has also been under consideration.

Full-base accounting presupposes strict discipline of foreign economy. Our legislation contains severe penalties for export supply failures, as well as for breaking contracts or failure to pay off credits taken. The quality of exports is to be checked by special State quality commissions and a special quality inspection by the Ministry for Foreign Economic Relations. The requirements as to the quality of imports have also been made more stringent.

Non-traditional forms of business cooperation, notably in the industrial sphere, are an important part of the new economic mechanism. In addition to the industrial, scientific and technological cooperation practised before, direct links and joint ventures are being organized.

Direct ties are being established with enterprises and organizations in the Socialist countries on a contract basis. They include cooperation in production, research and training personnel, and the consequent exchange of commodities. The partners themselves determine the scale, nomenclature and prices for the exchange, the Soviet enterprises receiving 100 per cent of the currency earned.

Direct ties that are profitable for the partners are also of great macroeconomic importance for the Soviet Union and other CMEA countries. They increase Socialist economic integration, widen its production level and are laying the foundation for a future CMEA common market. But their development has run into its own obstacles. The economic rights of enterprises vary in different Socialist countries. Differences in national prices often also make it difficult to arrive at a unified opinion in evaluating the level of profit in transactions. A further point is that wholesale trade is not yet developed, and USSR enterprises have now only small volumes of free product which can be sold directly. The situation may improve by 1990 when the share of wholesale trade in the domestic economic turnover becomes predominant and the CMEA countries start working on bringing their price system together.

The reform legalizes higher forms of cooperation, namely joint ventures. The rules for their organization within the territory of the USSR are the same for partners from Socialist and capitalist states. The Socialist countries can, in addition to joint ventures proper, also organize 'international associations' (which are needed for joint R & D, the results being shared).

For the reasons stated above, such forms of cooperation have not yet developed to a great extent. In mid-July 1988 there were still only eleven joint ventures with partners from Socialist countries and just seventy international associations and joint organizations. The focus is currently on joint ventures with Western partners, seventy of them being registered by the same date. The total sum of their statutory capital allocation was nearly 800 million dollars with one-third of the capital being foreign.

The use of foreign capital in the Soviet economy caused much ideological dispute. But it was evident that with the economy being internationalized, economic ties between the two systems, even though they were totally different from one another, could not be brought down to mere trade contacts. Lenin's works of the 1920s and the experience of other Socialist countries proved the exclusion of joint enterprises to be wrong. As a result economic expediency, supported by new political thinking, prevailed. From the very outset, Soviet investment legislation was planned as being balanced, giving due consideration to the interests of both sides.

In building up joint ventures, the Soviet side pursues the policy of better satisfying the country's economic requirements and has, in particular, the following goals: *(a)* to draw on modern technology and management experience; *(b)* to replace imports; *(c)* to attract additional money and materials;

and *(d)* to develop the export basis of the country. These goals are viewed as interconnected and complex, and have for the time being been attained. A number of joint ventures are based on Soviet as well as foreign technology.

The foreign partner is stimulated in this area by guarantees that his property will be protected and that profits will be received; by his immediate participation in the enterprise management; by a number of customs privileges and preferential duties; by getting priority in construction needs; by economizing on social payments to workers (the bulk of them being met by the Soviet Union); by the freedom of the enterprise from export-import operations and from obligatory State plan assignments; and by an internationally accepted system for settling accounts in the event of disputes.

While approving of the policy in general, foreign businessmen listed a number of problems. They mentioned the absence of information about industries and projects meant to draw foreign capital; the legal requirement reserving for the Soviet side 51 per cent of the statutory fund, plus the posts of president and general director of the enterprises; as well as the rule of currency self-financing (i.e. covering all expenses with currency income); and problems caused by difficulties with Soviet components. Their opinions are being studied. In June 1988 foreign businessmen received a list of more than 320 Russian projects open for foreign investments in the period 1988–95. This helped to overcome industrial investments being such a bewildering mosaic, and to coordinate them with the priorities of Soviet economy development. In order to guarantee the management rights of the partners, the joint venture plans include lists of issues which can only be decided upon unanimously. If the currency income of an enterprise turns out to be insufficient for a partner's profit to be transferred abroad, he is allowed to use the rest of the profit for buying Soviet goods; and his investments in start-up capital may now be made in any currency that he chooses. Things are more difficult with supplies, because a developed wholesale system is, again, needed to guarantee its flow. But by the time the majority of joint enterprises are functioning, the wholesale sector of the USSR's trade will have become much larger, such enterprises being supplied by the relevant ministries and organizations from their funds.

By the middle of 1988 sixty more commitments to open new joint ventures were signed and more than 300 foreign applications for beginning joint ventures were considered. Consideration was also given to the idea of creating 'special economic zones' in the USSR with privileged conditions for such ventures. There is therefore justification for hoping that the new channel of cooperation will occupy a sound position in the Soviet mechanism of foreign trade relations in the future.

A new approach to foreign economy policy

The restructuring of the USSR's foreign economic relations demands sound guarantees in the sphere of trade, policy and diplomacy.

Having analysed the international situation, Soviet diplomacy has put forward a concept providing for international economic security and has submitted it to the United Nations. The major idea is to rid international relations of any burden: to create a climate that will allow each country to maximize profits earned as a result of participating in the international division of labour and to minimize the risks involved.

In particular, the idea is for the international communities to unite their efforts to free international trade from artificial restrictions and discriminations; to solve the problem of debts through joint effort by debtors and creditors; to install in the world a new international economic order that will guarantee equal economic security for all countries; to realize the programme of 'disarmament for development'; and to solve the human problems facing the world today. Soviet diplomacy sees a way to such security – by means of dialogue with all interested parties. It does not claim a monopoly in its interpretation or in choosing priorities, which can vary. Indeed, the concept envisages a positive contribution by all states.

At the present moment, the idea is under discussion at the UN, understanding of international economic security being a part of a comprehensive system of international security involving the military, political and humanitarian spheres.

Being a part of the world trade system, the Soviet Union aims at participating in its main institutions or at closer contacts with them. The USSR is one of the countries that initiated the creation of UNCTAD and UNIDO, and it is ready to fully participate in GATT. In August of 1986 the Soviet Union applied to the GATT Secretariat to participate in the 'Uruguay round' of trade negotiations. It planned to outline its interests there, in order to accumulate some experience in international trade negotiations and to show a readiness to participate that might later help the USSR to join GATT. But the negative position of the USA, and to a lesser extent the European Community and Japan, saw the application rejected. Nevertheless, Soviet economic diplomacy is continuing with preparations to conduct negotiations with GATT and the USSR's reform of foreign economic relations will serve as a foundation for such negotiations, since it makes the mechanism of Soviet trade policy compatible with the rules of GATT.

The establishment of official relations between CMEA and the European Community opened the way for direct negotiations between the USSR and the EC regarding an economic agreement. The Soviet Union would want such an agreement to be as wide-ranging as possible, to cover both the full range of interests of Soviet industry and the full powers of the two communities. Such an approach corresponds to the policy of 'a common European home', and takes into account the tendencies of Soviet economic restructuring plus the reform of the EC. The goal is a 'unified market' by 1992.

The draft of the agreement worked out by the Soviet Union covers both traditional trade (including the principles of most favourable conditions and non-tariff restrictions) and the system of investment cooperation in industry, science and technology, as well as exchange of information, currency operations, business routines, rules for competition, exhibitions, and consultation procedures, etc. A joint USSR–EC commission is proposed to monitor the working of the agreement and to look for new directions in cooperation.

The idea of a wide-ranging agreement is considered in EC quarters as being an 'innovation' because until now the two communities have, with minor exceptions, concluded trade agreements only. However, the innovation has been dictated by the transition of the USSR from commodity exchange to a productive character for foreign trade relations and by new tendencies in world trade whereby more and more commodities are manufactured by internationally organized production processes. So, from the very beginning, the project was actively supported by business and industry.

At their meeting on 26 July 1988 the EC Council of Ministers gave their approval in principle to this wide-ranging approach.

In order to conduct negotiations with foreign countries while protecting the major interests of the Soviet Union, the USSR Customs Tariff is to be made more active so as to directly influence the pricing of imported goods in the domestic market. So as to be compatible with such negotiations, it is to be based on a practical system of commodity coding and description and is to be adjusted in some details in order to conform with the rules of GATT.

At the same time, a system of non-tariff controls is being worked out in order to regulate the USSR's foreign economic relations that will include licensing, technical requirements for imported goods (such as standards, ecology and health norms), rules for currency operations, and custom clearance, etc.

The same controls may be used reciprocally against discriminatory measures by other countries against the USSR in the sphere of trade.

The USSR is also actively involved in the restructuring of CMEA to advance the economic integration of the Socialist states. The CMEA members are searching for ways of bringing together their price-formulation systems, as well as full reciprocal interchange of each other's currencies and the introduction of a convertible rouble. The ultimate objective is to create a united market of CMEA countries. Specialists think that this way zones of free trade can be created in Eastern Europe and a CMEA customs union arranged.

As the political report of the CPSU Central Committee to the 27th Party Congress stated: 'The approach to mutually profitable economic relations should be on a large scale, it should face the future.' This is the primary aim of restructuring the foreign economic relations of the USSR.

Mikhail A. Ulyanov

Mikhail Ulyanov is a People's Artist of the USSR and President of Russia's Union of Theatre Workers set up under perestroika. One of the most popular Soviet actors, he first starred in films and on the stage in the period of the first post-Stalinist thaw. He will undoubtedly be remembered for his acting in the severe and dramatic film *Chairman*, in which he played the role of Yegor Trubnikov, chairman of the collective farms board, in the post-war years. The public was also greatly impressed by his interpretation of the role of Marshal Zhukov, in a number of films, and of Vladimir Lenin in a serial only shown on Soviet television twenty years after it had been shot. Ulyanov is an active publicist, motivated by the urge to participate uncompromisingly and passionately in the resolution of pressing social problems in the domain of ideology, moral education and defence of truthful art. Recently he has been in charge of the popular Moscow theatre named after Eugene Vakhtangov, where he has been a leading actor for many years.

Theatre and Perestroika

MIKHAIL A. ULYANOV

During my recent trips to the USA I saw for myself that every American knows at least two Russian words: glasnost and perestroika. And everybody wants to get 'first-hand' information about what is actually going on. I am no philosopher, no sociologist. Neither am I an economist. My sphere is the theatre. Therefore I shall speak of the subject which I am familiar with, without any claim to producing a detailed overall picture. But . . . there is a 'but'. The acting profession, to my mind, allows one to actively participate in what is happening in one's country and in the whole world. An actor conveys his own pain and his own joy, there are things he loves and things he hates, those he accepts and those he flatly rejects. One cannot just 'play a part'. A part for me is a way of expressing my own attitude to life. I cannot imagine the profession otherwise. This is, in fact, a job that has a civic responsibility. And as an actor and a citizen, I am sure my profession must have both heart and muscle.

Often, when speaking of perestroika, we use the expression 'the revolution is continuing', meaning the October Revolution of 1917. And these are not mere words. To my mind, they express the deepest meaning of the transformations that have put our whole society on the move, a vast country with a population of 280 million, occupying a sixth part of the earth. I am tempted to compare what has been going on with what was being planned and was on the verge of being done in the theatre in the early 1920s, and to judge from my own personal impressions. But I was born in 1927, in a remote Siberian town. So I was too young and, anyhow, how could I,

167

a provincial boy, be aware of the theatre of that epoch? And besides, theatre is something ephemeral. The performance exists while it is on; and when it is over, there are only reviews and reminiscences, it only lives in the mind.

But there is another outstanding and enviable kind of art, namely painting. Through painting I can revive the feelings prevalent both in the revolution and the theatre and in art in general. I can mentally follow an intriguing path. I stepped on this 'path' for the first time when I saw painting by Osmiorkin, Lentulov, Malevich, Kandinsky, Sudeikin. I was deeply impressed. I saw freedom, a rich variety of forms, art's surprisingly kaleidoscopic perception of life. I think something of the kind existed in the theatre of the 1920s. We know how many studios sprang up at that time, how many people sought new forms under the aegis of such personalities as Vakhtangov, Chaliapin, Stanislavsky and Isadora Duncan. The revolution gave freedom to creative energy and started a new epoch, the epoch of experiments, redundancies and carefree holidays.

Very often I hear the question: 'What can theatre do for a revolution?' The famous drama *Princess Turandot* staged in the 1920s springs to mind. That seemed to be a play for aesthetes, a play which did not raise any social questions, which was full of the gaiety and joy of a carnival. What had it to do with the revolution? But it was a revolutionary performance. Vakhtangov was a man of genius in his sense of time, and at a time of devastation and hunger, when Moscow's streets and houses seemed in deepfreeze, he anticipated the spring awakening of revolutionary possibilities. Many discoveries of those years were later claimed by other countries as their own. But all that had been introduced by Vakhtangov, Meyerkhold, Tairov . . .

Yet another reminiscence, this one from the 'stagnation' period. Some time towards the end of the 1960s my theatre and I were on a tour in Sverdlovsk. I went to see an exhibition by local painters devoted to contemporary themes. I had never seen such gloomy monotony.

We have arrived at such a situation not by chance and not because Russia lacked talent. For many years our art was being forced into a single channel. Into 'monumentalism', and endless praise and seeming lack of conflict. The creative palette was artificially narrowed, criteria were displaced, and militant incompetence and dullness suppressed talent and professionalism. The year 1956 brought some hope. But the thaw was followed by frosts. How many honest and talented films were shelved! And how many brilliant manuscripts mouldered away in writers' desks!

Not so many plays were forbidden at that time. But only because the battle was fought at the initial stage when dramatic material was chosen. What? Conflicts! Personal interpretation! Everything was under suspicion, even classics, not to mention modern drama. Administrative rule kept art in a steel harness and was leading the theatre into a blind alley. Traditionally Russian theatre had been a social tribune: its function was to tell people the truth about their life. But in those years it could be freely used only for endless eulogy.

Yefremov and Tovstonogov, Efros and Goncharov were working in the theatre at that time. Lyubimov was also with them . . . But most often they felt like the stepchildren of their time. 'There is nothing worse than the fate of a stepson living in an alien epoch . . .' These bitter words are taken from *A Lifetime and Fate*, Vasili Grossman's penetrating and powerful novel, which only reached the public forty years after it was written. Yes, that period of time loved only those to whom it had given birth. Nevertheless, the best of my countrymen, theatre people among them, hoped in their hearts for a spiritual rebirth and kept the same hope alive in the people. Despite bureaucratic commands and even reprisals, they were working at shaping social conditions for future changes. The 20th Congress of the CPSU initiated the exposure of Stalin's personality cult. The procedure was hindered in all possible ways, but not stopped.

And then came the 27th Party Congress. Its documents contain a thorough and detailed programme of democratic transformations. Needless to say, it was eagerly and ardently received. In the sphere of art, the changes started in the spring of 1985 found their earliest and most active reflection in the theatre. *A Silver Wedding*, *Dictatorship of Conscience* and

169

Speak Up – plays staged during that theatrical season – raised civic problems that even a year before would have been impossible to imagine on our stage.

Of course, theatre workers weren't the only ones ready to face the epoch. Perestroika did not spring up in a vacuum. It had been ripening within the people and stirred up the whole society. An impetuous process has started, very interesting, contradictory, but purifying. Complex and often painful problems hushed up for years have been brought up for discussion. These problems are now being solved. The very atmosphere has changed; we can breathe more freely. We are undergoing purification by truth. Our consciousness is being liberated, the people are becoming more active. Morning and evening there are queues at newspaper stands. People impatiently await the latest issues of magazine. 'Have you read this?' – the question is often asked even before people greet each other. All these things are tokens of change, of our awakening from the state of apathy, indifference and paralysis in which our society was submerged. In other words, things have begun to move.

Such movement has been slow, because alterations are taking place not only in the economic sphere but in public awareness, in the human soul. To my mind, it is here that the main frontline of perestroika and, consequently, the main theatrical frontline run.

A new way of thinking, consistently called for by Lenin and started recently, is a very difficult thing to acquire. For years our people were kept in a state of submission. The psychology of 'cogs in the wheel' was cultivated. As a result, many people grew used to not thinking at all, confining themselves to philistine satisfaction of daily needs. Withdrawal from social life seems to be our most serious problem. In fact, what has been going on is a call to the people to participate in the creative process and re-establish the moral principles initially inherent in our social structure. This is a call to them, through democratization and glasnost, through respect for the value and dignity of the individual, to return to the source of the great river of life, which from time to time grew shallow and some-times dried up altogether.

What can theatre, literature, or art in general do under these conditions? We are not in a position to introduce trans-formations directly, but we can do a great deal. We can help a man to get rid of fear and stand tall, support him in his search for his place in life. Make him think. I should even say: warn him and arm him with hatred of alien things, of any-thing that hinders moral purification and onward movement. This can be done only by art, and it is in this sphere that I see the most important role for art today.

There has been an intense struggle. The party has been overcoming considerable resistance to its new course. Mikhail Gorbachev in his book *Perestroika and the New Thinking* wrote: 'Revolution as we interpret it is always a creative process; but, of course, it is also a breaking up . . . In the same way peres-troika means the determined breaking up of the established obstacles for social and economic development, of the obsol-ete rules for the management of the economy, of dogmatic stereotypes. Perestroika touches upon the interests of many, of the whole society. And it goes without saying that breaking things up often leads to conflicts and to acute confrontations between the obsolete and the new. Of course, there are no bombs exploded and no guns shooting. But there is an oppo-sition of concrete participants in the braking mechanism . . . We have no political opposition, but that does not mean there is no struggle with those who do not accept perestroika for various reasons.'[1]

There are people who would like to use stereotypes as a cover, calling them 'adherence to traditions'. There are others who are simply afraid of the winds of change because of the real danger of losing their privileges. There is one more side to our problems – a liking for all things established, inertia and conservatism, which, unfortunately, are so typical of human nature.

I am especially worried by the position of those who think that glasnost inevitably leads to anarchy and chaos. What is the essence of the struggle of the supporters and the opponents of

[1] M. Gorbachev, *Perestroika and the New Thinking*, Politizdat, 1987, p. 49.

perestroika? The opponents do not want to deviate from the commonplace patterns, from the very dogmas that are the direct reason for the bitter situation our economy, culture and morality are now in. That was the reason for the debate in our press about an article proclaiming that one should love one's country and, because of that love, distinguish between 'useful' and 'harmful' glasnost.

What an amazing discovery – that one should love one's own country! It is exactly because I love my country that I want it to be worthy of the ideals proclaimed by the revolution. Enthusiasm, spirit, superhuman effort – we have lived through it all, and it cannot be wiped out. We won our victory over fascism in the most cruel and bloody war ever. We have great and indisputable achievements. But our people lived through the ordeal of the 1930s, 1940s and 1950s. We faced the year 1937. Shall we pretend those things never happened?

No, that is not right. To divide glasnost into 'useful' and 'harmful', to be afraid to face our own history, means to be insincere in our love for our country, to mistrust our own people. And if we get to the root of it, this is nothing but the striving of our bureaucracy to drive our life back into the rigid frame of directives, to keep the reins of government in its hands at any price.

The 19th Party Conference, to which I happened to be a delegate, vividly demonstrated how far we have come with glasnost during the years of perestroika. Now we know for sure what we have, because we remember what we had before. I participated in three Party congresses and in many CPSU Central Committee plenary meetings, so I can compare things judging from my own experience and not by hearsay. So I can state that never before during our lifetime has there been such a democratic approach to various aspects of most controversial issues, never before has there been such freedom of expression, such an atmosphere of free discussion. You could see that the people actually believed in the possibility of actively participating in running the country, of influencing all the aspects of our economic, social and cultural development.

The documents adopted by a Party Conference are not

laws, of course. They include general principles which form social and legal acts. They are the launching pad for the Party and the society that are undertaking to build a State based on the rule of law, a State which would guarantee all its citizens conditions and freedoms worthy of true Socialism.

It should be pointed out here that these general principles were a cause for heated arguments, there were a lot of ideas and opinions. There were ten times more people wishing to take the floor than time allowed. Versions and suggestions were discussed, compared, defended and rejected. Not long ago motions of that kind might have been accepted unanimously, which would have been a vote of total indifference . . . The ayes and nays meant true democracy.

Indeed, we must admit that we are only beginning to learn what democracy is about. We are staggering along, haunted by the fear of something bad springing up because of this unknown and unaccustomed openness in our society. The fear found expression at the Party Conference in a debate on the press and the limits of its activities. Calls to limit the activities of the press originated in the obsolete concept that the latter is the mouthpiece of the governing body, which is to judge on its own what is to be criticized and what is to be praised. The situation has changed now, our press has been gradually becoming the spokesman of the people, airing public opinion. This is frightening for the apparatchiks, as they are not used to any control at all. It is therefore only natural for them to defend the positions they have been losing, to accuse the press of giving inaccurate data and making real or possible mistakes in the process of exchanging opinions. The four days of sessions demonstrated this to be one of the most difficult and controversial issues touched upon by almost all of the speakers, myself included. I found it my duty to point out that there could be no development of democracy without wide and courageous participation by the press in critical discussions. And there is no need to be afraid of excessive criticism – what we should be afraid of is excessive boasting fraught with the return of stagnation.

Criticism is the air our social organism needs to breathe in order to continue its present active existence. When one is asleep or completely still, a small dose of air is enough. As soon as one starts hurrying and even running (like revolutionary perestroika), moderate doses of air are no longer enough; there has to be a rich flow of oxygen. The same is true of criticism, of glasnost and the – sometimes merciless – light it brings. In a direct dialogue with Mikhail Gorbachev during my speech at the Conference (which in itself testifies to the open atmosphere of the debate), we arrived at the conclusion that the press is a powerful weapon which should be expertly used in the interests of the people and the Party.

I was most pleased with the speeches that in their analysis of all aspects of our life combined sharp criticism and progressive ideas. The people who know what to do and how to do it are actually the foremen of perestroika, its most valuable possession. There are such people as Kabaidze, a machine-builder from Ivanovo, Iduck, a Chuvash kolkhoz chairman, Melnikov, a party worker from the Komi Republic. Their speeches reflect their own personal experience, certainly not a bed of roses, their readiness to defend their principles and ideas, and their sincere emotions. All the speeches of the representatives of the working class may serve as a real lesson for the cultural workers, and especially for those of our writers who allowed themselves an internecine dissension, mutual complaints and accusations, which found especially acute expression in the speech of Yu. Bondarev, one of our writers. The working people demonstrated at the Conference their ability to look into the heart of the problems – not just economic problems or the problems of production, but moral and social issues concerning the freedom of the individual, the freedom of creative work, the relationship between the individual and the society. They have put forward many concrete suggestions which may enrich our social atmosphere and enhance the development of perestroika.

The end of the Conference seemed to me to be rather significant in that the emotions and spontaneous, laconic speeches were somehow reminiscent of the revolutionary years. Yes, it was a real struggle, but not against each other; it was a struggle for the truth to emerge in the battle of opinions.

Truth is our most powerful weapon. There cannot be too

much of it. There can only be too many lies. It is dangerous
to forget that lies giving birth to 'blank spaces' in history bring
about blank spaces in the culture of the society,
and both taken together lead to blank spaces in the moral
climate of society.

Perestroika means fundamental restructuring, not just pol-
ishing things up or adding mere trifles. We have our reasons
for such fundamental changes. Had we really achieved what
we wanted, why should it have to be redone?

Everybody has to start perestroika with himself. And this is
extremely difficult. We have lived through uneasy years
deeply engraved in our destinies. We could be shut up,
deprived of any possibility of discussing grievances. We could
not publish what we wanted, we were deprived of our favourite work and thus of a creative life. We could be bribed with
prizes and privileges. And we grew quiet and tame and obedi-
ent. But we could not be deceived. We felt how false were the
elevated words of triumph and intentional understatements,
loud promises and studied cheerfulness. We understood
everything; the way we behaved is another matter, a matter
of conscience. But those who have accepted the ideas of perestroika as their own, as their own unique destiny, are no longer
afraid to look back.

Now is the time for discovering ourselves anew. And while
performing that demanding task we penetrate deeper and
deeper into Lenin's ideas and projects. This is where there is
no end to the work for those in the cultural sphere.

A vast theatre and cinema eulogy to Lenin has been created
in our time. What was dominant there? Some philistine, senti-
mental and tender feeling for 'an extremely nice man': so
simple, so modest, so full of attention to people. But for goodness sake, these are features characteristic of any educated
person. Does that mean that it is owing to these features that
Lenin became the leader of the Revolution and turned the
whole country upside down?

But as long as history itself was depersonalized and distorted, the image of the leader was totally deprived of individuality. It was thought that he had ready answers for all

occasions, never had any doubts and never had to search for answers. But that is not true. He also had to seek answers. It was a tortuous process of pondering over a new social formation never seen before. That was the extremely intense life of a man in constant search for ways out of ever more intricate situations not foreseen by any theory.

I assert that as a man who has had the good fortune of coming into contact with the image of Lenin three times. The first occasion was long ago, in the play *A Man with a Gun* at the Vakhtangov Theatre. The second was twenty years ago when we were working on the TV serial *Sketches for the Portrait of Lenin* by Mikhail Shatrov (by the way, this work, after having spent twenty years on the shelf, was shown on television for the first time a year ago and brought us a vast and appreciative correspondence from the audience). And, finally, there was my role in Mikhail Shatrov's play *The Brest Peace Treaty*. This play, too, had been awaiting its time to shine for about twenty years. Not long ago it was staged at our theatre by Robert Sturua, a Georgian producer.

Working with that wonderful master, a man with an incredible feel for the theatre's power and ability to influence, we got deeply involved not so much in a historical digression as in an attempt to compare the events of 1918 with the present moment.

Let me remind you of the facts. The year is 1918, the fourth year of World War I in Europe. Russia has been drawn into the war, and in addition there is a civil war brewing within. Lenin sees that the country has to get out of the war at any cost. The people are demanding peace, it is needed to save the revolution. Lenin's idea is to conclude a peace treaty with Germany. The treaty conditions laid down in the German ultimatum are not just hard, they are shackling. The decision to accept the Brest Peace Treaty becomes one of the worst moments in Lenin's life, a moment when circumstances turn out to be more powerful than the previous aims. Lenin puts the question of the treaty to the vote in the Central Committee and . . . finds himself outvoted. Under such circumstances what can be done by a man who knows he is right, that it is a matter of life and death for the revolution, and yet doesn't allow himself to use power in order to push his decision through?

The producer of the play and myself regard this as one of the most radical problems for democracy. This is actually what the play is about. And also about making a compromise for the sake of achieving peace. The plot of the play offers rich food for thought. The problem is that Lenin wants a peace treaty with a bourgeois State. The very idea seems a retreat, a step backwards. But the point is that Lenin's remarkable foresight was not his only unique quality. His was a mighty personality, a great mind endowed with both strategic and tactical flexibility, a mind devoid of the slightest traces of dogmatism.

We can sense the modern spirit of *The Brest Peace Treaty* in the realistic, sober and bold position of a political leader who faced life courageously without deceiving himself in any way. He never tried to soothe or lull. Gorky wrote about Lenin's love for people rather than ideas, about his bending and breaking ideas when it was in the interests of the people to do so. Something similar is happening now.

I would like to point out that the film *Sketches for the Portrait of Lenin* is just as pointed and the play *The Brest Peace Treaty* just as relevant now as they were twenty years ago. All that was needed then is needed now: consolidation of efforts, striving for truth, and struggle, an uncompromising struggle with dogmatism, revolutionary phrases, formalism, bureaucratic oppression and everything that has been deposited on our life.

Stanislavsky once said that the theatre is not aware of the present. The stage is a transition from the past to the future. While working on *The Brest Peace Treaty* we did our best to give that transition some milestones.

Earlier I mentioned that our theatre business had accumulated a lot of problems. The years of administrative tutelage have amassed such heaps of them that now we often have no idea what to start with. By 'we' I mean all those people whose official or moral duty it is to promote the development of our culture. And first and foremost I mean those people who are

177

at the head of our unions of theatre workers. These unions represent a whole system of public associations which includes the USSR Union of Theatre Workers and the fifteen unions in the Soviet Republics.

The very fact that such unions have sprung up and represent our theatre public is the direct result of perestroika. At the present moment our society has the historic task of handing some of the functions of State administration over to people's self-government. These creative unions, with their active support of perestroika, are meant to be one of the frameworks of such self-government.

Nevertheless, one should not forget that the restructuring of our theatre business, in fact the whole transition, is a process that changes as it goes. The trouble is that local cultural bodies accustomed to arbitrary rule and administrative pressure are often not ready to accept the new arrangement. There is also another problem. Our theatre world is passing through a period of truly revolutionary renovation – it is getting rid of administrative tutelage and is acquiring the right to handle independently not only creative tasks but, more and more often, economic problems too. While trying to do this, we discovered that we lack people ready to shoulder responsibility. That is only natural. We have not brought up such people; competence and creative independence did not find any encouragement. Now we are looking for such people, but there are not very many people like that here – neither in general nor in the theatre world in particular.

However, Soviet theatre is seething with new ideas. We are looking for new organizational forms, new economic procedures. We have started a many-sided economic experiment, with eighty-two theatres participating; various models of theatre organization are being tried on for size. A multitude of different youth societies, small theatres and studios are appearing – more than two hundred recently in Moscow alone. Under the wing of the Union of Theatre Workers so-called 'workshops' for theatre youth have sprung up. They are intended to help young and talented youth theatrical groups to perfect their art, with this creative Union covering the costs.

Of course, we have our sore points. Those of our theatre companies which have been participating in the experiment are starting to breathe freely, they are trying to solve their economic and repertoire policy independently. But alongside them, sometimes even in one and the same town, routine and hack work often prevail, and people often submit to outside pressure. Dozens of theatres are dragging out a miserable existence, nobody needs them – neither their own towns nor the areas where they go on tour. Their theatres are usually empty, their repertoire sometimes unthinkable. The government subsidizes such theatres, but with such a state of affairs this is a sheer waste. And what is even worse, working at such theatres, if I may use the term, cripples both the creators and those in the audience for whom these theatres offer their first acquaintance with the stage.

Quarrels are ablaze in theatres. Some of them have even begun to regard the Union and its leadership as a 'rapid-reaction force' or emergency fire brigade. And we do react, we rush to every call, we try to understand, to help, to set things right. But what do we find in the end? A situation typical of our theatrical life. I mean the forceful linkage of creative people, who for various reasons can no longer work together.

The disease has been spreading. One of the reasons for it is as follows: once we had our established theatre as the only model. It was a theatre with a stable repertoire, a long-term programme and a prominent producer as its leader. The pattern itself really is good, you can't deny it. But what about the dozens and hundreds of theatres lacking a stable programme because for years at a time they not only had no prominent producers as leaders but had to do without any professional producer at all? Such theatres opened not as a result of the creative effort of a talented person but because somebody upstairs wanted it that way. Leading producers were sent out to such theatres, but they did not know the town or the specifics of the company they were to run. Moreover, mediocre people were promoted at the expense of gifted but 'bothersome' people who were impertinent and tended to disobey.

Today we are pondering over the developmental strategy

179

of our whole theatre system. What seems to be most important? First of all, we are to give up uniformity. Our theatre must have a variety of forms. It goes without saying that we are to preserve the best of what has been accumulated over the years. But it is evident that we need different types of theatre: we must have a flexible system of creating theatre companies and an equally flexible and fearless system of dismissing or regrouping those companies which have exhausted their creative energy.

We can take different approaches. Some towns may have theatres existing as a kind of Socialist theatrical enterprise; in other towns actors may form associations. A theatre with an obvious leader must entrust him or her with its artistic policy; if there is no evident leader, a group of actors may conclude an agreement with a producer for a single play. A theatre may be run not only by a producer, but by a playwright, a critic, an actor. The only obligatory conditions are the candidate's devotion to the theatre, his competence and his ability to lead people.

The way I see it, much attention should be paid to the relationship between the theatre and its home town. Relations could be regulated by a special agreement fixing their mutual obligations. At the same time, a variety of social and economic problems should be solved in such a way as to restore the feeling both in the actor and in the theatre that this profession is dangerous, a feeling that provides no guarantees of a quiet life. In particular, I have in mind temporary contracts instead of lifetime hiring, which has been the practice until now. The right of creative work should be provided – but there should be an equal right to free art of people who are not willing to perfect their own professional skills.

The situation with producers and playwrights is particularly problematic. We trained many producers, but we trained them badly. The very idea of 'mass production' in such an area seems to me absurd, though in the general flow one continues to come across talented people. What is the situation like now and what do I hope for? People of my generation go on working, but we trail behind us the lives we have lived. This makes us less mobile, unable to answer many ques-

tions. A whole generation of forty-year-olds should be helping us. They should be breaking the mould, promoting new
approaches. But, as I said earlier, they are few and far
between. The long years of stagnation, suppressing everything individual and personal, have led to a vacuum. But a
younger generation has been growing, a generation with
quite a different way of thinking, allowing them to take a
detached view of our mistakes and our attempts to find a way.
I am sure that guided by our search they will have their own
say on the stage.

As far as our drama is concerned, I set my hopes on the so-
called 'new wave'. There have appeared such new names on
the playbills as Zlotnikov, Galin, Harrot, Slavkin, Petrushev-
skaya . . . These are playwrights who are occupied with comprehending the human soul and human motives and deeds
at the 'molecular level': they are trying to see in the molecule
the general picture, whereas our generation looked at things
from a general point of view, thus very often losing sight
of the human personality, the human essence, in our often
declarative plays and performances. When I look down from
my seventh-floor apartment at the people going to and fro, I
can't distinguish individuals in the crowd – yet the crowd consists of individuals. One can portray a crowd, or someone
from the crowd, and while penetrating into his inner world
perceive the whole world. Today, the process of perceiving
the microworld is more interesting for the actor and more
useful and important for society. Because, no matter how
global our problems are, they should not be allowed to push
the human face into the background.

I am sure that for us, the people of the theatre, perestroika
will turn into a mere waste of time and effort if it does not
lead us to the one result that matters. Namely, the radical
restructuring of our theatre through varied creative efforts
and new organizational forms, and the birth of all the necessary conditions, even unheard-of ones, for mediocrity to
retreat and make room for talent.

Our epoch has offered up great opportunities. After the
ruinous atmosphere of stagnation we are now breathing the

crisp air of *Sturm und Drang*, of passionate and pointed discussions.

The most urgent aspects of our life, our way of thinking and our self-awareness, have been put on the agenda.

Some of our former compatriots and colleagues demand proof that perestroika is not for show but for real. And some people try to frighten us with talk of glasnost lighting the way to the abyss.

I would like to point out that glasnost hasn't yet led anybody to catastrophe, whereas silence is a quick way over the edge. We have had that bitter experience. As to the proofs demanded, we can offer them only to ourselves. And each of us will be responsible. It has become clear that the process of democratization is not going to be smooth. 'Democracy comes ringed by storms', the famous Russian poet, Alexander Blok, said. And this is true, indeed. It is much easier to live without responsibility than to answer for one's actions and take risks. But we have no choice – neither the country as a whole nor any of us who live here.

I mentioned above that in the past year I visited the USA three times. I met American theatre workers and saw twelve plays staged in different towns. I also participated in the Chatoqua meeting between the Soviet and the American delegations and was a member of the Soviet delegation at the Washington Summit. Of course, I could not see everything – but what I saw was a holiday for the soul. The elegant Ronald Reagan, the embodiment of an eternal American respectability: the temperamental Mikhail Gorbachev, whose energy springs from his desire to overcome the stereotypes of hostility, animosity and fear. I watched the Soviet leader leaving his car and talking to Americans and being greeted by them. The scene was both symbolic and instructive. It turns out that we are equally worried about the future: that, even despite serious differences of opinion, it is possible to come to an agreement if we assume there is enough room on the globe for everybody and regard the idea as the only possible alternative to a confrontation that would threaten everybody with a nuclear holocaust.

Long ago, during my childhood spent in a beautiful, blessed spot (though, as I know, for many people the image of Siberia is of a place extremely cold and terribly frightening), the rest of the world seemed to me remote, unreachable and great. And great it is, indeed. But as we now realize, it is interdependent and therefore small – so small indeed that we hold the fate of our planet in our hands as well as our own fate. And it is precisely because we understand this that we are forced to take a serious look at each other, not to be afraid as we have been nor frighten each other as we have done. All of us live, suffer, hope in the same way. Human behaviour does not differ.

The theatre is the mirror of life. The American theatre finds itself in the same position as ours. A storm of information is pouring in on us, and we are in no position immediately to process what is going on into the images of art, we cannot answer immediately all questions asked by life itself. We have our perestroika to ask questions about, Americans ask about the problems of their modern society.

To my great joy, we now have a chance to interact in developing our theatre worlds. The gates have opened, not just for cultural exchange *per se*, but for exchange of experience, efforts, ideas. And I must say that our mutual interest is sincere.

Four delegations of American theatre workers have visited the Soviet Union. They have found something of use for them, and we in our journeys have discovered things for ourselves. Take, for example, one problem. Our theatre system was initially built on the idea of an established theatre subsidized by the State, whereas the American theatre is based on the contract system. We are now trying to introduce this system in our theatre because our subsidy system has offered too much stability and too little dynamic development. American actors, in their turn, are dreaming of greater stability, of more solid guarantees of future work. So both sides can learn from and enrich each other.

During their visits to our country our American colleagues discovered much for themselves. It is ironic that despite the massive flow of information, Americans know so little about us. As a rule, their ideas of our life and work are vague, prejudiced, or narrowly focused. (Indeed, the same is true of our vision of America.) It turns out that cultural exchange has more than professional value. It allows people to get acquainted with the life of another people. And then it becomes evident that things are much more complicated, much more logical and much simpler than they seemed from a distance. I visited Chatoqua and New York, Chatoqua is a small cosy town on the shore of a picturesque lake. There couldn't be a more peaceful place in the world. And then there is New York, a veritable Sodom and Gomorrah. So what is America like, the true America? It is somewhere between the two extremes . . .

The theatrical community in Houston is already familiar with the work of our producers Galina Volchek and the late Anatoli Efros. Now in Moscow, an American producer is working on a play at the Pushkin Theatre. It has been agreed that in the near future the Lithuanian Youth Theatre will perform in Houston and a Houston theatre will come to Lithuania. For the 125th anniversary of Konstantin Stanislavsky's birth, we have been preparing an exhibition dedicated to the great theatre reformer, who is known and appreciated in the theatre world of America. This exhibition is to be on in America for three years.

Joint conferences, symposia, and exchange of delegations, producers, plays and exhibitions – all that is covered by the Soviet–American agreement which is to be implemented in the years to come. No doubt, it will be of mutual benefit – both for the theatre and for mutual understanding and peace.

An English philosopher said that the greatest mistake is made by him who does nothing because he believes he cannot do very much. We have started out on a path which, I hope, will allow us to avoid that mistake.

Fyodor M. Burlatsky

Fyodor Burlatsky was one of the journalists dismissed for the publication of articles on theatre problems in *Komsomolskaya Pravda* in 1967 which sharply and painfully signalled the advent of the period of stagnation and repressive administration. At that time Burlatsky was on the staff of *Pravda* and had even participated in the work of the CPSU Central Committee. The end of the 'thaw' made some critics betray their ideals of justice and become time-servers – whereas others continued their critical analysis of the events and phenomena that had resulted in stagnation, despite the fact that they were working in isolation and deprived of the chance to publish. His own bitter first-hand experience and his knowledge of political personalities and the mainsprings and levers of power have enabled Burlatsky to publish significant essays, including political profiles of statesmen and party leaders, and to discuss expertly ways of implementing democratization. He is also a *Literaturnaya Gazeta* (Literary Gazette) reviewer.

Khrushchev, Andropov, Brezhnev: The Issue of Political Leadership

FYODOR M. BURLATSKY

How does the leader of our country come to power? What kind of policy will he pursue? What methods will he use? These are key issues in the process of democratization of the USSR. There have been no substantial changes in our political system since the time of the Revolution. But we have seen policy and ideology vary considerably – from Lenin to Stalin, from Stalin to Khrushchev, from Khrushchev to Brezhnev, from Brezhnev to Andropov. No matter which State position he occupies, the leader of the Communist Party has become the leader of the country. It has taken about five years for a new Party leader, irrespective of the course he has taken, to become dominant; for Stalin it was the period 1924–9, for Khrushchev 1953–9 and for Brezhnev 1964–9. Each time the struggle of the country's leader for authority has brought the Party and the State into a feverish condition and resulted in either hasty unilateral decisions or petrified political power.

I am going to illustrate my point mostly by discussing the era of Khrushchev, as I had a chance to observe the leader personally while working under Yuri Andropov in the apparatus of the Central Committee as an adviser and speech-writer.

The 1950s/1960s period of thaw was one of the most important and intricate in our history. Important because it foreshadowed the restructuring now under way in our country, and the current expansion of the democratic process. Intricate because it concerned a decade which was at first described as 'glorious' and then condemned as a period of 'voluntarism' and 'subjectivism'. It included the 20th Party Congress of 1956 and the 22nd Party Congress of 1961 where sharp political clashes reflected the change of direction. Under Nikita Sergeyevich Khrushchev the first steps were taken to revive Lenin's principles and purify the ideals of Socialism. It was then that the transition began from cold war to peaceful co-existence, and a window on the contemporary world was opened anew. At this major turning-point in history, society took a deep breath of the air of renewal and choked . . . either from too much oxygen or from too little.

How could it happen that after Stalin it was Khrushchev who came to power? Stalin seemed to have done everything possible to purge the Party of any opponents – real and imaginary, right and left. In the 1950s one of his aphoristic phrases became common parlance: 'There is a person, there is a problem; no person, no problem.' As a result, only the most seemingly loyal and dependable remained alive. How, then, did Stalin fail to spot in Khrushchev the man who would bury his cult?

In his later years, not long before his death, Stalin disgraced Molotov and Mikoyan, preparing for them the same fate as had befallen other leaders exterminated with their aid and support. The creation in 1952, at the 19th Congress, of the Presidium of the CPSU Central Committee which replaced the narrower circle of the Politburo, was a move towards getting rid of the next generation of overstaying comrades. But Stalin – and here is the paradox! – did not include Khrushchev in the line-up.

Was this the blindness of old age? Hardly. That brilliant exposer of tyranny Nicolo Machiavelli once remarked: 'Brutus would have become Caesar, had he feigned to be a fool.' One feels that Khrushchev in some way managed to pass himself off as an ideal subordinate, lacking personal ambition, and therefore a reliable instrument of another's will. The story goes that during the last vigil at the dacha in Kuntsevo which had been Stalin's home for the past thirty years, Khrushchev tap-danced a Ukrainian gopak. He wore an ornamented Ukrainian blouse and acted the jolly, swaggering

Cossack boy, one far removed from any claim to power. But clearly even then protest was welling up inside Khrushchev. And it spurted out the day after Stalin died.

Khrushchev came to power not by accident but rather by coincidence. It was no accident in the sense that he expressed the line within the Party which, in other circumstances and probably in another way, had been represented by such in many ways dissimilar figures as Dzerzhinsky, Bukharin, Rykov, Rudzutak and Kirov. Those were the proponents of the New Economic Policy, of democratization, the opponents of forceful measures in industry and agriculture, and particularly culture. Despite the cruel Stalinist repression, that trend never died. In this sense Khrushchev's advent to power was to be anticipated.

But certainly there was a large element of coincidence. If Malenkov had clashed with Beria, and if the 'Stalinist guard' had closed ranks in 1953 rather than June 1957, Khrushchev would not have been leader. Our history could then have taken a very different course.

Yet history made the right choice. Here was an answer to the real problems of our country. Our half-destroyed countryside, technically backward industry, acute shortage of housing, low living standards, millions of prisoners and isolation from the outside world all required a new line and radical reforms. And Khrushchev came precisely thus – as the nation's hope.

And so we were captivated by the 20th CPSU Congress. How did Khrushchev dare to make his report about Stalin, knowing that the overwhelming majority of delegates would be against its revelations? How did he summon up so much courage and assurance of its final success? This was one of those most rare instances in history when a political leader has risked his personal power and even his life for the sake of over-riding public interests. Among the post-Stalin leaders there was no other with the resolve to make a report about the personality cult. Khrushchev, and Khrushchev alone, was capable of doing it – boldly, emotionally, and in many respects unthinkingly. It took Khrushchev's reckless desperation to overcome the fear of change and decide on such a step. His personal evaluation of that moment, an evaluation made when he met foreign guests, is interesting:

I am often asked how it was that I decided to make that report at the 20th Congress. So many years we believed in that person! Elevated him. Created a cult. And suddenly such a risk . . . So, let me tell you a story I remember from childhood, from the time I was learning to read. There was a book named *Reading and Reciting*, which contained a lot of interesting stories. Among them there was a story by somebody whose name has escaped my memory now. It was about some political activists imprisoned in Tsarist times. There were Socialist-Revolutionaries, Bolsheviks and Mensheviks among them. And there was an old shoemaker in the cell named Yankel, who was there by chance. Well, they were electing the cell chief. Each party was putting forward its own candidate. There was a great row. What was to be done? And then somebody proposed to elect Yankel, a harmless person, no member of any party. They laughed at first, but then agreed. So Yankel became the cell chief. Later on it so happened that all of them decided to escape from the prison. They started digging a tunnel. Eventually the tunnel was complete. And then they started arguing as to who was going to be the first to use it. What if the prison authorities had learned about it and were waiting at its other end with guns ready? The first down the tunnel might be the first to die, then. Some of the Socialist-Revolutionaries were proposed, and they, in their turn, proposed Bolsheviks. That very moment old Yankel rose and said: 'Since you've made me your cell chief, who can be the first but me?'

And this is how I felt at the Congress. Since I was elected leader, I had to, I had no other choice but to speak the truth, like old Yankel the shoemaker, no matter what it cost me and no matter how much risk I was running. Lenin taught us in his time that a party which does not fear the truth will never perish. We derived lessons from the past and wanted other fraternal parties to derive such lessons too . . . Then our common victory would be assured.

Of course, it was more than just a matter of the sense of duty which the First Secretary mentioned. I on several occasions heard Khrushchev reminiscing about Stalin. Those were lengthy, sometimes hours-long, reflections-cum-monologues, as if he were having a conversation with himself, with his conscience. He had been deeply wounded by Stalinism. On these occasions everything boiled up: a mystical fear of Stalin who was capable of destroying any person for one false step, gesture, or glance; horror at the innocent blood which had been shed; a sense of personal guilt; and the protest which had been building up for decades and was now screaming to get out, like steam inside a boiler . . . Characteristic is a speech that he made at a 1960 Kremlin banquet for the participants in a conference of representatives of Communist and workers' parties.

At that time he was over 60 but he looked very strong, active and even mischievously gay. The broad double-chinned face, the huge, bold skull, the big snub-nose and the jutting ears were those of a peasant from a mid-Russian village. That impression of a simple country background was intensified by the paunch, and long arms that were always gesticulating. Only his eyes, small, grey-blue, sharp eyes which shone with kindness, authority and anger, revealed him as a deeply political person who went through fire, water and copper pipes and was ready for the sharpest turn of events.

That is how I saw him then and how I remember him. But most of all I was impressed by his words. What I heard then I also heard at least twice in a different setting, more intimate, with just a few people present. The amazing thing was that he retold the story almost word for word.

When Stalin died, we members of the leadership of the Central Committee went to the nearby dacha [country house] at Kuntsevo. He was lying in the divan and there were no doctors around him. In the last months of his life Stalin rarely used doctors, fearing them. Maybe Beria scared him or maybe he himself believed that doctors would weave some plot against him and the other leaders. He used then a major from his guard who had once been a veterinary's assistant. It was he who phoned to say Stalin was dead . . .

We stood there by the corpse, almost not talking among ourselves, each thinking of his own. Then we began to disperse. We got into cars in twos. Off went Malenkov and Beria first, then Molotov and Kaganovich. At this point Mikoyan said to me: 'Beria is off to Moscow to assume power.' And I said to him: 'While that bugger's still around, none of us can feel safe.' And it firmly registered in my mind that Beria had to go first. But how was I to talk to the other leaders about this?

Some time passed and I began to go around the members of the Presidium one by one. The most dangerous chat was with Malenkov, for he and Lavrenty Beria were pals. I went to see him and said, 'It looks like this: while that man's loose and holds the security forces in his hands, all of us have our hands tied. And nobody knows what trick he is capable of pulling at any moment. Look,' I said, 'he has brought special divisions up to Moscow.'

And I have to give Malenkov his due – in this matter he supported me, overcoming his personal feelings. He himself clearly feared his pal. And Malenkov then was Chairman of the Council of Ministers and led the sessions of the Presidium of the Central Committee. In other words, he had something to lose, but at the end of our conversation he said: 'All right, true, this cannot be avoided. Only it has to be done in such a way that it doesn't blow up in our faces.'

Then I went to Voroshilov. Klim Efremovich is here, he remembers. I had to reason with him for a very long time. He was very worried that it might blow up in our faces . . . Am I right, Klim?

Voroshilov was sitting nearby. 'Right,' he boomed. He was red in the face, either from embarrassment or from too much to drink.

'If only there is no war,' he added, irrelevantly.

'Well, war is another matter,' Krushchev replied.

Next I went to Kaganovich and laid it all out, and he asked: 'On whose side are the majority? Who stands for whom?

Will there not be some backing him?' When I told him about the rest, he too agreed.

And so I came to the session in the Kremlin. Everybody took a seat and no Beria. Well, I thought, he found out. This is the end for us. Nobody can tell where we'll be tomorrow. But in he came with a briefcase in his hands. I understood right away what he had there! But I too had something stored up for such an eventuality . . .

Here the narrator patted the right pocket of his broad jacket and continued:

Beria sat down, slumped back and asked: 'Well, what's the agenda today? Why have we gathered so suddenly?' I nudged Malenkov with my foot and whispered: 'Open the session and give me the floor.' Malenkov went pale and I saw that he could not open his mouth. So up I jumped myself and said: 'There is one question on the agenda: the anti-Party, divisive activities of agent of imperialism Beria. There is a proposal to remove him from the Presidium, from the Central Committee, to exclude him from the Party and to have him courtmartialled. Who is in favour?'

And I was the first to raise my hand. The others followed suit. Beria went all green and reached for his briefcase. I went zap! with my hand and grabbed it. 'Are you joking?' I say. 'Cut it out!' And I press the button myself. In run two officers from the Moskalenko military garrison. (I had arranged this with them beforehand.) I order them: 'Arrest this vermin, this traitor, and take him away where he deserves.'

At this point a terrible smell pervaded the room. Beria had soiled his pants . . . Yet he had always been so brave about grabbing others by the throat and lining them up against the wall. Well, the rest you know . . .

Later I learned that Khrushchev was crafty about one thing: he did not mention the role of Zhukov in Beria's arrest and, as we shall see later, he had his reasons. At this point in his story he took up a glass:

So, then, I want to propose a toast to these events never

being repeated anywhere. We ourselves washed away that dirty stain and we will make certain such things never happen again. I would like to assure you, comrades, that such things never *will* happen again and we shall all move forward together to the summits of Communism!

In general, Khrushchev was quite self-assured, always at ease and even boisterous. When he started talking, nobody, not even himself, knew what might come out. His speech was always deeply emotional and passionate. He found some difficulty in coping with this himself. In a way it was a part of his personality, but he sometimes used it for political purposes. He fired the imagination by using words which, had they been put on paper, would have made the Party boil with anger. But he managed to get away with these excesses as they were usually put down to emotion.

I remember a speech he made at a conference of the Central Committee not long before his fall. He was speaking about Mikhail Suslov who was also present. 'Look,' – he indicated Suslov – 'they are writing in the West about Suslov being an inveterate Stalinist and dogmatist who is awaiting a chance of doing away with Khrushchev. They are right, aren't they, Mikhail Alexandrovich?' And the man sat there with his eyes cast down, listening meekly to the charge. He got what he wanted in the end, too, though the conspiracy against Khrushchev was headed not by him but by Alexander Shelepin who had been supported by Khrushchev through a series of promotions. And Shelepin, instead of being grateful, planned to become leader himself.

Thirst for innovation and an active personality were Krushchev's distinguishing characteristics. He thought up a wide-scale programme for restoring agriculture and had regional and territorial economic councils set up throughout the country. He stimulated intensive housing construction and technical reconstruction of industry. He released the peasantry from collective-farm bondage by introducing a passport system for them, and raised pay for the low-income bracket. The new Party Programme, renovation of major laws, the changed principles towards the style of relations with the West, and even the famous corn saga all reflected his search for originality, his indefatigable sociability. Khrushchev's era was spiritual renaissance incarnate, though the process was obviously marred by inherited flaws in the system, was full of contradictions and often led nowhere.

It was Khrushchev who aimed to provide constitutional guarantees against relapses into the personality cult. He waged an uncompromising war for the purpose both inside the country and on the international scene, without taking into account the potential complications in relations with other Socialist countries.

Khrushchev attached principal significance to the ideological side of things, the need thoroughly to expose the personality cult and to tell the truth about the crimes of the 1930s and other periods. But this very truth, alas, was a half-measure, incomplete. From the outset Khrushchev ran up against the problem of personal responsibility, since many in the Party knew his role in the persecution of cadres both in the Ukraine and in the Moscow Party organization. Withholding the truth about himself forced him to withhold part of the truth about the others. Hence his information about the responsibility of various public figures, not to mention the liability of Stalin himself, for the crimes perpetrated was of a lopsided and frequently ambiguous nature. It was dependent on the political climate. For example, when exposing Molotov and Kaganovich at the 22nd Congress for persecutions during the 1930s, Khrushchev kept silent about the role of Mikoyan who subsequently became a reliable ally. When speaking of the 1930s, Khrushchev carefully avoided referring to the period of collectivization, as he had been personally implicated in the extremes of that time.

Khrushchev wanted every member of the Presidium of the Central Committee to reflect his views on the Stalin cult. At his bidding, each representative of the leadership who spoke at the 22nd Congress was to define his own position on the issue. But after the Congress it transpired that many of those who had made a great show of opposing the personality cult quickly reviewed their positions and reverted to their former attitude.

The matter of guarantees against any repetition of the personality cult and of its negative consequences occupied a major place when the Party Programme was drafted. I happened to participate in that work. I remember particularly how the note was prepared for the Presidium of the Communist Party's Central Committee to pass over from dictatorship of the proletariat to all-national dictatorship, which bore major import because the stereotype of dictatorship of the proletariat was used in the 1930s as a ground for the repression. The note was sent by O. V. Kuusinen and evoked quite literally uproar among many of the leaders. I was sitting in Kuusinen's office when one of the leaders ranted over the phone at him: 'How dare you attack dictatorship of the proletariat, the holy of holies of Leninism!'

It was only thanks to Khrushchev's energetic support that this idea was included in the Party programme.

One of the practical conclusions from the past was a need for interchangeability of personnel. This issue evoked the greatest number of arguments. The idea of rotating cadres, which emanated from the First Secretary himself, suffered a number of changes. About a dozen formulas for adequacy were examined. Khrushchev wanted to create at least some guarantees against excessive concentration of power in one pair of hands, against leaders overstaying their time, and against senility at all levels from grass roots to the top of the pyramid. With respect to the primary organizations, that did not evoke much dispute. But opinions differed cardinally with respect to rotation of power at the top. On this point Khrushchev, for all his authority, persistence and thrust, was forced to retreat.

The original draft fixed principles under which one could not hold the supreme leadership for more than two terms. That evoked violent protest from the younger section of leaders. They felt it most unjust that the representatives of the older generation, who had already sat out plenty of time, should try to limit the opportunities of the young. The next draft contained three terms in office instead of two, and that version was rejected too. In the final text the whole idea of creating a new procedure for changing cadres was unrecognizable.

On the other side, much was done at that period to provide legislative guarantees against violations of legality. The whole legislative system was reviewed and a start was made on a new constitution which came out later, in the 1970s.

Unfortunately, the laws adopted during this period were also vague. And sound constitutional guarantees against a régime of personal power, and relapses into such, were not enacted either.

Moreover, in a situation where all grovelled and sought to further their own interests, Khrushchev began to detach himself from the other Party leaders, to place himself above them, above the whole Party and the State. The few years from 1960 to 1964 saw a swift evolution in Khrushchev's self-opinion.

A very strange tradition of measuring the authority of a leader by the number of words he utters seems to have originated in Khrushchev's time. There could have been no such tradition in Lenin's time because other members of the government, besides Lenin, very often spoke in public or wrote articles and sometimes even books. As for Stalin, he preferred to speak seldom but on serious occasions, in accordance with the famous quotation from *Boris Godunov* by Pushkin: 'The voice of the Tsar should announce either a great holiday or a great calamity for the people.'

The problem of the guarantee against the régime of personal power met an unsurmountable obstacle – the narrow-mindedness in the sphere of political culture of Khrushchev himself and of that generation of leaders. In many aspects it was an authoritarian-patriarchal culture borrowed from traditional ideas of government within the boundaries of a peasant farm. Paternalism, arbitrary rule, interference in all manner of problems and relations, infallibility of the patriarch, intolerance of other opinions – such were the age-old ideas of power in Russia.

What happened after the June plenary meeting in 1957 was spectacular in this respect. As we all remember, some representatives of the 'Stalin guard' tried to banish Khrushchev from his post on a so-called 'arithmetic majority'. As a result of the voting, the CPSU Central Committee Presidium adopted a decision removing him from the post of First Secretary. But his keenest supporters managed to overthrow the decision. Marshal Zhukov played the major role in the defeat of the Stalinists on this occasion. During the sitting of the Central Committee Presidium he is said to have uttered the historic words: 'The army is against the decision, and not a single tank will move without my order.' In the long run, that statement cost him his political career.

Soon after the June plenary meeting, Khrushchev had Zhukov expelled from membership of the Presidium of the CPSU Central Committee and from the post of USSR Defence Minister. It was done in the traditional manner of that period, when Zhukov was on a trip abroad. He was given no opportunity to argue his case; in the same manner the Party and the people were not given any reasons for the removal of the most outstanding military leader of the Great Patriotic War from the political arena. And the reason for the banishment was traditional again – fear of a strong man.

A known weakness of Khrushchev as a leader also played a part in this. He had long been known as a man who 'preferred shoes worn down at the heels'. Even when working in Kiev and then Moscow, he had been considered a bad judge of character. He always preferred smooth talkers to genuine supporters of his reforms. That was why he surrounded himself with people like Nikolai Podgorny who paid lip-service to him and was ready to do everything he demanded. It was also the reason for his dislike of independent people with strong personalities. Khrushchev was too sure of himself to look for support from others. And that was one cause of his downfall. Those who in their heart of hearts did not share his reformative ideas, and regarded them as a display of his incompetence or even eccentricity, took the first opportunity to get rid of him.

There had been a time when Khrushchev was attracted by the more intelligent section of the apparatus. Take, for instance, his attitude to Dmitry Shepilov whom he promoted to the positions of a Central Committee secretary and Minister of Foreign Affairs. But Shepilov's behaviour at the plenary meeting of the CPSU Central Committee in 1957, when he supported the Stalinists, turned Khrushchev against the intelligentsia for ever.

Khrushchev's hasty manner, his wish to interfere everywhere and to decide everything, were also instrumental in spoiling his relationship with the intelligentsia. He was often a toy in the hands of his advisers and of opponents who were working for his downfall. I remember quite well that his visit to an art exhibition in the Manezh was provoked by a document specially concocted for the occasion. The paper contained almost no information about art, but it quoted true or invented opinions of writers and painters about Khrushchev's personality, referring to him as 'a fool on the throne', 'corn daddy', and 'a wind-bag'. Boiling with anger, Khrushchev went to the Manezh to dress down the painters. In the same manner, his secret opponents provoked him into the incident with Pasternak, made him have Academician Nesmeyanov retired to appease Lysenko, and had him quarrel with many a writer, painter and scientist.

Unfortunately, he was surrounded by advisers who blocked many wise reforms or replaced them with rash, untested organizational measures. This is what happened to the idea of fighting bureaucracy in economic management. The regional and territorial economic councils which replaced the State departments were quickly transformed into red-tape institutions which employed double the State personnel.

Thus the new system of economic relations failed to work out. Everything was done hastily, with many of those in the economic apparatus resisting the reforms and drastic changes because they, personally, were the ones to suffer. Who wanted to leave his long-occupied cosy Moscow study and go to some remote corner of the country?

As ancient wisdom has it, a man has to travel farthest when he does not know where he is going. But his step is uneven if he walks either too quickly or too slowly. That unevenness characterized many of Khrushchev's economic and social reforms.

His economic policy remained the most vulnerable spot. He

saw his major task in the transformation of economic management methods at the apparatus level, i.e. at Gosplan, in his new economic councils and in the Ministries; but he did not understand that thorough structural reforms were necessary to change the living and working conditions of those people who were directly engaged in the production process – the workers, peasants, engineers and scientists.

The situation was even worse when it came to restructuring the system of State management and Party leadership. Who 'fed' Khrushchev the idea of dividing regional Party committees into industrial and agricultural ones? My intuition tells me that it was done with the ill intention of finally undermining his authority among the Party leaders.

Khrushchev was accused of making these mistakes at the October plenary meeting of the CPSU Central Committee in 1964. A strange alliance of political forces had formed there, from those who were in favour of continuing along the course set at the 20th Congress to conservatives and hidden Stalinists – all of them united against the leader who had promoted 'to the top' most of their number. Later developments left no doubt that Khrushchev had been displaced not so much because of his voluntary and autocratic actions but because of his insatiable thirst for reform. The slogan of 'stability' put forward by his successors turned out later to be a long drag on reforms which were becoming more and more urgent. The very word 'reform', as well as any mention of the 20th Congress, became dangerous and cost many their political careers.

Time has not dispelled the numerous myths about Khrushchev in the Soviet Union and abroad. Khrushchev shared the fate of other reformers who failed to win support and recognition for their deeds from the majority of their contemporaries. The people who had once held Ivan the Terrible in high esteem and condemned Boris Godunov could not accept a public figure who, when compared with his predecessor Stalin, lacked charisma, a person who was earthy, mortal and apt to err. They despised Khrushchev for being a person of lesser stature, a man who, like Shakespeare's Claudius, saw the crown lying on a shelf and put it under his arm.

Meanwhile, the Western countries put Nikita Khrushchev on a par with John Kennedy and Pope John XXIII and traced the causes of the worsening of international relations in the late 1960s to the fact that these leaders, for one reason or another, had left the political scene. Many books on 'Khrushchevism' as a new trend in Socialism were published in the West.

One could reflect that no prophet is honoured in his own country, but that does not quite fit the case. The issue goes deeper and is more intricate. Probably the man who came closest to assessing Khrushchev correctly was the sculptor Ernst Neizvestny, with whom Khrushchev had engaged in his cavalry-style polemics at the Manezh exhibition hall. The tombstone for Khrushchev created by Neizvestny – a bronze head encased in white and black marble – aptly symbolizes the contradictory nature of the 'thaw' and its dominant figure.

Now, almost a quarter of a century later, when we compare the periods before and after 1964, we can see better the strengths and weaknesses of Khrushchev. His major accomplishment was smashing the personality cult of Stalin, and this turned out to be irrevocable despite later attempts to re-erect the monument. The failure of these attempts demonstrated that the effort had gone far and deep enough. The courageous decision to rehabilitate many Communists and people who were not Party members, who had fallen victims to repression and been executed under Stalin's dictatorship, restored justice, truth and credibility to the Party and the State. A powerful though not entirely adroit and effective blow was delivered at over-centralization, bureaucracy and petty official contempt.

Khrushchev's term in office brought a turning point in agriculture – purchasing prices were raised, taxes were drastically cut, and new technology arrived at the farms. For all the shortcomings, the development of land which had never before been tilled helped provide people with food. Khrushchev tried to push farms to use foreign expertise, to make them learn from the first agrarian revolution. Even his love affair with corn sprang from good intentions, although it was accompanied by naïve extremism. A damaging role was also

201

played by the trend towards giant farms and cuts in the permitted size of private farm plots.

I should also like to recall that Khrushchev's name is closely linked with the major advances in science and technology that enabled the country to build the basis for achieving strategic parity. All of us still vividly remember the meeting of Yuri Gagarin and Nikita Khrushchev, which highlighted the country's push into outer space. The policy of peaceful co-existence, proclaimed by the 20th Congress of the Communist Party after the shock of the Cuban missile crisis, eventually became a springboard for agreements and business dealings with the West.

One can also trace back to the period of the 'thaw' the origins of the Helsinki Final Act which fixed in law the borders that resulted from World War II and endorsed a new type of international relations, economic cooperation, and exchanges of information, ideas and people.

Under Khrushchev, the Party set out to solve many social problems. Urban and rural living standards slowly began to rise. But the planned social and economic reforms were choked off. The tragic events of 1956 in Hungary dealt a heavy blow to the hopes of the Soviet reformers, though not the least important factor was the self-confidence of Khrushchev, and his lack of attention to theory and political strategy. 'Khrushchevism', as a concept for the renovation of Socialism, failed. To use a favourite figure of speech of Mao Tse-tung, the Soviet leader's main opponent, Khrushchev walked on two feet: one foot was boldly striding forward into a new epoch, while the other was hopelessly mired in the past.

In seeking to explain why the reforms of the 1960s failed, one could also say that the conservative forces managed to triumph over the reformers because the administrative apparatus and society as a whole were not ripe for radical change. But this is too broad an explanation. We should try to identify the factors on which the conservatives capitalized.

In my opinion, one mistake was that the search for a philosophy for the reforms and ways to implement them was based on traditionally administrative and even bureaucratic approaches. Khrushchev usually delegated the study of specific problems, whether economic, cultural, or political, to the Ministries, State agencies and departments, that is, to the very administrative agencies which were being called on to curb their own powers. Of course, the apparatus found ways through direct, indirect, or ambiguous decisions to avoid checks on its power.

More or less successful reforms in both Socialist and Western countries are usually drafted by a team of experts, made up mostly of academics and public figures, who work under the guidance of the leader of the country. This was the case in Hungary, Yugoslavia and China. In Japan I met Professor Okhita, who is considered to be the father of the Japanese 'miracle'. In West Germany the outline of reforms was devised by Professor Erhardt who later became Chancellor.

Another factor was that then 'the people were silent'. Now, enriched by our experience with glasnost, we can see particularly clearly how little was done in the 1960s to inform people about their past, the problems they faced, and the decisions being planned, let alone to enlist the support of large segments of the public for the reforms. How often we heard then: 'And how is Khrushchev any better than Stalin? At least there was order under Stalin, bureaucrats were put in prison, prices went down.' It was no coincidence that most of the country probably sighed with relief and hoped for a change when the Party Central Committee met in plenary session in October 1964.

And the last factor was Khrushchev himself. He was a man of genuine and sharp political intellect, a man who was daring and enterprising, but who failed to resist the temptation of self-praise. 'Our Nikita Sergeyevich!' – didn't this phrase mark the beginning of the end for the genuine opponent of the personality cult? The people who jumped on the bandwagon drowned him in an ocean of flattery and eulogy, receiving important posts and the highest awards in payment. And it was not by coincidence that the worse things became, the louder and more lyrical became the choir of flunkeys and flatterers chanting about a 'Golden Age'.

October 1964 found me at a country house among a group of representatives of two Central Committee international departments. At Khrushchev's request we were busy preparing an important document on international policy. We were in a rush. The Central Committee secretaries came in several times a day to inquire whether we had finished. Consuming vast quantities of coffee and other stimulants, we were painfully engaged in hatching another paper. All of a sudden the telephone went dead. Nobody called that day. The next day started in the same manner. Then an old pal of mine said to me: 'Why don't you go to Moscow to find out what's up? The silence is rather odd.'

So I returned to Moscow, to the CPSU Central Committee office on Staraya Ploshchad. The first thing I sensed was precisely that odd silence. There was no one in the corridors, as if everybody had gone with the wind! I looked into some work-rooms where small groups of people were whispering together. Then I came across somebody in the corridor – the head of the Czechoslovakia department, as I remember, a fussy fellow, a former Komsomol worker. He said: 'What have you been doing, sitting about and writing things? Here people have been seizing power!'

'What kind of people?'

'Look, Kolka Myesatsev is already Chairman of the State Committee for Radio and Television!'

And Myesatsev had been the deputy head of our department up to the moment. Now I could learn some details, at last.

The Central Committee Presidium was in session for the second day running. Khrushchev had been criticized and offered retirement 'of his own free will'. There was also a rumour that somebody had put forward a suggestion that he should retain the post of Chairman of the Council of Ministers, but either the motion had not been passed or the rumour was false. The October plenary meeting resolved 'to accept Khrushchev's appeal for retirement of his own free will' . . .

After the plenary meeting Yuri Andropov, the head of my department, spoke to his workers and gave us some details. I distinctly remember his major point: 'Now we are going to be more persistent in following the course of the 20th Party Congress.'

But at the same time I was puzzled by a reproach he made to be, personally, for the first time in the many years we had worked together: 'Now, I hope, you understand why *Pravda* has not published your article.'

In fact, the article was not my own. It had been an editorial prepared by me, and it was entitled 'Stalin's Personality Cult and its Inheritors'. The article had been approved by Khrushchev personally. But the newspaper had been abstaining from publishing it for several months. Why? After the October plenary meeting it became evident that it had been held back deliberately.

Somehow I could not put two and two together. If we were going to follow the course of the 20th Party Congress, why hold back an article against the personality cult? Maybe things were not that simple!

Soon I had occasion to meet Leonid Brezhnev. And I could see for myself that there was not going to be any movement forward. No headway was what awaited us. Some arrangements, such as the regional and territorial economic councils, were broken up. But there was no obvious return to the pattern of the early 1950s. (I did not like it, and asked to be transferred from the Party apparatus to do some creative work. Perhaps I behaved more abruptly than was acceptable in their code of rules. They got even with me later on . . .)

I had worked with Andropov for nearly five years, and was at the time an adviser and later the chief of the advising group of the CPSU Central Committee department headed by him. Andropov belonged to a next generation of leaders. Contrary to Khrushchev, he had not taken part either in the Civil War or in the ideological struggle of the 1920s and 1930s. He became a leader after the Great Patriotic War, about the time of the 'thaw'. In fact, the 'thaw' was the only period when people like Andropov could emerge on the political scene – people who ardently supported the 20th Party Congress, but were circumspect enough not to get tied down to a single political course.

Andropov was possessed by one passion only, and that was

politics. From what I could see, as well as from what his other comrades said about him, his working day never lasted less than twelve hours. He started working at 9 o'clock in the morning and finished at about 10 or 11 p.m. He worked on Saturdays and Sundays, and during his vacations. And all that despite the fact of having blood-pressure jumping up to 200 or 220 even then. (He wore copper bracelets on both hands as they were thought to reduce blood-pressure.)

Such a way of working was not the result of necessity. It was actually his passion. A passion for political work. His life reflected the life of the Party, of the State, of the country, and attempted to embrace the problems of the whole modern world.

This did not mean, however, that he confined himself to business and political documents. Quite the contrary. In Hungary he studied the Hungarian language, in Moscow he tried to study English (though he did not seem finally to master it). He loved reading books, particularly volumes of political theory. I remember once, on entering his work-room, noticing Hegel's *Philosophy of Legislation* on his table. Slightly embarrassed by my obvious interest, Yuri Vladimirovich launched into a comparison of Hegelian and Marxian dialectics. But soon he left that subject and moved on to an analysis of Hegel's ideas on political history, displaying a brilliant memory and an independence of thinking which some of our professional philosophers might have envied. There was nothing that could surprise him, except perhaps some extra information on the concepts of the great philosopher of the past.

I remember getting him interested in a discussion of Rousseau and his 'social contract', and Rousseau's opinion on the contradictory nature of human progress which leads to the degradation of morality and humanism. He liked to deviate. But he could not be distracted for long, and he soon plunged back into his work on some 'little speech' which in my opinion was not important at all, and in my eyes was not worth dropping an intellectual discussion for. In Yuri Vladimirovich's estimation, any political task always towered way above any other thing.

Yes, he was a person specifically built up by nature and polished by experience to be a 'man of politics'. Politics were not only a passion for him, but a true vocation, like music for a composer, marble for a sculptor, the stage for an actor.

History deprived him of a chance to realize himself, his ideas and concepts as the country's leader. The vessel of life broke at the moment when it was filled to the brim with a thirst for action, and with all the knowledge he needed to attain his purposes.

Andropov was extremely reluctant to leave the CPSU Central Committee apparatus. When saying goodbye to his comrades after he was appointed Chairman of the State Committee for Security (KGB), he promised to return to the Party Central Committee. That was his dream and his constant intention. But in fact he returned only after sixteen years, after Mikhail Suslov's death. It was indeed Suslov who insisted on transferring Andropov from the Party apparatus, because he was afraid of Andropov as an obvious candidate for the post of a Politburo member dealing with international affairs. Brezhnev, who was a master of compromise, may well have arranged the move – satisfying Suslov's demands by transferring Andropov to the KGB, but at the same time appointing him a candidate for the Communist Party's Politburo membership.

Unlike us, young advisers from scientific or journalist quarters, Yuri Vladimirovich understood perfectly not only what was to be done, but also how difficult it was to do it under the circumstances in which the party and the country found themselves. In other words, he, like probably no one else, realized there were hard political limits which turned into insurmountable blocks to urgently needed reforms.

His political shrewdness may be illustrated by the following incident which took place in Hungary in 1956 and which I was told about by some people working with him at our Embassy at the time. Several months before the Hungarian events, Andropov warned the Hungarian leaders of what might ensue. He informed Khrushchev of the forthcoming explosion and suggested effective measures to prevent it. By the way, that was why, after the Hungarian events, Andropov was appointed head of a CPSU Central Committee department.

The year 1956 was the reason for Andropov developing a certain 'Hungarian complex'. He was always watchful and even suspicious when something was happening in the Socialist countries which did not fit into the Soviet pattern. He displayed a typical reaction once when I wrote an article on the Yugoslavian self-management programme.

I had visited Yugoslavia in 1961 with a journalists' delegation. We saw a dozen enterprises and State economic institutions, some scientific and medical centres and unions of art people. On my arrival back in Moscow, I wrote an article where I told the truth about what I had seen. And did I get a dressing-down from Andropov! Somebody had told him about my 'seditious' writing on Yugoslavia. Andropov demanded the article be delivered to the hospital where he was undergoing a medical examination. There he wrote a long letter to me, several pages in the clear handwriting so typical of him. The letter asked me not to have the article published, considering our relationship with Yugoslavia at that moment and the evaluation given to its Communist Party activity at the Meeting of the Communist Parties in 1960. He did not dispute the truth of what had been said in the article, but pointed out the political inexpediency of publication.

I was somehow discouraged, because I had not touched upon any ideological problems, and the article was more of a feature story. Probably my straightforward description of the day-to-day experience of self-management at industrial enterprises, with all its peculiarities, achievements and difficulties, did read unexpectedly or even strangely. I could not ignore Andropov's opinion. So I asked for the article back and pushed it into my desk drawer, for ever.

But later, when our summit delegation went to Yugoslavia, it visited a Belgrade enterprise where the delegates were made acquainted with some peculiarities of the Yugoslavian system of self-management. We were told about the work of the administration, the system of hiring people on a competitive basis, how the workers' councils operated, and the problems they had with the enterprise management because of its incompetence which considerably influenced the production process and everything connected with it.

Then our First Secretary took the floor and proceeded to make a sensational statement which was in all the Yugoslavian newspapers and the bourgeois press, but seems never to have been mentioned by our own newspapers.

He said: 'I find Yugoslav self-management an interesting experience. Each country has to choose its own way of development, in accordance with its own traditions, its own culture. There is nothing wrong in the workers' councils, but our country has chosen another way, that of widening the rights of the trade unions and of the working collectives.'

The statement was met with a storm of applause, especially from the Yugoslav leaders present.

I looked at Andropov, wishing to see his reaction. But he was busy writing something down in his notebook. I do not know even today if the First Secretary had had the statement approved beforehand or if it was delivered as an impromptu speech.

In his theoretical writings Andropov was bold and creative; he searched for maximum application of new science and technology. That was especially evident when he was elected General Secretary of the CPSU Central Committee. But back in the 1960s he had already expressed all his major ideas for modernizing the economy and the style of Party and government work. Let me remind you of his speech 'Leninism Enlightens our Path' (22 April 1964). He stated then that every turn of history enriched the theory of scientific Communism, filled it with new ideas and conclusions and raised it higher and higher. Only people who did not realize that could refuse the present generation of revolutionaries the right to think independently, or intimidate all those who wished to have their own say in Marxist-Leninist theory with the bugaboo of revisionism. He said that the need for bold and creative steps for Socialism had never been more acute than in the post-war period.

It was no fluke that after Andropov was elected General Secretary of the CPSU Central Committee he succeeded in formulating in such a brief period of time so many problems important for the economic development of the country and in indicating pathways to their solution.

One could write quite a lot about Brezhnev – if one were to go through the speeches and reports he delivered or the articles and books not written by him – or very little if one tried to remember what his personal opinions were. He almost never expressed himself without the aid of a document prepared for him by somebody else. Being unsure of himself as an ideological and political leader, he was always seeking some support. At meetings he was never the first to speak. He preferred to listen to others and to share the opinion of the majority, or, if in doubt, to stall on the issue to avoid a delicate subject, or to hush it up. His was a typical 'weather-cock' leadership, the top of the apparatus iceberg with nothing there but a Torichelli vacuum. That was why he was so convenient and pleasing for his retinue.

I suppose we are as yet in no position to evaluate objectively the rule of Brezhnev which lasted for nearly twenty years. The epoch is still so close at hand, so painful for all the participants, the criteria for such an evaluation are still so vague. But one thing is evident: the period of stagnation gave birth to Brezhnev, and he was a typical embodiment thereof. He obtained power by chance; it just dropped into his lap as a result of a peculiar correlation of forces. Alexander Shelepin, the main conspirator against Khrushchev, was still in no position to claim the leading role at the October 1964 plenary meeting of the CPSU Central Committee. In supporting Brezhnev, he expected soon to overcome a weak leader. And he was mistaken. Brezhnev was powerful, not as a personality, but as a speaking-trumpet for the bureaucracy. Shelepin himself, with his neo-Stalinism and his Napoleonic ways, was rejected by the apparatus.

I happened to witness one of the most dramatic clashes between those two persons. It happened in the spring of 1965 when we were getting ready to celebrate the 20th anniversary of our victory in World War II. We were working at the documents necessary for a Brezhnev report on the subject. Suddenly it turned out that Shelepin and his 'Komsomol members' (he had been the first secretary of the Central Committee of the YCL) were also working on the subject. Brezhnev's assistant asked me to analyse Shelepin's version of the report, and later on Brezhnev himself came into our workroom (it was not far from his study) and asked: 'Well, what has he piled up there? Copied some dissertation, hasn't he?'

I started diligently explaining the essence of the Shelepin position as reproduced in his paper. I tried to demonstrate that he differed substantially in his attitude from the course proclaimed at the 20th Party Congress – on the problem of the Stalin personality cult, on peaceful co-existence, on the concept of a peaceful transition to Socialism, on the relations with China and Yugoslavia – sixteen points, all in all. Brezhnev was listening attentively and even with a strain, his lower jaw dropping a little.

And then he said: 'That is difficult for me to understand, I am no specialist here. My area is organization and psychology . . . You see to it yourself.'

Nevertheless, during the discussion of the report later on, he refused even to mention the 20th Congress of the CPSU in order to appease the majority, but positively appreciated the role of Stalin in Great Patriotic War.

He was a conservative person by nature, and a very careful one. That left an imprint on the whole period of his leadership. Vital problems were put off, though both economics and society were accumulating elements of stagnation and crisis.

Of course, in Brezhnev's time some wise decisions were adopted too. Our international policy started towards the détente which had the Final Act adopted in Helsinki as its culmination. In the domestic sphere, a transition from the extensive to the intensive stage of economic development was declared, but it was not supported by any practical steps, as Brezhnev had a bureaucrat's fear of such movement.

But on two occasions Brezhnev displayed a resoluteness not typical of him in general: in Czechoslovakia in 1968 and in Afghanistan in 1979. The latter action had a dramatic effect on the détente which had been so difficult to achieve. I suppose, however, that Brezhnev's comrades-in-arms once more played the most important role in those decisions. As far as I know, there was no serious analysis, no discussion of the need to send the troops into Afghanistan. Things were decided within a small group of leaders, at the level of emotions and not of serious policy. Besides, we must remember that after 1974 Brezhnev, who had suffered from a serious illness, could not fully participate in taking important decisions. More and more he became a toy in the hands of the apparatus, a puppet who found it difficult to cope with reciting speeches and reports which contained so many loud words and so little real politics. At the end of his life Brezhnev is rumoured to have asked to retire from his post of General Secretary of the CPSU Central Committee, but everybody was against it as they were afraid of cataclysms. And it was all so convenient under Brezhnev, so free, and no control at all. What else could they desire?

And now some conclusions. The experience of the past has demonstrated that the mechanism for electing a leader has serious flaws. Otherwise how could it have happened that at the most difficult period of our own and world history a great country such as ours acquired such leaders as Leonid Brezhnev and Konstantin Chernenko, who were hardly fit to be leaders on a regional scale. And after the death of Chernenko there was a real danger of Victor Grishin coming to power, which would have turned stagnation into a quagmire from which we would not have emerged until far into the next century.

During the discussion of the CPSU Central Committee theses for the All-Union Party Conference, I put forward the idea of switching over to a presidential way of electing the country's leader, which involves the election of the General Secretary of the USSR Communist Party directly at a Party Congress, with further balloting for the post of President of the USSR through a direct and secret ballot. The two mandates, of the ruling Party and of the sovereign people, would provide the country's leader with the authority necessary for him to implement his policies. On the other hand, it might raise the leadership requirements to those of a worthy candidate known to the people. A maximum of two five-year terms in office would be a guarantee against the establishment of personal power.

The decisions adopted at the 19th Party Conference included the principle of recommending for the post of the Chairman of the USSR Supreme Soviet the General Secretary of the CPSU Central Committee, who should ballot for the post at a congress of Soviets. The Conference decided that the Chairman of the USSR Supreme Soviet would perform the functions of the head of State.

Presidency implies sharing power. Our experience says that concentration of power in the hands of one organ (no matter if it is a State or a Party organ), as was noted by Lenin, leads eventually to extreme concentration of power in the hands of one man, as was tragically displayed in Stalin's time and turned out to be so ineffective under Brezhnev. This means that discarding the ideas of great revolutionary democrats of the past on division of legislative, executive and judicial powers (I should like to add here – and of Party power) has been a mistake.

The situation could be radically changed if we made the Supreme Soviet into a constantly sitting Soviet Parliament. It would gather regularly for autumn, spring and winter sessions and function permanently. Then its deputies would have a real opportunity to express the pluralist opinions of society, to prepare laws carefully, and to control the executive organs, first of all through the distribution of finance and resources.

Our juridical system also needs serious reconstruction. We must increase the number of people working for courts, raise their salaries and their social status, and make courts independent of local Party and State organs. Effective defence of the violated rights of a personality through the courts and without delay must become a rule. This may be considerably helped by a jury of people's assessors on most important matters (jury trials); by abolishing the death pentalty (as was done by Lenin in the 1920s); by abolishing imprisonment for so-called anti-Soviet propaganda (less harsh measures might be enough); and by a sharp restriction of penal sanctions for all criminal acts in accordance with the principle 'law is effective when it is inevitable but not cruel'.

We must have coherent laws and a precise procedure for enacting social pluralism of opinions, glasnost, freedom of views, of conscience, the right to associate and to create non-formal organizations, and the right to have demonstrations and meetings excluding both administrative tyranny and crowd orgies.

An important decision has been taken on building up a Committee for Constitutional Supervision which will have the right to call off a law, a decree, or an instruction if it does not accord with the Constitution.

The main thing is to have the functions of the Party organs changed. The principle is familiar from Lenin's times: the Party is to engage in political leadership, and the State organs must do the management; work collectives and their associations must be self-governed. As the majority of the personnel in the Soviet, economic and social systems are Communists, there must be no direct pressure upon them for any purpose. As Lenin put it, to manage things indirectly means to manage them correctly. We must work out a system of non-direct but effective methods for the Party organization to influence the other institutions within our political system. Cutting down the functions of the Party apparatus to at least one-third would allow it to concentrate on the major problems of political leadership and ideological educaton.

Such are some of the lessons of our past concerning the problem of leadership in our political system. The 19th Party Conference has laid a sound foundation for the development of the democratic process and for the development of a Soviet parliamentary system. The immediate future will see new laws adopted, which will aim at putting these ideas into practice and bringing about a new political culture for the whole nation and for its officials, a culture based on principles which organically combine Socialism and democracy.

Georgi A. Arbatov

Georgi Arbatov has had first-hand experience of warfare – indeed it was the war that formed his convictions and patriotic views. Arbatov joined the Communist Party at the front in 1943 and by the end of the war was already a senior lieutenant. Although a military career lay ahead of him, he was deeply conscious of the horrors of war and the value of peace. As a result, he entered the Moscow State Institute of Foreign Relations and successfully combined diplomatic work with research. He quickly gained first a Candidate's and shortly afterwards a Doctor's degree. Subsequently, he was unanimously elected a fellow of the USSR Academy of Sciences. Arbatov has to his credit more than 400 publications, including monographs, booklets and articles in Soviet and foreign magazines. In 1967 he set up the Institute of US and Canadian Studies, which he has headed ever since. Arbatov is President of the United Nations Association in the USSR and a member of the independent commission on disarmament and security (the Palme Commission). He is one of the few scholars to be elected a member of the CPSU Central Committee and deputy of the USSR Supreme Soviet.

Such Different Meetings . . .

Soviet–American relations and the four summit meetings

GEORGI A. ARBATOV

Dissimilar as Mikhail Gorbachev and Ronald Reagan's meetings were, they were united by a common idea, a common purpose. They were born as a result of realizing the sheer impossibility of drifting further towards a dangerous confrontation – and the two countries had been getting closer and closer to it since the early 1980s. Therefore these meetings were united by the desire to find a road to safer, normal relations.

Today, after these four meetings, we can say there has been a turn towards such relations. And though there are still many unsolved problems, one should not underestimate how deep and how important the improvements have been.

The transition itself, the very possibility of there being four summit meetings in three years, meetings so different but so successful in general, could only have come about through deep changes in each of the two countries. It is about these changes and each of the four summits – and I happened to participate in all of them as an expert – that I should like to write in some detail.

The present thaw in Soviet–American relations was preceded by severe frosts, which at times seemed to be another ice age in politics. I would call them a second cold war. The sharp drop in the political temperature after a brief period of détente had its reasons. And perhaps it would be logical to speak about them first. So, what were the reasons for the second cold war?

I shall start with the United States, because it was that

217

country which proclaimed a new cold war in the election platform of the Republican Party in 1980 and then in the first statement and actions of the Reagan administration. I see the reason for détente's quick replacement with a freeze, above all in those difficulties which the process of readjustment to new realities demanded of American policy and of the American way of thinking as a result of certain internal and external transformations in the USA's environment. The essence of these transformations lay in the fact that the epoch of American exclusiveness was coming to an end. Some aspects of that exclusiveness were imaginary, but some of them were quite real. Indeed, for a long time the USA had been much less vulnerable than many other countries as far as external dangers and cataclysms were concerned, and therefore it was actually independent of what went on in the world around it. After World War II its strength was increased by an overwhelming military force (the atomic monopoly) and an economic power, giving the country freedom of action in the world economy and politics unprecedented for any single country. The 'American Age', or the 'American Era', seemed close at hand.

It was not surprising that it was so difficult for the Americans to adjust themselves to the new world realities so obvious even in the 1960s. That was when the USA, remaining a great world power, began its transformation into an 'ordinary' state. It was ordinary because the Americans not only lost their chance for global hegemony, they entered into a relationship of *mutual* dependence with other countries. And they turned out to be as vulnerable to many threats as any other country.

The American reaction was quite painful – and as a human being I can appreciate the emotion; for a long time the Americans did not want to face the fact. But even when they accepted it they went on trying to see if there was any chance of restoring their privileged position. Various circumstances led to intensification of such moves and steps by the time the 1980 election campaign rolled around. This contributed to the victory of the extremely conservative forces which were promising 'to make America as powerful as before' and, of

218

course, to restore the rest of her traditional values. That was the basis of Reagan's platform.

In fact, a kind of 'counter-reformation' of both external and internal affairs was promised.

That was the slogan in the first years of the Republican administration. And though at times the policy seemed to many people to be a success, to bring progress, soon both the USA and the world realized it was all rather euphoric.

Counter-reformation had brought no success either in the economy, in domestic affairs, or in foreign policy. From what I could see many Americans were of the same opinion. They had to face the same questions, with which they were imperiously confronted by history itself, the same painful problem of readjusting to new world realities, to a situation where it is impossible to attain any political goals by military force. This brought reduction and limiting of armed forces and arms, and the need for normalizing relations with the USSR, back on the US national agenda.

I would like to pay tribute to President Ronald Reagan and his administration. They realized what was happening, they learned their lesson and made up their minds to wheel around in their policy.

But the stage for a new historic act was not set by the American side alone, where both good and bad things were concerned. The Soviet Union had its own share of responsibility for the erosion of détente, the thaw which had given rise to so many hopes in the 1970s. It was guilty by the very fact of permitting stagnation of its internal affairs, of having come to the brink of economic, social and spiritual crisis which gave its enemies reason to hope that the slightest pressure would get rid of the very problem of co-existence. On the top of that, there were serious mistakes and miscalculations in our international policy.

The Soviet Union, naturally, always stood for peace. It did not want war and fought (as much as it could) the threat of a nuclear catastrophe. But besides common purpose, there are definite steps, tactics, political art. Here things were looking bad.

The problem of the incongruity of Soviet foreign policy

with our country's real needs, its long-term interests and abilities, was analysed by Mikhail Gorbachev at the 19th Conference of the USSR Communist Party. In particular, he criticized the undemocratic procedure of adopting decisions, when even the most serious of them 'were made by a fairly small group of people without a detailed collective discussion and analysis'. This could only lead to an inadequate reaction to international events, to the policies of other countries, which in turn would inevitably give rise to mistakes. Somehow (and that was one of the biggest mistakes) we allowed the other side to impose upon us its own 'game rules' as well as its own platform for political struggle.

In this connection Mikhail Gorbachev spoke at the 19th Conference above all about our being obliged to attain military parity with the USA, while at the same time allowing ourselves to be dragged into the arms race. We accepted too many challenges in the sphere of military rivalry and sometimes were too eager and too enthusiastic in that rivalry. We tried to match each American military programme with a similar programme of our own, ignoring differences in our economic resources as well as strategic and political realities. Sometimes we ignored common sense. The idea of 'asymmetric' reaction established itself in our consciousness only recently.

Things were not much better with talks. For a long time we reconciled ourselves to the fact that they were slow, unproductive and hopeless. Sometimes we were not critical in accepting Western military concepts (in particular, the concept of 'nuclear deterrence'). In general, we attached too much importance to the military aspects of security.

Now, in the period of glasnost and perestroika, we have been trying to comprehend our mistakes and miscalculations in domestic as well as foreign policy. We are doing this not only to perfect our foreign policy, but to overhaul it thoroughly – and the 19th Party Conference made that point.

I do not want to overstate what we have done – there is nothing we would like to avoid now so much as boasts, lies, illusions. But I think there is reason to state that for a little over three years we have managed to achieve a great deal, foreign policy included. Perestroika has favourably influenced it, along with many other things. And now I am going to speak about the four Soviet–American summit meetings, so different and yet united by a common idea . . .

The situation was changing in the two countries in different ways. In the USA, changes went on at a leisurely pace, little by little; in the USSR they were impetuous and rapid, in the mainstream of a perestroika that was astonishing the world public. But in both countries the process was speedy enough to bring them both to a turning point in a couple of years.

Here I must confess that if in April 1985 (we see that as the start of the epoch of perestroika) somebody had told me that the same year would see a meeting between Gorbachev and Reagan, to be followed by three more summits in the next two and a half years, I would not have believed it. Nor would I have believed that in such a brief period of time we would manage to swerve from the path of inevitable confrontation on to another path opening up chances for gradual, but real movement towards normalization. I humbly admit my mistake now. But it is a rare occasion when I can be so glad to have been mistaken. (Frankly, I console myself with the thought that others would have been wrong too; of course, I am in no position to speak for astrologers.)

So, the first summit meeting was in Geneva. If my memory doesn't deceive me, it was the first time a group of experts had been called together on the eve of a summit, a group including specialists on the problems of foreign and military policy (among them Velikhov, Sagdeyev, Zhurkin, Primakov, my other colleagues, General N. F. Chernov and others), public representatives and writers. Their task was to answer questions which might be asked by the heads of the Soviet delegation in the course of the talks. In particular, these people took part in a couple of interesting conferences in Geneva. Moreover, the experts were allowed to talk with the media, something quite new for Soviet foreign policy. They left for Geneva some five or seven days earlier than the delegation itself and were given considerable opportunities. Geneva was filled to overflowing with reporters.

After the first 'blows' dealt by Gorbachev personally (I must say, after many years of Soviet silence, they were deafening) – I have in mind his *Time* magazine interview, his talk with French reporters and his speech during the visit to France in October 1985 – that was the first concentrated action of Soviet open diplomacy. This diplomacy was now compared to what had been happening for many a year; but at the same time it was not new, it was returning to the initial Soviet practice of the first years after the Revolution of 1917, when Lenin was still alive.

As the West had quite forgotten those years, it was caught unawares. I do not want to quote, but almost unanimously the Western media concluded that the Russians had won a great propaganda victory (there were even calculations: a score of 10:1). Was it true?

Today, looking back at the events with three years' experience, I should say there was a grain of truth in it – because for quite a time both the Soviet Union and those who officially, half-officially and unofficially had spoken about foreign policy on its behalf did not look very convincing in a public political debate. Now it turned out that we could learn fast, that we were not meek in discussions, and what is more, we even took the initiative. And it was not for the sake of eloquence, but, above all, because we had something to say, because there appeared many points on which we did not need to keep to our defences (the weak spot in a lot of our public speeches).

At the same time I should answer the same question in the negative – public debate during the Geneva summit was not just an exercise in propaganda. There was something greater than that behind it. That was the first display of serious improvements and shifts in the Soviet mentality (later named the new thinking), as well as in Soviet policy, which became so evident to the world public and press.

At the same time the Western mass media did not see the second point. Somehow it was understandable – the new political thinking and a more mature foreign policy corresponding to the times were at the initial stage of their development.

The West did not realize many other things. In particular, many people in Washington, aware of the energy, the power

222

and the political skill of Gorbachev as a politician, were afraid
that the Soviet leader would inflict a shattering defeat upon
President Reagan, taking advantage of the obvious weaknesses of age. But it never occurred to the Americans that
Gorbachev had no intention of 'winning' the meet. He did
not look upon it as a duel, or a tie-breaker. He understood
perfectly that he had to cut short the major developmental
tendency in the relations between the two superpowers, and
that it was an incredibly difficult and complex matter requir-
ing prolonged effort. It was quite evident to him that the
problem could not be solved in one go, that a durable bridge
had to be built patiently and persistently. His tactics evidently
matched the job. From what I could see Gorbachev was quite
satisfied with his first meeting with the President of the USA.
And in my opinion he had every reason to be satisfied. There
had been a talk, the summit dialogue had started. And the
documents signed in Geneva were not bad at all, though they
contained no definite obligations. It was important that the
two leaders had admitted a victory in nuclear war to be
impossible, coming to the conclusion that it was senseless to
wage such a war. The two leaders also agreed that it was
necessary to give up all attempts to achieve unilateral advantages. That was a good and sound beginning for building up
mutual understanding on such a basis.

I think the opponents of improvement of Soviet-American
relations saw that. If they hadn't there would not have been
such active attempts in America to create new difficulties
immediately after Geneva, to introduce new 'irritants' which
might make us react sharply to US actions, to heat up the
situation and to force it back into the 'pre-Geneva' state. This
is how I interpret the demand for a 40 per cent cut in the
Soviet delegations to the UN, the entry of American warships
into Soviet territorial waters at the Crimean shore, the demonstrative speed-up of nuclear explosions in response to the
Soviet unilateral moratorium. There were also a number of
other actions, not to mention the 'superfluous rhetoric'.

Moscow got the message, answered hostile attacks as it saw
necessary, but tried not to yield to provocation. And it per-
severed in its course. So much is obvious from Gorbachev's

speeches during that period. And most important, the USSR was going full speed ahead in establishing the new thinking; a new international policy was being hatched.

The year 1986 started with Mikhail Gorbachev's January speech containing the programme of doing away with nuclear arms by the end of the twentieth century.

The 27th Congress of the CPSU became a milestone, with the new concept of general security and a number of other major international ideas shaped there.

While persisting in its attempts to develop a dialogue with the USA, the Soviet Union became much more active in other political directions, above all, where the countries of Western Europe were concerned. Within the framework of the Warsaw Pact, serious work started on correcting military doctrines and working out new proposals on reducing regular arms and military forces in Europe. The USSR Far East policy also grew more active. In particular, there were serious improvements in our relations with China. Contacts with Japan were resumed at a high level. Gorbachev's visit to the Soviet Far East turned out to be a very important event, the Soviet leader taking the opportunity to put forward his new ideas on security in Asia and the Pacific.

By the end of the summer the world political barometer was rising. But the USA came up with new problems. Each step on the way to normalization had been difficult. But at that particular moment the struggle for the President's 'soul' seemed to intensify. This is how I interpret the growing attempts to put a strain on Soviet–American relations with the autumn coming – and another summit meeting had been planned for that autumn, a meeting which even at that time looked very important for Reagan. One such attempt was the arrest of G. Zakharov, an official at the Soviet mission at the UN, and his incarceration without following existing procedures. Soon after that N. Daniloff, an American journalist, was arrested in Moscow. That was an occasion for a loud anti-Soviet campaign. Everything that had been achieved in the previous year seemed to shatter . . .

Against this background, from out of the blue, there came

news of an agreement (on Soviet initiative) to hold another summit in Reykjavik in October 1986.

That seemed the most dramatic meeting of the four – mostly because the Americans had underestimated Gorbachev, had not taken the new Soviet policy seriously. They were therefore caught unawares, not by the Soviet leader's 'insidious surprise', but by the fact that his proposal embraced everything that he had said in his statements and speeches and during the talks that the other side had not listened to. The document handed to Reagan at the very beginning of the meeting – a draft of 'Directives to the USSR Minister of Foreign Affairs and to the USA State Secretary' – summed up our proposals on restricting various types of nuclear weapons and offered a joint agreement.

Nevertheless, Gorbachev's proposal caught Reagan, Shultz and the whole American group by surprise. At first they were in no position to answer at all. Then came a decision – let the experts work on it. Their meeting was scheduled for the evening of the first day, so that the discussion of the major problems of disarmament could be continued the next morning. Meanwhile other problems were discussed.

In the evening the session of the experts started. The American group was headed by Paul Nitze; it included the whole Geneva delegation headed by Kampelman, officials from the Council of National Security. The Soviet group was headed by Marshal S. Akhromeyev, head of the General Staff; it included V. Karpov (head of the central department of the USSR Ministry of Foreign Affairs for disarmament talks), Academician Velikhov, myself and our ambassador, V. Falin. The sitting started around 8 p.m.

Several hours passed before we managed to discuss the text of the 'Directives' in earnest. Our American colleagues started with prolonged hesitations, endless exchange of papers and notes. Then they asked for a consultation break. The 'time-out' lasted for about an hour.

Little changed afterwards. We weren't getting anywhere. All of it looked rather strange. I was sorry for Nitze – it was late in the evening, his colleagues were sending him notes all the time, they were whispering to each other, going to and

225

fro, and finally they took another time-out, for an hour and a half.

When they returned they handed us an 'alternative' text which turned out to contain the American proposals put forward in October and rejected by the Soviet Union. It was then that Marshal Akhromeyev said it was late, and since the discussion was going nowhere, it would be best for our delegation to go home and tell our leaders that we had failed even to get the talks started.

The statement had an effect. And the discussion of the Soviet proposals started at last, and started, logically, with the first chapter – on a 50 per cent reduction of strategic offensive arms. Richard Perle should be given credit – he immediately noticed an inaccuracy in our proposals. The number of our carriers was a little larger than that of the Americans. 'You want to freeze the inequality with the 50 per cent cut', he accused us. Soon it was our turn to ask for a time-out; we went to the *George Otz*, the ship where our delegation was staying, to discuss these questions with our leaders. The problem of the carriers was quickly solved – we made our position more definite by stating that the 50 per cent reduction should lead to both sides having the same number of both carriers and warheads (the Americans had put forward figures of 1,600 and 6,000 respectively, to which we agreed).

Things got moving after that; the two sides were quite quick in agreeing on the first chapter, including the problem of shorter-range ballistic missile sites, the question of control still remaining the stumbling block. (I must say I got a lot of pleasure out of a discussion between Marshal Akhromeyev and Perle. The former insisted on the need for on-site inspection; the latter was resolutely against. How quickly times change, I thought, not without a dose of malice.)

The second chapter (on medium-range missiles) could not be agreed upon because of the British and the French missiles (the next morning Gorbachev agreed not to take them into consideration and agreement was reached). As to the third chapter, the problem of the strategic defence initiative (Star Wars) turned out to be an insuperable obstacle. And because it was so late (about 6.30 in the morning) we decided to end our session and go home, so as to report the results to our leaders.

The next day the most dramatic turn of events came. I was not personally present at the talks between Gorbachev and Reagan, but know by hearsay that during the discussion of the Soviet draft of the 'Directives' (with the additions and corrections made after the night session) there was a moment when Reagan suggested that ballistic missiles be eliminated. Gorbachev answered with a counter-offer – to do away with all nuclear arms.

And for the first time in the nuclear age at the summit level of two superpowers there started something which not long ago would have seemed impossible: the possibility of the total elimination of nuclear arms was being discussed. I suppose it terrified some of the President's men, all the more so as the discussion at first took a serious turn and it was decided to have one more, additional conference after lunch. One can imagine that the conference was not an easy one. Reagan was under constant pressure from his retinue and even took some of his words back . . .

Meanwhile tension grew behinds the walls of Hofdi House among the experts, assistants and journalists. At 6 p.m., when I entered the press centre, it was crowded. The reporters did not take their eyes off the TV screen: it showed Hofdi, its door shut, mysteriously shut. But then came the moment when it opened, one person emerged, then another, a third, then Reagan and Gorbachev. Gorbachev (he performed the role of host that day) saw Reagan to the car. They looked upset, and the journalists immediately understood – things had not worked out! Later the reason became known. The SDI had again been the stumbling block. There came a moment when the President had gone silent, breaking off the discussion by rising from the table.

Gorbachev's conference was quite interesting. He was very emotional, it was evident that he was taking things very much to heart; and indeed, the historic arrangement had been so close, and at the very last moment fell through! (The same mixture of distress and resentment was displayed by George Shultz at his meeting with the press.) But as Gorbachev spoke, it became more and more evident that, despite the resentment, he had made up his mind never to turn back to the past, to a situation where the tables of the disarmament talks, in his own words, were piled up with mothballs and there was no progress at all. In this respect Reykjavik was supposed to become and, I think, has in fact become a kind of watershed. And that's the main thing. I got the impression that, after cooling off a little, the Soviet leader was rather serious in his evaluation of the very possibility of a more favourable outcome to the talks: even if there had not been the problem of the SDI and Reagan had agreed to do away with nuclear arms in the next ten years, he would either have been forced to take his 'yes' back or would have been removed from the political arena (such things have happened in American history).

Thus, though nothing had been signed, there was a political result. After Reykjavik many things changed in Soviet–American relations. But it became evident gradually; all the more so as immediately after the summit there started a battle over interpreting Reykjavik, and the USA tried to distort the meaning of what had taken place there.

And this was understandable – there appeared more and more obstacles on the way ahead, more and more new proposals were put forward (on the Soviet missiles in Asia, on control, and so on). But the Soviet Union displayed great flexibility, it made serious concessions. And by the summer it became generally clear that even in 1987 it was quite possible to conclude an agreement on total elimination of middle-range and shorter-range missiles.

Now I shall turn to the Washington summit. The meeting was the most predictable of all and it brought the least surprises. That was only natural – the agreement had been prepared beforehand and the most heated arguments at the meeting were connected with some paragraphs of the communiqué on the parameters of the next treaty on the 50 per cent cut in strategic arms. An agreement was reached to attempt to work out the treaty in the near future, so that it could be signed at the next summit in Moscow, in the middle of 1988. These were the obvious results.

But Washington had some hidden offshoots as well – the dialogue was being developed, personal contacts between a whole group of leaders of the two countries were being established. And, most important, the Soviet leader, and through him the Soviet Union, had become more familiar to many an American in person and to the public through the media. They had seen the Soviet Union at a time of great transformation, of perestroika and the shaping of a new political thinking. Three days was not a long time, mind you. But it turned out to be instrumental in improving the atmosphere of Soviet–American relations.

Unfortunately, the treaty on the 50 per cent cut in strategic arms was not ready by the Moscow summit. We were quite disappointed by the fact, as well as by the hold-up in ratifying the treaty on eliminating medium-range missiles.

Nevertheless, I think the Soviet Union had every reason for being so intent on arranging the Moscow meeting at the appointed time. It was important not to stop the dialogue, especially on the eve of the US presidential elections, with the international situation so unstable, combining great dangers and threats with new possibilities. There was a substantial difference between Washington and Moscow in this respect. Washington wanted to see results of the shift in Soviet–American relations and in the struggle to reduce nuclear arms materialize first. The Moscow summit would have gained a lot as a result of an agreement on a radical cut in strategic nuclear arms. But it could take place even without signing such an agreement. It could be justified by the very fact of mutual understanding growing, the dialogue continuing, the movement towards the end of the cold war speeding up.

In a way the Moscow summit terminated a whole stage of the development of Soviet–American relations and became a kind of bridge linking it to the next stage. It is difficult to speak of final results in the couple of months after a summit ends – as a rule, the meaning and the consequences of major political events don't shine through at once.

The Moscow summit, like the one in Washington, was not

as unpredictable as the first two meetings had been. But that doesn't mean it brought no surprises. There were some.

I, personally, had not expected the people preparing Reagan's trip to Moscow to try to impart an ideological and even a confrontational shade to it by making a point of the traditional topics of 'dissidents' and 'refusniks'. That was the reason for a certain toughness, but soon the initial idea was overridden by the natural logic of events.

The irresistible wave of shifts in the domestic and foreign policy of the USSR overwhelmed even the obdurate anti-Sovietism, anti-Communism of Reagan – he is known to have 'recalled' his thesis on 'the evil empire'. It marked the beginning of the end for traditional American concepts of a whole range of aspects of Soviet life and policy.

It was also important that the major problems of Soviet–American relations, disarmament in particular, still remained on the agenda. The talks minimized real obstacles and pretexts preventing the conclusion of new treaties. This has not only brought our positions closer on a number of questions, but has brought to light the fact that effective disarmament measures are prevented first and foremost by a lack of political determination, political will.

This is primarily caused by a fear born after the agreement on medium-range rockets had been concluded: what if the next disarmament steps turn out to be a fatal blow to the whole infrastructure of the cold war – the straw that breaks the camel's back?

The 'camel' has indeed been overloaded, even from the economic point of view. The question of who is to pay for the reckless arms race has been sounding louder and louder. The USA wants its allies to loosen their purse-strings. The allies, naturally, are reluctant to do so, all the more so as economy is closing in on policy here. While demanding that the Europeans take up a larger portion of the burden of NATO expenditure, the Americans tell them: there should be a time-limit for us to carry on paying the lion's share of your defence spending. But at present doubt has been growing in Western Europe as to whether the military threat is really great enough to justify the fantastic sums demanded.

There have been shifts in the USA, too, on the home front. Under the influence of economic difficulties (the growing national debt and deficit as well as escalating social problems), the changes in the USSR in connection with glasnost and perestroika have been watched with particular attention. And the public's idea of what the priorities are seems to be undergoing transformations. Problems at home come to the forefront, and not the idea of increasing military might; people are inclined to think more of improving relations with the USSR and signing agreements on reducing armaments.

In my opinion, the Moscow summit will back up these moods. In particular, the new concepts the meeting introduced into the interpretation of the problems of reducing conventional arms and military forces will be very important for Europe. For about forty years, Western Europe has been taught to think of Soviet military supremacy as the Big Bad Wolf, the main obstacle on the road to security. I am not going to insist that we never gave cause for such statements – with former US nuclear superiority, with their policy of surrounding the USSR with military bases, it was probably even natural for us to retaliate by increasing conventional forces on the European continent.

But now the situation is quite different. In the last two or three years, the USSR and its allies have put forward a whole system of new proposals shaping a profile of radical changes for Europe. The West was trying simply to ignore them. But the Moscow summit lifted the curtain of silence. Unfortunately, the Americans did not decide to include that understanding in the text of the communiqué. But Gorbachev told the world about it by having the major points published: the Soviet Union was offering a solution which would rid the Western countries of their anxiety and fears. Let me remind you of these major items: exchange of data on conventional forces and armaments and their exhaustive control by all methods including on-site inspections; exposure and elimination of asymmetries; reduction of military forces by 500,000 men on each side as a first step; and such transformations in the military doctrine, structure and deployment of forces as would make them of use only for defence and not for offensive operations.

The meeting has also demonstrated how quickly the intellectual level of Soviet policy has grown, incredibly quickly. (Let's hope that other countries will soon espouse the new political thinking.)

Four summits, all so different and at the same time so indivisible in political meaning . . . What is their general outcome?

In answering this question, I would like to point out that we have successfully passed the first crossroads, we have turned off the road of increasing tension and aggravation of military rivalry leading to unavoidable danger of a confrontation. And this is very important. For since the early 1980s we have been on that road.

But now we are facing another crossroads, a second fork. One of the roads is quite familiar, it lies somewhere between the cold war and a cool, restricted, indefinite peace, a peace seeming to admit that a nuclear war, as well as any other Soviet–American war, is unthinkable, but with military preparations in full swing and the rest of the attributes of power policy and the cold war left intact.

The second road is total renunciation of the cold war. The second road implies giving up any attempt to solve controversial issues by military methods, acccepting peaceful co-existence as the universal principle of international relations, pledging non-interference in the internal affairs of other nations and recognizing their right to freedom of social and political choice – with all these norms looked upon as basic, inalienable and universally obligatory.

Which of the roads are we going to take?

It is difficult for me to answer this question, because the present American policy is contradictory; because, while admitting a nuclear war to be unthinkable, it hass not given up power as a foundation for its foreign policy.

Moreover, there have been attemmpts to put down the posiive changes in Soviet–American relations to 'American power', to the increasing military force of the USA.

In this connection the following question is relevant. Has

232

the USA become stronger in the 1980s, has it managed to change the military balance with the Soviet Union in its favour? No, it has not. The military balance has not changed, judging from available data (including American, Soviet and European sources). It has been all the more stable as the chances of politically effective use of military force have sharply narrowed. At any rate, this is true of conflicts larger in scale than Grenada or the Falklands. All the great powers, the USA included, have seen that for themselves.

But other indications of the might of a state have become much more important. And this is where the USA has had to retreat, and not least because of excessive military spending. America has not become stronger over the years, and we have not become weaker compared to pre-Reagan times. Something else has changed – we have grown bolder in facing the truth and, consequently, have grown more realistic and wwise. The same is true of the American leadership in the past few years. It would be odd to deny it. You need two to tango.

The 1980s have brought to light one more common Soviet–American interest besides preventing a nuclear war – to lower military and foreign policy spending in order maximally to concentrate their power, their means and their attention on solving domestic problems, economic problems the first among them. And it is only natural in our day and age that these have become top priority in all countries, small and large, rich and poor. But it is not enough to have a common interest, one's conduct has to be adjusted to it.

The shifts have opened up new vistas for all of us – for the USSR, the USA, Western Europe, and other countries as well. What matters now is to make good use of them, without losing any time.

Nikolai Chetverikov

Although Nikolai Chetverikov graduated from the 'Alma Mater' of Soviet diplomats, the Institute of International Relations, he did not go on to become a full-time professional diplomat. He does not regret this, preferring to follow his dominant passion for public activities and journalism – although he has also held some high-ranking diplomatic posts in Soviet embassies abroad. For some time after graduation he was on the staff of the TASS central branch. He was appointed its representative in Belgium and Luxembourg during the period of the cold war, and much of Soviet opinion about the situation in Europe at that time was based on his reports, as he was the only Soviet journalist in those countries. Since then, much water has flowed under the bridge. He travelled and worked abroad for twenty years, in all. Then he was recalled to Moscow and promoted to replace Valentin Falin as First Deputy Head of the International Information department of the CPSU Central Committee. Then he became Chairman of the Board of the USSR Copyright Agency – the organization in charge of cultural exchanges with foreign countries. Recently he has been working hard as Secretary of the Board of the USSR Union of Journalists and Chairman of the newly established All-Union Board for Ethics and Law – a kind of professional court of honour for Soviet journalism.

Samizdat Without the Halo

A commentary on the role of culture in perestroika

NIKOLAI CHETVERIKOV

Traditionally an epigraph is supposed to come from a classical source, something which has long been in literary circulation. But what is written below is best prefaced, contrary to that tradition, by the words of Alexander Gelman, a contemporary Soviet playwright: '. . . Yesterday we did not even dare to think of what we are discussing in our newspapers today.'

Indeed, only yesterday an attempt at objective analysis of such things as samizdat would have seemed impossible to many people. Today we are witnessing shifts in the public consciousness on a scale our country probably has not known since the Great October Socialist Revolution. The tasks put forward by perestroika are truly revolutionary – in essence, depth and magnitude: to improve the well-being of the people and their culture; to clean the sediment off our social ideals; and to create an atmosphere of moral purity and high standards at all of society's levels.

Our literature has always been at the cutting edge of public opinion, objectively reflecting social problems demanding immediate solution. This is even more so today, when the principles of democracy and glasnost in everyday life, while opening up new vistas for the creative intelligentsia, burden it with new responsibility as well.

Literature and art, journalism and non-fiction even more so, are joining in the uphill struggle against distortions of the human soul, against blearing of the mind and numbing of the conscience. They are fighting to affirm the new thinking, which includes a reappraisal of human values.

Glasnost, the driving force of the purifying and renovating process going on in Soviet society, sharply outlines the eroded borderline between good and evil. It entrenches humanism and moral principles in human relations. Naturally, it is not supposed to be interpreted exclusively as freedom of speech, as often happens. In the Soviet Union glasnost is understood not only as the right of every citizen to express his opinion on all social and political issues freely and openly, but also as the duty of the ruling Party, and of all the bodies of power and management, to observe the principle of openness in making decisions; to involve broad strata of the population in these processes and to be responsible for their actions.

Thus, glasnost is a guarantee of the real participation of citizens in discussions of all the country's problems, in working out and making decisions touching upon the interests of the whole of society, and in seeing them through. Besides, glasnost is intended to assist in the revolutionary reconstruction of our society; in creating a new image of Socialism. Hence there is a principled course for developing the art of criticism, which can be an effective instrument of perestroika – but only if it is based on the whole truth and concern for justice.

At the present stage of perestroika this progressive and creative mission of critics stands out, with critics having gained momentum in their role as exposers. Now it is not enough to reveal social diseases, they have to be treated with the 'bitter medicine' of criticism, and the reasons for their existence have to be traced.

An evident decline of morality among our fellow citizens is a cause for alarm. Some cannot withstand the thirst for affluence – only for himself, this very moment, at any cost.

Devaluation of moral values has been promoted considerably by the impoverishment of our mass culture – I am not afraid to use the term 'mass culture' because I interpret it quite differently from our zealots of elite culture. I do not mean 'second-rate' culture, which, ostensibly, is the only culture demanded by the unassuming, unexacting public, but a truly noble culture freely accessible to the widest strata of our society, a culture made by the people for the people and

meeting the whole spectrum of their interests and requirements.

It is evident that this will happen only if culture is created
by bright, talented individuals capable of depicting the whole
truth of our complex and controversial life and the world
around us. The diversity of forms, the artistic search and
penetration into truth, competition, initiative and innovation,
plus continuity, become the guarantees of progress in culture,
which was slowed down during the years of despotic reprisals
and the stagnation period.

An objective appraisal of the cultural process in our country
cannot be uniform, though. For even that hard and bitter
period in Soviet culture and art was marked by many brilliant
works by honest and talented masters.

We have no right to forget that it was the period when such
great creative Titans as Sholokhov and Tvardovsky, Sho-
stakovich and Prokofiev, Eisenshtein and Dovzhenko,
Meyerkhold and Okhlopkov, lived and worked. That was the
time when such stars as Ulanova and Plisetskaya, Ulyanov,
Yefremov and Glazunov began to shine – it is impossible to
enumerate all who have gone and all who are still with us, all
who have worked at creating and multiplying the world fame
of Soviet literature, cinematography, music, theatre and fine
arts.

It would be as inexcusable to forget about the cost at which
selfless art and civic courage sometimes forced their way
through, despite the persecution and reprisals of the Stalinist
period, despite autocratic approaches, despite the bureaucratic system of management in the sphere of cultural development, a system prohibitive by its very nature. It is only
natural for bureaucracy, whatever its form, no matter where
or when, not to admit the new and to be inert in its thinking.
In our country the commanding style which in the 1930s sub-
stituted for the Leninist principles and norms of management
armed the bureaucrat with power at the State level, with the
order. It is always easier to condemn, to denounce a new
phenomenon that does not fit in with habitual concepts, than
to study it, to appreciate and – if necessary – to oppose it with

something which would surpass it in artistic value, purity of ideals and social benefit.

Bureaucracy passed off its natural narrowmindedness as the absolute truth, thus establishing its infallibility as well as the stability, necessity and inevitability of its existence. Our bureaucrat was bristling with an arsenal of orders, local resolutions, instructions, rules and schedules – acts that were against the law (sometimes even unconstitutional), which strictly regulated nearly every step to appease someone up above.

Remember the methods used to mould 'a harmonious personality' not long ago, when, for instance, in Sochi, a famous health resort, women who risked wearing trousers were not allowed on buses, and in Moscow streets self-appointed keepers of the peace and morality grabbed the few Elvis Presley fans they could find and cut off their long hair with scissors.

In the same line our cultural life was trimmed, squeezed into the same pattern established 'once and for ever'. On the whole it inevitably led to the erosion of artistic criteria, when obsequious sensitivity to somebody's attitudes and to the status quo passed for talent and creative individuality. Extraordinary works deeply penetrating the inner self of their characters, full of civic pathos, appeared from time to time too, but they only underlined the general dullness and monotonous mediocrity of series production by slippery craftsmen in literature and art. Wasteful generosity with titles and prizes, decorations and honours, not always deserved, encouraged time-serving and disoriented the artistic tastes of the public.

On the other hand, such a situation stimulated the most active part of the audience to fill in the gaps in their spiritual life in whatever way they could, as far as their intellectual ability and cultural level allowed. They tried to find ways to compare their spiritual life with reality. A part of the creative intelligentsia found their own means of self-expression.

It is difficult to say now whether demand gave birth to supply, or whether supply stimulated demand, but one can say with certainty that all these reasons and others, taken together, favoured the emergence of samizdat.

The etymology of the term and its geographic origin, so to speak, are not open to question – the Russian language is rich in such capacious and accurate words embracing whole phenomena. But it is impossible to give a precise definition of the concept.

In fact, we should speak of two versions of samizdat. The first version implies the publication of a work by a Soviet author abroad outside the framework of the copyright service. (Since 1973 these functions have been performed by the Copyright Agency of the USSR, VAAP, which mediates contracts on publishing the works of Soviet authors abroad and defends their rights.) In this case the author only lacks legal backing, but there is nothing illegal in his actions. In the second case samizdat may be interpreted as independent reproduction (by any accessible means) of some work of art, literature, or science on Soviet territory. It may be the work of either a Soviet or a foreign author. This is what happened with James Hadley Chase whose works were published in Russian in collections of stories and in magazines, but not in sufficient quantity to satisfy his ardent Soviet fans.

Some lawyers are inclined to regard this version of samizdat as illegal, because in their opinion the legal capacity of Soviet citizens does not include publishing activity. However, there are no legal acts in the Soviet Union giving anyone an exclusive right to publish, juridical persons included.

Nevertheless, samizdat (especially in its first version), as it was not covered by any instruction, became the object of struggle in which the usual methods were applied: at best it was hushed up, but it sometimes happened that the authors of writings published by samizdat were oppressed and persecuted.

This was largely because in the West, where samizdat is given an evaluation disproportionate to its role in the life of the Soviet people, the appearance of samizdat books and their distribution was connected with so-called dissidents who, without exception, were proclaimed to be political opponents of the Soviet system.

All the authors who were published in samizdat were regarded as dissidents, though many of them were acting precisely from devotion to Socialism, did not want to put up with deviations from the Leninist conception of Socialism, and wished to see it cleansed of the rusty layers of bureaucracy and sluggishness, of mercenary interests, unscrupulousness and clannishness.

Some people in the West regarded these writers, sometimes prominent, as anti-Soviet and carried on an insidious campaign using their names. Radio stations broadcasting to the Soviet Union and other Socialist countries tried to pass off critical appraisals of drawbacks hushed up in our country as evidence of our system's insolvency as a whole. And here it must be pointed out that glasnost, which has done away with 'taboo themes' and 'prohibited zones', leaves these dishonest attempts with no chance of success. Now the Soviet audience receives so much fresh news, objective, true to life and not retouched with ideological half-truth from the Soviet media, that people no longer feel a need to tune in to a foreign wavelength. They are not interested.

All these famous wavelengths also tried to back those renegades who actually spoke out against the Soviet system; they deliberately set them alongside honest writers calling for renewal of the system in order to strengthen it. Much effort went into making the Soviet creative intelligentsia quarrel and split, into setting it in opposition to the Communist Party and to the people, and that was what made samizdat so vulnerable. Even in our country many people regarded samizdat as illegal, nearly subversive – official disapproval dominated public opinion when there was no glasnost. We are not going to be severe judges, either of them or ourselves: the habit of looking back, of self-censorship, was imposed upon us for years. Even now the postulate 'Everything is allowed which has not been forbidden by law', so indisputable in its logical simplicity, is finding it very difficult to get established in the public consciousness . . .

Samizdat, as we can see, was becoming an impostor in international exchange, adding its own substantial distortions to the West's picture of Soviet reality, a picture which was incomplete and not always true to life.

For reasons which seem quite evident, the overwhelming

majority of samizdat publications contained pointed criticism, touched upon areas of our life which, owing to bureaucratic efforts, were regarded as 'prohibited zones'.

Persistent in his mistrust of the common people – 'they will not understand' or 'they will interpret it wrongly' – the bureaucrat spoke in defence of the spotless image of Socialism, but acted in defence of his post using all the means at his disposal. Instead of engaging in a decisive struggle to denounce and uproot negative factors, which sooner or later, but inevitably, would demand that the bureaucracy admit its own mistakes, and moreover, unconditionally admit the faults of an administrative-commanding style in general, bureaucrats preferred to hush up many of the faults. They were not just ignored, their very existence was not admitted. At the same time these faults were skilfully commented upon, with reference to samizdat, by far from benevolent foreign radio stations giving their own interpretation of the 'truth' about the Soviet reality.

Thus the public in the West received through samizdat either one-sided information or facts out of context, and these formed the basis for their conception of Soviet life; all the more so as the Western propaganda machine, speculating on great natural interest in the Soviet Union, actively advertised samizdat as a reliable source of the 'truth about the Soviets'.

The publishing policy of our country was often subjective, it was not always guided by the artistic value of a work – and that accounted, in particular, for literary and artistic works by foreign authors penetrating the country's market through samizdat. We must confess, some Western writers were shown much kindness by high-ranking but not always competent officials, and were published in the country in huge editions which were not always justified. If we count the number of Soviet editions of *Spartacus* by Raffaelo Jovaniolli, he might be regarded as the outstanding Italian prose-writer of all times – though I don't think Italians would agree with that.

At the same time, the Soviet reader's access to works by other writers who had not pleased our bureaucrats (such as Graham Greene, to name but one) was artificially restricted, with our bureaucrat as mistrustful and touchy as his brethren all over the world.

One more factor that has nothing to do either with politics or ideology should be mentioned, as it created the conditions for samizdat to arise. I have in mind the huge, rigid structure of the editing and publishing process and the extremely poor financial backing and technical level of our publishing business, which has yet to reach modern standards.

I must say that in the course of restructuring our publishing industry some radical steps have already been taken. The practice of publishing books at the expense of the authors is to be introduced by the State Publishing Committee. This is not an uncontroversial measure, to my eyes, because it clears the way for writers without talent but with lots of money. Moreover, as the newspaper *Sovietskaya Kultura* informed us, some writers call the 'Statute' on this kind of publishing 'a classical example of a widely announced right being turned upside down and made fiction'. Whatever the case may be, the innovation is going to assist the democratization of the Soviet publishing business to a certain degree, making it more mobile. The 'rapid reaction programme' providing for urgent issue of books arousing the greatest interest has been welcomed.

I cannot help mentioning the Copyright Agency of the USSR (VAAP) which has made a decisive turn in its work. It exports and imports the copyrights for scientific papers, books and works of art; it offers manuscripts by Soviet authors, written specially for the occasion, to foreign publishing houses, all of which undoubtedly assist in acquainting readers with the urgent problems and revolutionary changes in Soviet society.

Measures of that kind seem to be enough to ensure that samizdat will fade, if not die altogether. But let us remember that these measures became possible only after Mikhail Gorbachev proclaimed from the highest rostrum the main slogan of perestroika: 'More democracy, more glasnost, more Socialism.'

That was when samizdat lost its raison d'être – at least, in the form known in the West. Technically, samizdat exists even now – we know of many extremely interesting articles reflecting the most pressing problems being xeroxed, retyped and copied out by hand, despite the fact that at present the USSR has about 8,000 newspapers with a total circulation of over 180 million! But here, as we can see, the quality of samizdat and the reasons for it are quite different. And even our most inveterate enemies could hardly see it as anything but existence of an acute growth in the social activity and self-awareness of the Soviet people, who are for perestroika heart and soul, and who most sincerely welcome the establishment of democracy and glasnost.

The brighter the light, the darker the shadow. This is how it goes in nature. But under the lamp-post of glasnost and truth there is no room for even a shadow of the samizdat which was so pleasing and convenient for certain Western interests. 'Requiem' by Anna Akhmatova and 'By the right of memory' by Alexander Tvardovsky, *The Quarry* by Andrei Platonov and *The Fatal Eggs* by Mikhail Bulgakov, *Life and Destiny* by Vasili Grossman and *The Children of the Arbat* by Anatoly Rybakov . . . Nikolai Gumilyov's poetry and Boris Pasternak's prose . . . *The Executioner's Block* by Chingiz Aitmatov and *A Sad Detective Story* by Victor Astafiev, *A Golden Cloud Spent the Night* . . . by Anatoly Pristavkin . . . The ardent journalism of Ivan Vasiliev, Nikolai Shmelyov, Andrei Nuikin, Yuri Chernichenko . . . Posthumous recognition of Vladimir Vysotski, 'legalization' of Alexander Rosenbaum and Boris Grebenshchikov . . . An exhibition of the graphics of the tempestuous Salvador Dali and publication of novels by sarcastic George Orwell . . . I shall not go on with the constantly growing list of works which may be not equal in artistic quality, but which have been drawing a picture of our world so rich and versatile that they make people ponder more and more often on a new appraisal of their interdependence, their mutual destinies and their responsibility for the future.

Some of the books by Soviet authors mentioned above (in particular, those dedicated to the dramatic events of our past) were hastily proclaimed 'sensational' in the West.

The reader must understand that it was the Stalin period that was meant, a versatile period marked by daring achieve-

245

ments and inestimable losses, by ruthless conformism and unbending courage. An appraisal of this chapter of our life, which can neither be rewritten nor removed from the life-experience of our State, has been given in Party documents which reflected a position well thought out and historically substantial. This stand has been taken by a Party that holds sacred the memory of all comrades – Communists, many a son and daughter of the country, victims of mass reprisals. But we have to return to the role of Stalin and his personality in our history – there is still a turmoil of opinions.

Some people remember marching into battle with the words 'For our fatherland, for Stalin!' on their lips, and demand a pure gold monument to him. No matter how blasphemous it may sound, there are voices asking that these people be 'understood'. From my own personal experience, somewhat restricted compared to the scale of society's as a whole, I can say that they either cannot or do not want to realize that the heroic deeds of that period as well as our great victory over fascism cost the whole Soviet people superhuman effort. (This was not so much owing to as despite Stalin's policy, which was anti-Leninist and anti-Socialist in nature.) When, intentionally or unintentionally, we substitute the history of administration, with its progress and failures, for the history of the people, they see rehabilitation of Stalin as justification for their own life.

Much more dangerous are the forces which, speculating on such sentiment, try to defend Stalin with the deeply hidden purpose of perpetuating the Stalinist social and administrative structures, norms of Party and social life, and arbitrary decision-making where debatable problems or the future of the people were concerned. When they attack critics and glasnost under the guise of protection of our history and our reality from slander, the opponents of perestroika ostensibly strive to protect the public, especially the younger generation, from disillusionment with the noble ideas which they say could be undermined by 'too much truth'.

In fact, they set up all-round defences of the cult of official hierarchy with its insatiable desire to rule over ideas and feelings, to decide the fates of the 'people below'. And this is where all means are used, including references to foreign authorities, unpardonable, tactless references that can hardly be called naîve – to Churchill, for instance, as Nina Andreyeva did in her letter to the newspaper *Sovietskaya Rossiya*, an epistle that was interpreted by the vast majority of Soviet people as a manifesto of anti-perestroika forces.

We must be no less careful in our appraisal of publications whose authors are vying with each other to embellish Stalin's closest associates.

However, anyone can see that only with the help and instigation of Stalin's retinue can the 'great leader' cult and the repression mechanism thrive. Attempts to free these people of their share of guilt prevent our society from correctly evaluating its history, from learning instructive lessons.

Some people are trying to overstate Khrushchev's merits. But assertions that he, who enjoyed Stalin's favour, was trusted by him and shown much indulgence including high posts, stood apart when the reprisals broke loose, are meant for extremely simple-minded souls.

While admitting the role of Khrushchev in exposing the Stalin personality cult, one should not forget that the 20th CPSU Congress was an objective step in the development of Soviet society, predetermined by historical development, and was not brought on exclusively by Khrushchev's 'willpower and courage'.

Nor can we forget about the negative personal role of Khrushchev with respect to the creative intelligentsia. He could not see that Soviet writers and artists were offering their intellectual and creative potential in support of his well-meaning initiatives, and he pounced upon everything that was not to his personal liking.

Such 'activity' can hardly be justified.

Those who proclaim themselves to be 'more leftish than Gorbachev himself' are playing into the hands of the conservative opponents of perestroika. They are trying to make their extremism seem radical, and their 'leftism' revolutionary. While carried away by war-cries, they exhibit insolvency in concrete actions – and the lesson of Boris Yeltsin is an obvious case in point. Their actions discredit perestroika with the same kind of breach between slogans and everyday life which caused so much moral and psychological damage during the stagnation period and led to apathy and nihilism among our youth.

As you can see, it is not at all easy to make out what has been happening to us. All the more so as our science in general has not yet responded with fundamental works containing objective analysis of events of the past, the recent past included. This mission is now being performed by writers, journalists, film directors (above all, via documentaries) and playwrights. I admit they are too emotional sometimes; they are understandably eager to let everything out, to unburden their souls. But they are doing it sincerely, with the ardent temperament of real publicists. Hence the heightened interest in works of art and literature touching upon problems thrilling for everybody, in the media broaching upon painful themes among which the number of taboos is shrinking. No, people are not after 'cooked-up facts' – they are looking for the truth, the best medicine for society's ills. We are drawn not so much by a desire to expose these manifestations of evil and vice, but by the need to analyse the reasons for them, to find ways of eliminating them.

A return to Lenin's concept of Socialism, a restored belief in the moral force and spiritual health of the people, the decisive course of the Communist Party towards establishing Socialist pluralism as an immutable fact of public life, are all undermining the self-declared belief of the bureaucrat in his exclusive right to judge what we do and do not need.

The renewal of Soviet culture, however, does not merely involve opening up the hiding places where it has been forced to seek refuge. The task is to create such a moral and psychological atmosphere and such conditions for the everyday work of creative unions and societies as would allow all talented works, fully reflecting the people's life and deeds, the real Socialist and humanistic ideals, to find their way to the reader and the audience. That is how the contribution of the creative intelligentsia to improving the Socialist state, to creating a powerful and rich culture, itself becomes rich and powerful, reflecting the talent and Socialist emancipation of our peoples. Accordingly, cultural policy is now based on democracy and glasnost, i.e. upon discussions of everything which constitutes our life.

What is left to samizdat under these conditions of spiritual purification and renewal? Evidently nothing but dirty daub and obvious anti-Sovietism. But this is quite another matter . . . Soviet law includes clauses under which propaganda of war, outrages on national sentiment, racism and pornography are punishable. Society has a right to protect its views and moral foundations; therefore it is inadmissible to use glasnost to impair the interests of the Soviet State and human rights, to advocate violence and religious intolerance. Yes, the time of bans has gone, let us hope, for good. There is more and more of what we call Socialist pluralism – a favourable climate promoting original thinking and free competition of ideas.

For many years our society was kept on a spiritual diet, its progress determined 'from above'. Now the revolutionary process of renewal involves the masses in creative public activity, which is the only real Socialist way to the future. And it demands of everybody activity, independence and initiative in decision-making. And most important, it opens up a real possibility of sharing one's ideas and feelings.

Democracy, the power of the people, is unthinkable without glasnost. For an artist, in particular, democracy in its Socialist interpretation is also freedom to discuss everything that is important to him, and freedom to choose live themes and paints for depicting it; only the truth can be the judge here. Life may be slandered only by lies; the truth purifies it and elevates it.

I mentioned earlier the statistics on the number of our newspapers and their circulation. You may add to them over 1,500 central and republican magazines, with a total annual circulation of more than 2·7 billion copies, over 80,000 different books and booklets published annually, and vast cinema, theatre and television audiences. I repeat: none of the former taboo themes are left. Magazines, publishers and studios decide for themselves what they are going to make public. So now that the word is reaching out to the people with an energy multiplied by the years of forced silence, its value is rising immeasurably.

Glasnost is an inseparable part of a normal spiritual and moral atmosphere in society. It is the driving force of society's moral potential, the instrument of the people's will. Glasnost is irreversible, an invincible weapon against gossip and rumour – a mighty and cutting weapon. This is why it requires careful handling. Do not look for hidden appeals to limit glasnost in my words – this is just a necessary warning to anyone taking the rostrum offered by democratization of our socio-political life to be highly responsible. Today it is extremely important to use the rostrum not only to list facts about society, but to ponder on them, to seek the roots of the problems. At the present stage it is especially important to see from the rostrum what positive things there are, to study them and to utilize them, to make them the property of the masses, to help new approaches get established, and to reinforce perestroika. Glasnost is, in fact, the voice of the people, and it must be raised in order to multiply good around us – in the name of victory over evil.

Reporters' gullibility, superficial evaluations and bias are fatal to the policy of glasnost. Falsities and lies may bring any good intentions to nought or turn them into the exact opposite. Sometimes we come across unchecked news published, vain claims to monopoly on the truth, intentionally lining up the facts to fit into their concepts. Such unscrupulousness, to put it mildly, leads authors who seem, at first sight, to have the best intentions, into the camp of perestroika's opponents who write off the fruits of Socialist democracy and glasnost as slips and miscalculations. Glasnost, evidently, is also a test of our sense of civic duty, conscience and feeling of responsibility towards people.

The Soviet Union is rightfully proud of having achieved total literacy in such a short time, historically speaking. But, as Lenin pointed out: 'You cannot go far on literacy alone. We need a tremendous rise in culture.' It is clear that without general culture, true democracy, true democratism cannot be achieved. This is why the spiritual culture of Socialism is there not only to decorate society, but to be an integral part of it, its intellectual and cultural potential. A breakthrough into the future, a transition of Soviet society to another qualitative state, may be attained only on a wide front that includes the spiritual sphere.

The Soviet intelligentsia, which Mikhail Gorbachev called 'the priceless spiritual capital' of our State, has a great potential of civic responsibility. Its reference points correspond to the political line of the Communist Party, and to the interests of the people. By reaching a new level of thought and responsibility, scholars, writers and artists try to enrich spiritual life, to make Socialist thought versatile, which will aid the advance of perestroika.

Perestroika has acquired world importance. And it is significant that the period after the historic April plenary meeting coincided in time with an evident thaw in international relations, with the beginning of the process of real disarmament after the Soviet–American agreement on medium-range and shorter-range missiles.

A steady course towards consolidating democracy, broadening glasnost and increasing the openness of Soviet society will assist in the development of cultural exchange and cooperation, of spiritual dialogue between peoples, which is so important for mutual trust and confidence. The truth about perestroika, as Mikhail Gorbachev has pointed out, meets the interests of world peace and international security.

Our literature and art have acquired new strength, new hope and new stimuli as a result of the 19th Conference of the Communist Party of the USSR. The historic forum was instrumental in winning for the ideas and aims of perestroika the support of a creative intelligentsia who, in their best works, bring the truth of revolution, the truth of Socialism, to the people.

Tatyana I. Zaslavskaya

A peasant's granddaughter and professor's daughter, Tatyana Zaslavskaya grew up to become an Academician and a distinguished Soviet sociologist. She started her research in the Siberian academgorodok, specializing in a topical problem – 'Social Mechanisms of Economic Development'. Her first conclusions indicated that the study of public opinion and social responses in this large country was still in embryo and that the leadership did not rely on public opinion, so came to grief both in industry and in agriculture through failing to take hold of the social and economic levers of success. The years of sharp criticism and vigorous debate made Tatyana Zaslavskaya the highest authority in sociology, President of the Soviet Sociological Association. Perestroika has measurably increased her scope and she has headed the recently set up National Centre for the Study of Public Opinion on Socio-Economic Issues.

Friends or Foes?

Social forces working for and against perestroika

TATYANA I. ZASLAVSKAYA

Throughout the long decades of the stagnation period, Soviet sociologists kept hoping against hope that their vital school of thought would gain recognition and the right to exist and develop at its own pace. Their hopes failed. Many sociological establishments (institutes, sections, laboratories) were suppressed and disbanded in the 1970s, and many talented scholars suffered. The scholars of Leningrad, who in the late 1950s and early 1960s had stood 'by the cradle' of emerging Soviet sociology, had a particularly hard time. Professor Vladimir Yadov, the best known and most respected sociologist in this country, was literally booted out of the Institute of Socio-Economic Problems attached to the USSR Academy of Sciences, and labelled a slanderer of Soviet reality. Professor Boris Firsov, another prominent expert in the field, shared the same fate. Though the main targets were Moscow and Leningrad scholars, we in remote Siberia didn't have an easy life either. We had to fight stubbornly for the right to continue our research, to poll people on the painful issues which affected their immediate interests. Such polling was referred to as 'provocative' at the time, meaning that we sociologists were 'suggesting' to people that they were short of housing, that shops didn't have enough food on sale, that public transportation malfunctioned, and so on. As if they couldn't see all that for themselves!

As for the results of our research, to be honest, nobody wanted them. Reports were sent to the top Party bodies, raising the same issues over and over again. New volumes of

255

research, describing the difficulties people were facing in their everyday lives, and registering the absence of any positive shifts in public opinion, kept landing on the shelves of archives. But these findings were rarely reported in the press, and when they were, the rewards were thorns rather than laurels.

Today, by virtue of the growth of glasnost and democratization, sociology has been given a prominent role in overhauling the entire system of social relations, while public opinion and its function in management is particularly emphasized. One can understand why by tracing the relationship of perestroika with interwoven social interests, and looking into the strategy of the social management of perestroika.

Perestroika and social interests

The working class constitutes the largest group in socialist society. Restructuring of social relations is in its interest. If the restructuring is successful, the working class will benefit by better satisfaction of its needs as regards goods and services, by availability of additional labour activities, by democratization of industrial management, by more efficient handling of social issues, by acceleration of housing construction, and by improved rights when fighting against bureaucracy.

But perestroika also brings certain disadvantages to the workers, which cannot be ignored: inevitable price increases for stable foodstuffs and services up to the level which will make their production and supply non-deficient and profitable; stepped-up rent rates for surplus housing over the State-guaranteed minimum; and so on. A potential cutting down of redundant jobs raises a spectrum of problems no less involved. This is a natural result of perestroika, the 'social price' which has to be paid for the acceleration of social and economic development in this country, for getting rid of our backwardness.

Perestroika holds different promises for different groups of the working class. Let me begin with the advanced group, which comprises well-trained, highly skilled, innovative, politically and creatively active journeymen, employed as a rule in hi-tec industries. Under the command administrative system the abilities of that group were not used to their full capacity; they mostly 'did as they were told', and remained barred from really creative functions. That group stands to gain more from perestroika than the others. First, they are more interested in getting rid of 'levelling' than the others, that is to say, they are interested in decent and equitable remuneration for high-quality and conscientious labour. Secondly, they are efficiently involved in contract and lease teams, and task forces, set up for particularly sophisticated jobs. Thirdly, those skilled workers eagerly join co-ops, which give them a better chance of self-fulfilment. Also, this particular group of workers usually provides the driving force for self-management bodies, for public organizations, and for the councils of labour collectives. They take an active part in the election of managers, in the struggle for better glasnost in management, and so on. On the whole, this particular group of the working class provides a reliable social base for the reformist activities of the Party.

A lot of the foregoing is also true of the numerous groups of averagely skilled workers whose labour is averagely equipped technologically. These also show a major interest in contract and leased forms of labour. True, paying for results rather than for virtually just time spent in the shop separates conscientious workers from shirkers more markedly than ever before. The first get equitable remuneration, the second, who are fairly numerous, stand to lose as compared with the old ways. But nobody prevents them from starting to perform efficiently. A lot of workers are engaged in all kinds of supplementary labour activities on a cooperative or family basis. They have both the potential (skills and raw materials) and need for supplementary income, as their income level is lower than that of the preceding group.

Taking advantage of the social and economic acceleration, this massive group of workers will probably soon begin feeling the negative effects of accelerated technological progress, and of the new system of management as well. Some of them will have to start looking for new jobs. That will hardly be an issue in major cities, at least not right away. But in the first place, new jobs are liable to be inferior to their old ones, and secondly, things may get somewhat difficult in small towns and in the country. Major problems will emerge for elderly and poorly skilled workers, who have lost the retraining potential, and for the limited mobility groups (mothers of families, and elderly people).

On the whole, the hard core of the working class stands to gain more than to lose from perestroika. That is why supporters of perestroika form a majority of the working class. But many workers contribute little to social activity and initiative, because they are more used to doing as they are told than acting as they see fit. Also, to emerge as an active champion of an idea, a person has to understand that idea in depth, having examined it in the light of his or her own conscience, values, needs and interests. But the bulk of the working class do not yet have a deep understanding of the concept of perestroika; they have not yet grasped how its measures interrelate, or how much it supports their own basic interests. This is hardly surprising; along with cadre workers, the working class comprises many who are poorly educated, badly trained, and limited in their social and political outlook. For that matter, socially passive people abound within the working class, alongside the convinced supporters of perestroika. Some of them take a sceptical position, and do not trust the mass media. ('So, what else is new? Didn't work before, won't work now either.') Others are indifferent to the current changes and believe that the restructuring of management is of concern only to leaders and experts. Still others hold conservative views, and hark back to 'the good old days'.

Another stratum of workers is worth mentioning. These occupied various privileged positions under the old order, and are wary of perestroika for that reason. This heterogeneous stratum possesses a unifying feature: its members are used to getting 'free' incomes, unearned bonuses and privileges unjustified by the level of their professional skills. An opportunity to take more from society than they give back corrupts people. For that matter, the obvious priority of private and group interests over collective and public ones is typical of that stratum.

Who specifically constitutes that stratum? First, that part of the working class which is employed by privileged agencies and departments, and thus traditionally supplied with more comfortable labour conditions, better wages, and larger benefits from the public consumption funds – not because of better performance, but because of the specific employment. Secondly, workers in jobs which are especially short-staffed; these have been able to pressure their foremen into 'setting up' high wages, irrespectively of their performance. The third segment I see consists of unabashedly hack workers, whose 'performance' amounts to converting quality raw materials into unusable products. The fourth segment are those workers who have considerable 'graft' incomes – those employed in car maintainance, public catering, services, the State trade system, collective farm markets, and so on. 'Tips', 'compensations', 'considerations', and often direct extortion provide a major if not the basic share of their incomes. The fifth type is similar; these are the workers who profit from pilfering, or major thievery of raw materials and finished products. It is common knowledge, that light, food and construction enterprises and agricultural industries are still being badly hit by systematic organized thievery.

Naturally, the stratum of the working class, employed mostly in the services, who have been partially corrupted and bought by higher social groups, are not interested in perestroika. The worst part of this group are openly conservative, reactionary even. Its best part, who recognize both the unseemliness and the instability of their position, take a passive stand, displaying a fatalistic attitude to perestroika. Like, if they take away some privileges, they won't just take them away from me, so it won't be all that frustrating. On the whole they are foes rather than friends of perestroika, but not firmly convinced foes, and they do not constitute a major social force.

It is clear from what has been said so far that the mechanism for retarding perestroika is not created by bureaucrats alone. Members of the working class, the leading force in our society, contribute to that mechanism as well, and in no small degree. Thus, according to the sociological research carried out by the Academy of Social Sciences early in 1988,

> only one in four or five rank and file workers supports the economic reform without reservations, expects positive results within two or three years. Others doubt its success, or expect results in the distant future. Only a quarter of those polled deem it necessary to restructure their own ways.[1]

Collective farmers constitute the second largest group in Soviet society. Basic patterns of economic reform fully correlate to the principles of agricultural as well as industrial cooperation.

However, during the entire post-war period all traces of cooperative relations were persistently eroded from the collective farm sector, beginning with freedom in economic decision making and ending with the way income was generated and shared. The process of spreading the realm of Statehood over collective farms went on relentlessly, with collective farms being turned into quasi State farms, run by the same bureaucratic methods with the same low economic yield.[2] I am positive that if some thirty or forty years ago collective farms had been allowed to perform under economic conditions endemic to their nature, not only would we not be suffering from food shortages today, but we would be in a position to export foodstuffs.

For collective farmers perestroika means coming back to Leninist ideas of the development of cooperation, 'unStatehooding' collective farms by liberating them from the guardianship of bureaucratic management, restoring the almost

---

[1] *State and Trends of the Development of Economic Consciousness at the First Stage of Perestroika*, Academy of Social Sciences with the CC CPSU, 1988, pp. 50–51.

[2] Numerous Soviet experts on the economics of agriculture (V. Venjer, A. Nikonov, L. Nikiforov, M. Lemeshev, A. Yemel'yanov and others) opposed turning collective farms into State ones, and sought to prove that under Socialism collective farm production was more profitable than that of State farms; but their voices were drowned by the chorus which maintained that the collective farm form of property was 'lower' than State ownership, which made it imperative to quickly 'erase the line' between State and collective farms.

extinct collective farm democracy, developing self-management, and providing real opportunities to search for profitable economic structures and efficient production methods.

The long-term strategic interests of collective farmers
undoubtedly lie along the lines of perestroika. The issue of
their immediate tactical interests is more complicated. The
previously existing economic relations, though inefficient,
infringing upon the freedom of farms and causing waste,
provided at the same time certain social guarantees by securing compensation for losses even for the worst of the farms,
along with pretty good pay-offs for their efforts. It is true that
collective farms were denied any economic rights whatsoever.
But as they carried no responsibility for the results either,
they ran no economic risks.

Is this a typical picture of stagnation? Yes; but people have
got used to it, and have lost the habit of running things on
their own, and taking risks. That is why perestroika causes
serious concern among a sizeable number of collective farmers. Attitudes are similar to those shown by the working
class: the more efficient, creative, self-assured and skilled collective farmers support perestroika, eagerly form contractual
relations, and by sophisticated and efficient labour get results
which are far better than those of the past. More inert collective farmers, mostly those employed on farms with poor
material and social development, doubt that any positive
shifts are possible unless supported financially by the State.
There also exists a broad stratum of collective farmers who
do not even try to grasp what perestroika is all about, because
they believe it is of concern only to 'the bosses'.

More than one-third of collective farm products are supplied from peasants' individual allotments cultivated on strips
of land assigned to them by a collective farm. The attitude of
the Soviet State towards these allotments has undergone
many changes, ranging from encouragement to forcible suppression.

By opening up opportunities for all kinds of individual and
family endeavours, perestroika has given a 'second wind' to
peasants' private allotments. Collective farm families contract
to raise scores of pigs, oxen and other animals, either on their

261

own premises or using public facilities which they repair themselves. The collective farms supply these families with forage, veterinarian services, and so on, and then buy the products on previously contracted terms. Under this kind of management the private sector in fact merges with the public one. Both peasant families and collective farms benefit, and the whole of society benefits as well. The move towards using the potential of the private sector more fully is in the interests of the peasantry and enjoys their sincere support. Unfortunately not all local leaders share that line. Many of them obstruct the development of private allotments rather than supporting it.

On the whole, collective farmers stand to benefit from perestroika no less than the working class. Their vanguard, like the vanguard of the workers, constitutes the social base for economic reform, and the main bulk are loyal supporters of perestroika.

Middle-level managers, engineers, technicians and scientists constitute a stratum of the technological intelligentsia. At present, admittedly, the socio-economic standing of this stratum is at discrepancy with their public role. The number of technical specialists exceeds public need considerably, while their efficiency falls badly behind the world level. It is no coincidence that the majority of technical specialists are actually employed in the capacity of unskilled clerks, involved with all kinds of paper work. Their labour is devoid of anything creative, and their wages and social standing are low.

As far as the better-skilled, creative, efficient segment of the technological intelligentsia is concerned, they more than any other group suffer from bureaucratic management. They are tied hand and foot by regulations, and do not see their discoveries and research put into practice for years and sometimes decades.

Those specifics determine the ambivalent attitudes to perestroika on the part of that group. To the best and brightest, perestroika promises both better opportunities to introduce the fruits of their efforts into practice, and better incomes and prestige. Technological specialists along with workers take on contracted and leased jobs, and start cooperatives to produce sophisticated goods and those which are in short supply. The majority of them actively promote glasnost and further democratization of society.

On the other hand, this stratum of the intelligentsia is badly infected with scepticism about the reality of changes in economic relations. For that matter, many specialists sincerely sympathize with perestroika, but still do not believe that the retarding mechanism can be eliminated.

Last but not least, there is quite a sizeable group of technological intelligentsia, who are used to receiving their meal tickets and good salaries, but have virtually no responsibility for end results. People of that group either have lost whatever skills they had, or never had them in the first place. They are simply unable to perform under the new conditions, and naturally wish they could last till their pensions under stable conditions.

I include the following personnel in the economic management group: general managers and chief specialists of enterprises, industrial associations, construction and transportation organizations; directors of State farms, chairmen of collective farms, and managers of such major industrial units as shops, sections, and so on.

Managers enjoy high salaries, abundant bonuses and numerous privileges allocated from public consumption funds. Moreover, they have ways of manipulating production resources and finished products to gain some private benefits along with the public ones. Their social and material status is high, but their labour is extremely difficult, intensive, and fraught with enormous physical and moral pressures. Perestroika drastically changes management's *modus operandi*. Managers get a considerably freer hand to work creatively in economic, organizational, scientific-technological and social fields.

But that is one side of the coin. The other side has to do with the necessity to change radically the traditional ways of management, to move from the execution of orders 'passed down' from the top to an independent, sometimes risky, organizational and technological quest. The new conditions increase both the professional and the personal demands on managers, and their work becomes even more involved and responsible. This alone is enough to push a segment of managers to a conservative position, and make them mark time as far as actual changing of management ways is concerned.

To these factors must be added all the confusion and breakdowns caused in many industries by first attempts to implement new ways. These artificially expand the circle of managers who are not happy with how perestroika is proceeding. While supporting its concept in principle, they believe that perestroika isn't really happening, and that many reforms are in reality strengthening rather than weakening the command and administrative structure. Thus, when asked to what extent their positive expectations of the economic reforms have been justified, only 9 per cent answered 'basically justified'; 49 per cent said 'partially justified'; 21 per cent said 'not justified at all'; 21 per cent found it difficult to answer. In the same group, 38 per cent believed that decision-making at the enterprise level was poorly thought out; 44 per cent believed those decisions were too broadly based. Thus scepticism and disbelief in the final triumph of perestroika were common, and many chose to reserve judgement.

Perestroika is bound to result in better material standards for gifted and skilled managers. But only those managers who can utilize the new methods to speed up and improve production stand to gain real benefits.

Perestroika affects the interests of managers too strongly and too immediately to leave room for indifference. But their attitudes are complicated and contradictory. First, attitudes are distinctly different because of differences in socio-personal types and ways of socio-economic thinking. Secondly, managers better than others differentiate between the theory of perestroika and the reality of changing economic relations in practice. While supporting the former, they often deplore the latter.

The next group is composed of trade, public catering and service executives, along with executive personnel of the agencies which distribute material wealth from public consumption funds. This group organizes the exchange and distribution of social produce assigned to public funds. Their relationship to the means of production is nothing special, but they occupy a special position with respect to consumer wealth produced in this country. While not legitimate proprietors, they possess quite broad powers in managing the produce meant for public needs, and they naturally have ways to manipulate that wealth for their own ends.

The wages of this group do not exceed the average level. At the same time, according to sociological research data confirmed by numerous press reports, this is the very group who possess the largest amount of amassed wealth, including seashore houses, foreign-made cars, gold, jewellery, works of art, major money savings, and so on. A considerable if not the major part of their income comes from illegal sources, that is, it stems from different 'games around deficit': profiteering, bribery (when distributing housing, for instance), so-called 'sorting out', when low-quality goods are sold as high-quality ones, channelling products from the State-run trade system into the cooperative one to be sold at higher prices, and the like.

The well-being of this group is immediately connected with the administrative-bureaucratic mechanism of economic management which creates the deficit of consumer goods. No less important has proved to be the weakening of Socialist legality, merging with corrupted Party, soviet and law and order officials, lack of glasnost in management, and the atmosphere of impunity and permissiveness surrounding those vested with power which has prevailed for quite a long time.

Perestroika of social relations cuts the ground from under that group. Self-accounting and self-financing make enterprises interested in precise accounting of the profits made by sale of their products. The transition from rationing to free trade in resources destroys the monopolies of those who used to distribute those resources. Glasnost and the consistent development of democracy, along with control on the part of the working people, facilitate the uncovering of shady dealings which have gone on with impunity for years.

Finally, cooperatives along with individual and family labour activities create competition for State-run retail sale, catering and service enterprises – and the more the better.

The old system is coming to the end. That is why the segment of this social group which is deeply 'rooted' in the old system opposes the changes by all available means. First of all, they aspire to compromise the idea of perestroika in the eyes of the working people. It is no coincidence, as the media testify, that shops are empty in many cities, while supply bases are full of produce. People who managed to obtain railway or airplane tickets to Moscow, or some southern health spa, are surprised to see that the trains or planes are half empty: transportation isn't being used to full capacity. What is this, if not outright resistance to perestroika on the part of those who carry immediate responsibility for the distribution of material wealth in society, for making goods available to consumers?

Perestroika promises hope for expurgation and cleansing to the honest, morally sound segment of this group, and opens up ways to work professionally and with dignity, and reap normal labour rewards. But on the whole the atmosphere is not favourable there. The fields of distribution and exchange of goods will in all probability remain a major bulwark of conservatism and reaction in our society.

Petty cooperators and persons engaged in individual labour activities may be regarded as one social group. Their role in the organization of public labour consists in initiative production of goods and services needed in the country, basically with the help of industrial, labour and intellectual resources which are not available for public production. Petty Socialist entrepreneurs seek to fill in those 'holes' and 'gaps' which regularly occur where there is cooperation between major agencies and enterprises.

Petty producers independently possess and manage their means of production. Unlike those employed in the public sector, they derive income from the sales of their products (goods or services), at market prices which are subject to demand and supply. A cooperative, or an individual entrepreneur, will break even, put aside a development fund, and spend the balance. This kind of making and disposing of income resembles that of a collective farm, but petty cooperators have less stable incomes, as they are more dependent on the market. For that matter incomes become more distinctly differentiated according to the level of entrepreneurship of each collective, and are higher on average. On the other hand, petty entrepreneurs still lose out on access to public funds compared with other groups (in terms of housing, pensions, social security in case of illness, and so on).

The stratum of the populace interested in further development of petty entrepreneurship is quite extensive, and comprises not only those who have already started working, but also those who are still only examining the field of their potential endeavour.

All these people are allies of perestroika. Not only does perestroika let them improve their income, it also leads to better fulfilment of their potential. The most progressive segment of that group view their activities not only from a purely private base, but also from a broader public angle, as their practical commitment to perestroika; and they list themselves among its active supporters.

Another part of the same group is concerned with rapid self-enrichment, often without any regard for law or morality.

The position of a humanitarian intelligentsia under a régime of muteness, spiritual stagnation and social decay was unfavourable in material as well as moral and spiritual terms. That position was characterized by humiliatingly low wages, severely limited supplementary incomes, minimal social prestige and, finally, the impossibility of individual creative work whether in education, in the medical professions, in literature, in the arts, or in research.

Today we see many of these persons among the group who have carried universal human and Socialist values through all the difficulties of the epoch, and thus have prepared the ground for perestroika. We may consider such singer-poets as B. Okudjava and V. Vysotski as initiators, ideologists and forerunners of perestroika, along with the social scientists who put forward the ideas of perestroika even during the stagnation, or the writers and journalists who courageously spoke out against bureaucratic perversions of Socialism. Even now the most radical members of the humanitarian intelligentsia regard perestroika as a social revolution, designed to bring Soviet society back to the Leninist path of Socialist construction. The humanitarian intelligentsia welcome perestroika *en masse*, first of all because of the greatly increased freedom for spiritual creativity, secondly because the development of glasnost and democracy open up discussions of painful social issues which facilitates their practical handling.

One gives due to the humanitarian intelligentsia for their fight against stagnation, but one cannot close one's eyes to the fact that they also did much to support the prevailing state of affairs. The conservative segment of this group, who served as agents or often even authors of previously accepted dogmas, cannot be forced to change their views radically by waving a magic wand. They feel nostalgic towards the past, and they view current reforms not as steps forward, but rather as 'a retreat from Socialist principles', and they are indignant about 'excessive' glasnost, too many open accounts of the past, and so on. A notorious letter by Nina Andreyeva to the *Sovetskaya Rossiya* editorial board served as a conspicuous example of that kind of view. Though such people mostly speak in favour of perestroika publicly, in reality they do not accept it and adopt conservative or reactionary positions. Incidentally, a number of speeches at the 19th Party Conference – to cite only that by the writer Yu. Bondarev – serve to confirm this point.

While our society stagnated, officialdom acquired enormous political power. That group kept spreading rapidly, and in effect dominated society, gradually distancing itself, from all other groups behind ever more rigid social and political barriers. Command methods of rule over the lower echelons, unhesitating execution of orders from the top, formal and bureaucratic ways of handling issues which immediately affected people's interests, the curtailment of direct contacts with working people – all emerged as increasingly typical of that group.

Under the new conditions, officialdom is supposed to undergo radical changes. Giving up bureaucratic ways of management, enlarging enterprises' rights and developing industrial democracy will make many apparatus functions redundant.

The strength and the field of influence of the apparatus will diminish – which is hardly inspiring for those who are still a long way from retirement age.

Serious problems will emerge for that part of officialdom which stays in the apparatus. Under the new conditions the very essence of the Party's political leadership is supposed to change. The Party must learn how to act on the basis of spiritual power, the power of ideas. That idea, in a nutshell, was expressed at the Party Conference clearly enough.

It must be added, that executives of the apparatus are probably the staunchest agents of the ideology of the stagnation period. Many of them still believe in the efficiency of command management, fail to comprehend the real implications of the plan for the market, and keep hoping for the return of the good old days.

Regrettably, conservatives still constitute a majority in the apparatus. Their left wing grudgingly agrees to go for a certain degree of democratization in government, but the right wing is openly reactionary. They do not wish to give up anything, not the least crumb of their power, and they choose to ignore the articles criticizing them published by the central press.

This is not to say that there are no progressive thinkers and competent specialists among officials, who not only support but creatively prepare and develop the concept of perestroika and actively promote its implementation. But most of them do all that because of ideological considerations, in opposition, rather, to their narrow group interest.

The group of political leaders of society includes the top power echelon of the Party and the Government. The obvious dominance of centralism over democracy in governing society has predetermined the exceptionally important function of the top political leadership in shaping the course of this country and handling her most vital problems. The principle interests of representatives of this group are of a political nature, where two components may be distinguished: public and personal. Their personal interests are primarily manifested in aspirations to preserve and maintain their own powers. But political leaders preserve and strengthen their positions in quite different ways: either through highly efficient theoretical and organizational efforts, and sophisticated handling of complicated poltical issues; or through setting up private clans, whose members support each other by virtue of social and family connections. Those who opt for the first way require the highest level of political, economic and social awareness, along with civic courage, unbending will and a deep conviction of the historical necessity of perestroika. The people recognize such qualities in Mikhail Gorbachev, in some of his closest lieutenants, and in a number of other leaders.

At the same time the group in question still contains quite a number of people who have been shaped by the period of social stagnation and are used to administrative command rule. While paying lip-service to perestroika, they maintain the old ways in reality and persistently frustrate all attempts to democratize society. Cadre turnover tends to improve the situation somewhat, but proceeds slowly and not all that successfully.

To provide a more comprehensive picture of the structure of contemporary Soviet society, it is necessary to look at the numerically small but influential and dangerous mafia of organized crime, which incorporates the corrupt segment of trade and service workers, shadow economy tycoons and the corrupt area of officialdom, including law and order agencies.

In this case we are not talking in terms of petty pilferers, profiteers and bribe-takers, but in terms of major criminal families, who have imposed and maintained a régime of lawlessness in 'protected' areas over the years. A proportion of that group have been uncovered, tried and sentenced, but the other part have gone underground. However, they cannot afford to wait passively, and perestroika can have no more implacable foes, who will stop at nothing. Here we are confronted not with just conservatives, but with fierce reactionaries, to whom fundamental Socialist values are alien.

The strategy of social guidance of perestroika

Up to now I have analysed people's attitudes towards perestroika as functions of their objective positions in society and their involvement with certain social groups. But in reality the views and conduct of individuals towards perestroika depend upon many private circumstances.

Thus levels of skills and training are of major importance, along with levels of awareness of ongoing processes, political and practical background, scope of vision and the depth of perception of private, group and public interests.

Age factors prove to be of considerable importance in attitudes towards perestroika; generations shaped during different historical periods develop different attitudes. I find the highest social activities among two age groups: young people (those no older than 35–38), and elderly people (no younger than 55–60). Those are the generations who happened to 'take a gulp of freedom' while still young (before they turned over 30–32) – in the first case after 1983, in the second in the middle 1950s and early 1960s.

Subjective attitudes to perestroika also depend upon personal creativity. Creative people are usually distinguished by high energy, radicalism of political thought, and a leaning towards revolutionary reshaping of reality. Persons of the opposite type are more inert and passive.

Also of great importance are personal experiences, such as involvement in reform-making, level of involvement in the old system of social relations, maturity of social ties, and satisfaction with the acquired position. Finally, individual attitudes towards perestroika depend upon such human qualities as honesty, integrity, decency, ability to feel for those with less advantages, and so on.

For those reasons, inside a single class, social stratum, or group one meets people whose attitudes towards perestroika not only are not identical, but are even opposed. Workers who run neighbouring machine tools, scientists who work on the same problem, officials who run the same bailiwick, are often 'on opposite sides of the barricades' where perestroika is concerned. Thus the differentiation of the populace along the

271

lines of perestroika seems to be of a two-dimensional nature. The groups which are elements of the social structure of society are differentiated by dominant types of attitude towards perestroika. At the same time there are persons with different attitudes towards perestroika within each of them. I see the following as the most conspicuous types of those attitudes.

1 Ideologists and movers of perestroika. This group comprises people convinced of the necessity of a radical revolutionary remodelling of the social relations inherited from the past. They realize that no acceptable alternative exists to that remodelling, and that any digression from the mapped course, any delay, not to mention any 'quiet folding up' of perestroika will threaten the fate of Socialism both in the USSR and elsewhere. People of that group are distinguished by practising what they preach: not only do they speak in favour of perestroika, but they also fight for it, not sparing their strength or health. They are the standard-bearers of perestroika, who tackle the worst problems, overcome the biggest difficulties, and thus blaze the trail for others. This group is not all that numerous, but its historical role is enormous. It is a kind of 'yeast' on which the 'dough' of public growth raises.

2 Followers of perestroika. This more numerous group contains people who unequivocally support the concept of perestroika, who share its ideas or even develop them creatively, and seek to implement them in reality. They are the best, the most progressive, energetic and creative part of Soviet society, who are prepared to work to capacity in order to support renovation and promote the prosperity of this country, improving their own level of life by the same token. This group comprises people of democratic and humanistic persuasions, dedicated to ideas of Socialist justice. When confronted by retarding mechanisms, they engage with the foes, but due to their disunity do not always win. Many of them experience major difficulties and frustrations, but do not as a rule change their convictions.

3 Social allies. In this group I would class those who are not dedicated followers of the concept of perestroika (just because they do not know what it is all about, or doubt or disagree with some of its provisions), but are personally interested in other specific aspects of ongoing reforms (like the emergence of co-ops, individual labour, better rights for labour collectives, better glasnost of management, acceleration of scientific and technological progress, etc.). The attitude of these groups towards perestroika is less stable and reliable than that of those mentioned earlier. Their attitudes are more a product of the difficulties they have met when trying to assert their interests.

4 *Quasi supporters of perestroika.* Those are people devoid of either deep moral principles or strong political persuasions. They are ready to serve any master, to assert any 'truths', to organize people to handle any problems, as long as they incur the bosses' favour and get promoted. To judge from their words, those people ought to be registered among the most ardent supporters of perestroika. But as soon as they notice that the political atmosphere in this country shifts unfavourably, they immediately quieten down and reserve judgement. Their danger lies in their unscrupulousness, combined with a high level of visibility. Regrettably, the leading cadres of this country are quite generously littered with such people.

5 *Watchers.* This group unites people who in principle support the concept of perestroika, but who have had negative experiences of early attempts of social reforming, or of current reforms. They prefer to watch from the sidelines, sympathizing with the perestroika camp, but not believing in its ultimate victory. Their own position is not stable either, and depends to a great extent upon the actual development of perestroika. Each tangible success reduces their scepticism, each failure refuels it. On the whole, the group in question may be reasonably well regarded as a potential reserve for perestroika.

6 *'Neutrals'* are a socially inert part of the populace, who have not as yet developed any definite attitude towards the processes going on in the country. Locked into their own private or narrow family interests, lacking in culture and social experiences, they are distinguished by social passivity.

7 *Conservatives.* This group comprises persons who were

shaped during the periods when democracy was suppressed, and the command and administrative management flourished. Their outlooks have been permanently affected by social stagnation. For the most part they are convinced of the omnipotence of 'His Majesty the Plan', of the un-Socialist nature of the market, maintain that World War II was won by Stalin's genius, and so on. They have to adjust to the new conditions, and thus they have to pay lip-service to the necessity for certain changes, and often use the perestroika vocabulary. But in the narrow circle of 'their own' they brand the concept of perestroika as 'anti-Socialist'. This group applies profound and quite effective efforts to hold back the transformation of society, and to prevent perestroika from gaining momentum and becoming irreversible. Conservatives are the main social component of the mechanism which slows perestroika down.

8 *Reactionaries* do not accept the ideas of perestroika for even more fundamental reasons. Inasmuch as the conservatives juxtapose the ideas of perestroika with their own dogmatic concepts of the 'advantages' of Stalinist 'barrack Communism', the reactionaries are basically alienated from Socialist and humanist values. Some of them live by pure greed, unembarrassed by legal or moral considerations. Others, corrupted by their unlimited power over scores of thousands of people, aspire to preserve or restore a situation in which no action on their part is ever judged.

Other attitudes towards perestroika also exist. Thus, a certain proportion of young people fail to tell real values from false ones, and blindly follow false leaders and 'innovators'. They believe they are serving perestroika, but in reality they damage it.

Now, what is the correlation between these groups, distinguished on the one hand by their objective positions in the system of social relations, and on the other hand by their personal views and convictions?

The movers of perestroika are the progressive political leaders and economy managers, along with the radical part of the socio-humanitarian intelligentsia, advanced workers and peasants.

The followers of perestroika are the most widespread group. They are found within all social strata except the most conservative ones, which indicates the extraordinarily broad social base for ongoing reforms.

The allies of perestroika are workers, peasants and petty entrepreneurs.

Quasi followers are found in all groups of the intelligentsia involved with management, and among officialdom, while workers, peasants and craftsmen do not need to display any such political mimicry.

The position of interested observers is typical of many strata. The groups whose performance demands a more definite standline are exempt from it. Those are political and economic leaders, managers, advanced workers and peasants, and petty entrepreneurs.

A neutral attitude towards perestroika is typical of the most inert and passive section of manual workers.

Both conservatives and followers of perestroika are to be found in almost all groups, except advanced workers, peasants and petty entrepreneurs – who wouldn't have thrown in their lot with perestroika had they been of conservative mettle.

As for open reactionaries, they are concentrated in a small number of groups, which ought to be given special attention in the process of guiding perestroika. Those are: first, the corrupt part of the Soviet and Party apparatus; secondly, executives of trade and services; thirdly, the part of the working class in the pay of the aforementioned groups; and finally, organized crime.

That obviously makes for quite a complicated picture. On the one hand society has split into groups, considerably (often diametrically) differing in their views on perestroika. The mass media provide daily coverage of the struggle of social forces pro or contra transformation of social relations, which provokes most lively discussions and emotions. As society becomes more deeply involved in perestroika, the groups of 'neutrals' and 'observers' gradually diminish, while the confrontation between the dedicated followers and the consistent opponents of social renovation emerges in the most obvious way.

On the other hand, we have seen that people's positions on perestroika are determined by their social affiliations, but not all that rigidly. In this connection the general arrangement of social forces around perestroika is somewhat 'vague', At the same time Mikhail Gorbachev and other leaders of the Party keep emphasizing the not just deep, but positively revolutionary, nature of ongoing perestroika. From the point of view of those tasks which await decisions, the forthcoming transformation of social relations can hardly be described as anything but a relatively bloodless (though blood was shed in Sumgait) and peaceful social revolution. Therefore, we speak in terms of preparing a strategy for guiding not just a regular though complicated evolutionary process, but a revolution which will drastically transform basic socio-political structures and lead to a radical redistribution of powers, rights, duties and freedoms between classes, strata and groups.

Two kinds of question arise in this connection. (1) What are the social and class priorities of the revolution? In the interests of which social groups is it being waged? (2) What kind of social price must Soviet society be prepared to pay for successful perestroika? I shall discuss both of these points briefly.

I do not believe that analysis of the distribution of social forces has given any grounds for viewing perestroika as a social revolution of, say, workers and peasants against Party and Soviet officialdom, or trade and services executives. From my point of view, this is a revolution of the radical democratic part of this society against its conservative and reactionary part, while the groups who have still not determined their positions are becoming increasingly involved in the struggle. I cannot agree with the opinions voiced by some authors, that perestroika meets the interests of all social groups equally, that class and social contradictions no longer exist in our society, that all social groups 'are on the same side of the barricades'. If all social forces were on the same side of the barricades, there would have been no need for barricades to exist. Whereas the barricades (by which I mean lots of invisible but clearly felt boundary markers) obviously divide society into the group of movers, followers and allies of perestroika on the one hand, and the group of opponents on the other. It is to be expected that each of these two groups will gradually consolidate, and recognize that its interests are in opposition to those of the other. It is in this sense that the question arises of what 'social price' this society may, must and subjectively is ready to pay for getting rid of its backwardness, for expurgation, moral renovation and accelerating development.

Is any revolutionary transformation of society possible without considerable social struggle? Certainly not, as this transformation drastically changes the relative and absolute positions of classes, strata and interest groups, so that some gain at the expense of others to a certain extent. To deny the inevitability of, not just contradictions, but the heated struggle of group interests as well in connection with perestroika, is to ignore reality. Whereas it is obvious that even the present early moves towards revolution are giving rise to extensive social struggle.

Given the fundamental opposition of interests of the democratic and the reactionary wings of society, attempts at conciliatory approaches to social conflicts often result in truncating the essential ideas of perestroika. I believe that the whole complex of problems which reflect the slow progress of perestroika, and the dissatisfacion of working people with the results achieved so far, ought to be considered from precisely this angle. The guiding strategy of perestroika should be to contain and defuse possible and probable social conflicts. But one-sided emphasis on social compromises, and inordinate fear of stepping on the toes of the groups who obviously do not care for perestroika, may create a brake which will slow down both the depth and the extent of the process.

There is no such thing as a free lunch. Revolutionary perestroika of society cannot be achieved without payment, either. Perestroika will cost intense struggle and profound conflicts of group interests. This is what political leaders should expect, this is what should be made clear to the populace, this is, finally, what should be accepted by anyone who has not already been scared off by the word 'revolution'. And the social strategy for perestroika must be to guide the social ship across the ocean to the desired shore of perestroika with minimal losses and damages.

Valentin M. Falin

During the war, when still in his teens, Valentin Falin worked as a turner at the Krasny Proletary plant in Moscow. Subsequently, he became a diplomat, his career reaching a diplomatic climax in 1971 when he was nominated Soviet ambassador to the Federal Republic of Germany. He held this post till 1978, when he was promoted to First Deputy Head of the CPSU Central Committee department. Although it would seem that new promotions were close at hand, his career suffered a number of setbacks and for some time he stayed in the background. From 1983 to 1986 Falin was one of *Izvestiya*'s political reviewers and since 1986 has headed one of the largest news agencies, APN. Valentin Falin has to his credit numerous publications, both in this country and abroad. The 27th CPSU Congress elected him an alternate member of the CPSU Central Committee. He is Vice-President of the USSR Journalists' Union, a member of the Presidium of the Soviet Fund of Culture and State Prize Winner for 1982.

Glasnost : Getting at the Roots

VALENTIN M. FALIN

'In the beginning was the Word . . .' Well, probably there was one. Anyhow, we are told that Earth's civilization started with the Word. But did glasnost also emerge from the primeval mud? That is the question. Which raises another even more difficult one: what is glasnost?

Every country has its own custom. Socrates invited: 'Speak, I want to know thee.' A weather-beaten Arab objected: 'The ten wisdoms are to remain silent nine times out of ten, and speak only the tenth time – a little.' Goethe went further. He believed people would have kept their mouths full of water to prevent speech if they had known how rarely what they said was understood. Our Russian Koz'ma Prutkov was a first-rate dialectician. 'Think before you speak,' he taught. 'Maybe you won't speak at all if you do.' His followers are legion.

To whom and to what should we give credence? To what kind of glasnost? When we talk, not of individuals, but of human communities, referred to as states, and of relations between those states, which are governed by people, not by gods. Not just by people, either, but by relatives, according to science. The latest hypothesis populates all continents with decandents of the same mother – Eve. Which does not pre-vent, but rather helps, heated discussions and battles involv-ing a temperamental application of freedom of speech, as befits relatives. Or is the Patriarchy to blame for everything? Who knows? Verily, he who knows us does not look like the one we know.

What freedom of speech has not suffered! Especially since, long before atomic energy, greed and perfidy split the word, took the soul out of it, and turned a natural means of communication into (to borrow Harold Lasswell's terminology) one of 'the main three weapons' – the other two being economic and military might. Thus he who is concerned with human well-being cannot remain indifferent to what this weapon is loaded with, and what charges the word intended to guide human thought and endeavour.

To render war impossible, everyone will have to cleanse his mentality of the ideas of violence, and his vocabulary of the stereotypes of hatred and enmity. This may prove more difficult and in a way even more important than material disarmament, or just disarmament. To eliminate enmity one has to overcome one's own mistrust and bullishness, and accept unconditionally that a bad friendship is better than a good fight. We don't really have any choice. Either we learn the art of good neighbourliness in a dialogue of good faith, or we doom our civilization to degradation and extinction. We ourselves, and nobody else, programme our future today. And that of our children, and their children's children.

Let me state this as explicitly as I can. Man must accept his own mortality once and for all, whatever exotic technologies he invents, whatever new physical laws he discovers. Even if wars are waged by robots, it will be people who will be claimed as victims. Security depends on the natural intelligence of political leaders, not on the man-made intelligence of weapons. Objective interests of development require that this truth be publicly recognized and acted upon.

We will not be forgiven if, blinded by prejudice, or just through inertia, we miss the turning that each policy which wishes to remain fully realistic is seeking. Situations do occur where vanities have to be set aside, when the basic issue of 'to be, or not to be' comes forward and supersedes everything else. What are the concerns then? According to N. K. Rerikh, a famous Russian artist and scholar, people try to save what is most precious to them: their children and their knowledge. This is in order to avoid the extinction of mankind, to avoid Nature having to look for another species able to start all over again, from the intelligent Word.

Is it only the Soviet Union which is confronted with the dire necessity to restructure, to get busy with a profound reassessment of axioms, structures and beliefs; to analyse critically each step made, both long ago and quite recently? Can it be that elsewhere theory and practice link up with ideal visions and realities so perfectly that no gaps are left, that all dreams come true, and all that remains is to rest on one's laurels? Such a thing as a non-problem, no-conflict society has never existed. Nor can it exist at turning points in history, when conventional wisdom is of an optional value at best, and one has to get by on one's own inner strength.

It is no exaggeration to say that the new thinking knocks upon virtually every door in this world. Not every door opens to admit it though, even as a guest. The new thinking has moved into our Soviet house because people of a new type have emerged as leaders of the Party and the country.

True, nothing is stronger than practical ideas. But it is also necessary to be able to hear how the grass grows; to separate the seed from the weeds; to feel the concerns of society and to share its dreams. The word, too, must come from within. Otherwise convictions degenerate into empty talking, and glasnost and freedom of speech degenerate into mere demagoguery.

'Glasnost and freedom are interlinked,' said Mikhail Gorbachev,

– but they are not identical. One may put it this way: freedom of speech is a necessary prerequisite for glasnost, but glasnost is somewhat bigger than that. We understand glasnost as not only the right of every citizen to voice his or her opinion on all social and political issues, but also the duty of the ruling Party, and all bodies of State administration, to adhere to the principle of openness in decision-making, the duty to be responsible for their actions, to respond to criticism with deeds, to consider the advice and recommendations of labour collectives, public organizations and individuals.

And the General Secretary concluded:

Glasnost, the way we see it, emphasizes conditions under

which citizens may really participate in discussing all affairs of the country, in decision-making on the issues which affect the interests of society, and in control over how those decisions are carried out.

Developing those thoughts, Mikhail Gorbachev emphasized at the 19th Party Conference that 'there is no renovation without glasnost', and that without glasnost we would not have been able 'to create a new morally political atmosphere in society, to push the ideas of perestroika forward . . . Glasnost', the Soviet leader said,

> means pluralism of views on any issues of domestic and foreign policy, free comparision of different opinions, and discussion . . . Glasnost isn't compatible with any monopoly of views, with imposing new dogmas instead of those we give up now, with pursuing group interests, or particularly with distorting facts and settling personal grudges. It is entirely undemocratic to deprive those criticized of the opportunity to answer the point of criticism.

For the moment, this is the most coherent presentation of the Soviet stand on what virtually emerges as the hard core of debates on the role and place of an individual in the contemporary world, on his or her right to self-expression and participation in establishing norms to guide actual actions in domestic and foreign policies, if not in the specific actions themselves. To state the obvious, I will add that what Mikhail Gorbachev described is not what Soviet society has become yet, is not what has already emerged and taken roots in Soviet reality. No, this is something we have still painstakingly to work for.

But now, since the 19th Party Conference passed the special resolution 'On Glasnost', which specifies the further development of glasnost as one of the basic political priorities of the Party and the whole of society, it is easier to pursue these ends. Glasnost has been institutionalized as the indispensable condition of the democratic nature of the Socialist system, its human orientation; as the efficient guarantee against deformations of Socialism, built on the foundations of all-people

control over all social institutions of power and administration. The conference viewed glasnost as the indispensable
condition for Socialist self-governing of the people, constitutional rights, freedoms and duties, and irreversibility of
perestroika for the sake of democratic and humane Socialism.

Overnight transformations of such magnitude occur so
rarely that those precedents which did exist look like dreams
in retrospect. I will not plunge far into history, just state the
fact: seventy-one years ago, post-February Russia was the
most democratic country in the world, not by formal parameters either, but by the most real ones. In October of the
same year, 1917, the capitalist world shuddered and then was
infuriated because of the social and political glasnost displayed by the Soviet Republic. That glasnost called all spades
spades: the imperialist war was called imperialist, enslaving
nations was called oppression, the system of barbaric exploitation of working people was called inhumane.

Incidentally, the 'classic democracies' were badly upset by
the determination of Soviet power to make public all the State,
diplomatic and economic secrets of the overthrown régime,
to make available to the masses the real information on how
policies under Tsarism had been made behind their backs
and against their interests, who had made them, and what
alliances were operating.

London and Paris, Washington and Tokyo, scores of other
bourgeois capitals read the Soviet variant of democratization
and glasnost, the call upon the working people to take over
the fortunes of the country, as the rebellion of the rabble.
Our intention to educate the masses socially and politically, to
make them able to understand the realities and do everything
with their eyes open, was interpreted as an impermissible
attack on 'the established order of things'.

Really, something unheard-of was happening in post-
October Russia, and retrogrades viewed it as 'outrageous'.
Not only did the Bolsheviks expose the inner workings of the
Autocracy and its institutions, but they destroyed the seven
seals which hid from the uninitiated the intricate mechanics
of brainwashing, the alchemy of making and waging wars,
and partitions of the world. Unbelievably, the secrets of

secrets crowded the front pages of the Soviet dailies, and filled magazines, books and documentary publications to the brim. The stormy sky crashed on an Olympus accustomed to social calm. Social and property castes were dismantled. The former slave raised his head and emerged as his own master.

Try to recall what was used to scare a citizen in 'a good society' in those times. Not Soviet military power, because nothing of the kind existed. Not any political or economic expansion – no grounds existed for those either. The mortal danger was seen to lie in the ideals of people's rule, social justice and national equality.

Attempting to protect their territories and colonies from 'the diabolic temptation', imperialist countries started to wind rings of hostility and disinformation around Soviet Russia, to apply armed pressures and blockades. They attempted to bar us with 'cordons sanitaires' and all kinds of curtains. They attempted to keep Moscow at a distance from world problems, and to consider Soviet interests in them at the very last turn, if at all.

It may be said that it is easier to give away someone else's secrets than one's own. True. Even the Bible speaks of 'the speck in thy brother's eye, and the beam in thine own eye' . . . But Lenin did not call for a one-gate glasnost game, nor in fact did he call for any glasnost games at all. He wrote in his early book *What Is To Be Done?*: 'It would have been ridiculous to speak about democratization without glasnost, and such glasnost at that which would not be limited to members of the organization alone.' According to Lenin, glasnost means a truthful conversation, to the point, 'without boasting, or literary swordsmanship'. Glasnost, as Lenin emphasized, is 'the sword which will itself cure the wounds it has inflicted'.

After the October Revolution Lenin insisted that the widest possible information on the activities of the soviets, the administration and public organizations be made available to the masses. He wrote in 1921: 'We need complete and true information. The truth should not depend upon those it is supposed to serve.' Lenin took care to have regulations published which would provide for glasnost and restrict to the *minimum minimorum* the list of secret data. Unfortunately, he did not have enough time left to do more.

What happened, happened. I am not raising this issue to start another endless argument about the East's and the West's faults. I believe it is more important to emphasize something else: the events of that epoch are meaningful because they testify to the ability of the spirit to triumph over force. The Soviet example was turned down as something 'illegal', but it could not be ignored. Under the influence of this example, world politics underwent changes, along with the philosophy of security, the structure of the world community, and even the domestic scenes in the citadels of the 'Western democracies'. Damning the Bolsheviks, the leaders of the latter had to release the pressures from their own steam-boilers, and smooth off the corners from their most uncomfortable social issues. Just because the USSR was there.

Therefore, for a certain period in history the Soviet Union did indisputably call the tune in the affairs of real non-commercial glasnost, and our political and ideological opponents could only either adjust or try to hinder and slander us. So there was a time when we did not hide our heads in the sand but challenged, and sought competition with, anyone who dared to engage us in the realm of human rights.

When did it happen that we ourselves deviated morally and politically from probably the most precious gift given to us by the October Revolution – from the right and means always to be sincere, to speak only the truth and nothing but the truth to ourselves and to all others? When and why did the living become hostages and victims of mythology, which stymied first the thought and then the deed? When the backbone of our science, culture and journalism ceased to be creative, and turned into an apology for itself, who usurped the power and turned everything upside down in the State, society and the Party?

I have a simple answer: when Lenin's successors broke away from Leninism both ideologically and morally; right when the intricate political mathematics were replaced with primitive 'whatever you say'. Guided by the need to make 'all memos and decisions of the Central Committee' available to every party member, the CC published *News of the Central Committee of the Party* from 1919 to 1929. At varying intervals, usually once a week, or every ten days, they published the documents of the CC, reports of all of the CC departments, accounts of organizational work in the provinces, and articles and addresses by Party leaders. Every Soviet citizen had the right of free access to any non-secret documentation, information and materials on the activities of a local soviet, its executive council, and services; he or she could be aware of the duties and performances of State agencies, and could be present at the functions arranged by State and public organizations where conditions permitted such participation.

Lenin left the bridge and left this life. Then the trouble started. The Party Rules accepted right after the October Revolution aimed to develop glasnost in the performance of all Party agencies. But the 16th Party Congress held in December 1925 cancelled the precise terms of the CC's accountability to local organizations and only obliged the CC 'to account regularly'.

The turn towards elimination of internal Party democracy and glasnost occurred in 1927. The *News of the CC* ceased publication in 1929. By the mid-1930s it was all over with glasnost, and freedom of discussion. The mechanism of lawlessness and tyranny, programmed by the power-happy dictator, started working to full capacity.

Alas, the warning made by Marx about 'the ever-present danger of the government usurping class dominance' had no effect. Lenin's Testament, which insistently advised the Party to have Stalin replaced, was left unheeded. Yes, he who claimed 'to make all classes happy', he who thought himself to be the owner of the philosopher's stone, and guardian of eternal truths, appeared. The Living God was infallible by definition, could not make mistakes, or meet bad luck, not to mention defeats. Even technical catastrophes or natural disasters were not allowed to happen in the country which he ruled autocratically. As he soared out of the reach of his adversaries and the envious, only complete adulation and applause, parade marches, and triumphs – in statistical data and on newspaper pages, as well – were permitted.

But what of defeats or failures which could not be hidden, or dealt with under the cover of silence? Then look, not for the woman, as the French advise, but for the 'enemy of people'. Find him, make him confess his mortal sins, and have him destroyed for the glory of 'The Only and Indispensable One', who believed in his own exclusiveness, and made others believe too. And not only the Soviets and their friends, either. Just look up Winston Churchill's message to Stalin dated 17 February 1945, and read the concluding lines: 'I pray for long life for You, so that You may guide the destinies of Your country, which has displayed her greatness under Your leadership . . .' Quite a panegyric, as good as any offered by the homespun eulogists who fed us all that stuff.

It may be asked whether coming back to our senses hasn't taken us too long. That is a reasonable question, and it is not easy to answer. At first sight, it seems simple: get the portrait off the wall, pull the nail out when you can lest another portrait take the place of the old one, and that's it. That was how Nikita Khrushchev saw de-Stalinization, or something like that. Khrushchev started out feeling very strongly about this. Over the years my job brought me in touch with him, and I have grounds for saying that Nature endowed him richly. If only his fundamental education and culture had been as strong! Then he might have looked for the answer to Stalin's riddle beyond the dictator's personality, and penetrated the system Stalin devised to implement his beliefs, which were absolutely alien to Socialism the way Lenin saw it.

Inability or lack of desire to get to the bottom of things or to provide questions with adequate answers, along with proneness to hare-brained plans and instability – why else should Khrushchev have indulged in persecution of the Church, 'art criticism', and persecution of co-ops and individual labour? – these were the primary reasons for the collapse of the reforms of the 1950s. Khrushchev's successors stuck at a similar watershed, when they started looking for consolation in brushing up the wording for non-existent deeds, instead of dealing with the main illness, which was the gap between deeds and words. 'Real Socialism', 'the economy must be economic', and other 'theoretical' revelations of this kind imitated activity, served as political mimicry. They did not change the course of things, and could not meet with any positive response from the populace. The illnesses were driven deep inside and the country plunged into lethargy.

How to start, which link to pick up in order to free the public mind and the ship of State from the fetters which bound them and drew them off course? The new Soviet leadership has opted for what they think is the only right thing to do – to turn to the best teachers, which are real life and the people's wisdom. The leadership has had to tackle a great burden: analysis of the entire seventy years of the Party's history and that of the country, using all the data and not making any allowances. To do that they have had to remove the blindfolds from their own eyes, to fuse politics and morals, to compare the interests of class, and of individuals, of the country and of mankind, in order to find common denominators; to open up numerous banned zones which have been created over the decades, and to do all that without sparing ideological and other relics, without fearing to wake up the ghosts.

The highest manifestation of glasnost under concrete Soviet conditions was raising one basic question for national discussion: have we got the Socialism for the sake of which we perpetrated the October Revolution and suffered so many hardships? Did we choose the optimal alternative out of the ones available to us after the Civil War was over, and the last aggressor had been driven from our land? Was Stalin our fate, immanent to the Socialist system, or did he violate that system and the world view upon which the system was based? What is the optimal choice for society today, and how should this choice materialize in practice? What is necessary to exclude the possibility of relapses into Stalinism from all realms of our existence, and on all levels? Are reliable guarantees for that possible unless we make structural changes in the system itself?

This is the pivot around which passions are rampant and spears get broken, and all with the biggest glasnost. All the rest are details. Important, bright, even conspicuous specifics. The public organism may feel uncomfortable without them, but still will keep functioning, and even gaining weight. Not only is this the pivot, but it is the finest tuning-fork to verify the ongoing processes, to read the aspirations of different groups and individuals, the anatomy of words and the meanings of arguments. There is no hiding it: people often use the same formulas, slogans and mottoes to express mutually opposed ideas and interests. I mean, you won't find a general or a politician in this world who, while preparing for war, won't swear he thinks in terms of defence only. Thus mankind 'kept defending' till two world wars, and will keep defending till the third one, if it doesn't come to its senses. That war will be the last, as nobody will be available to pick up the seeds of future conflicts from the battlefields. In a similar fashion there are only a few people in the USSR who would openly speak up against perestroika. According to the latest sociological research, four-fifths of the populace approve of the changes in the country. Inconveniences of sorts do spring up here, when instead of basic restructuring some people attempt to wash the spots off the 'well-tested' patented means under the cover of a formal vote 'in favour', and impose these means as the only 'orthodox' ones, using their profound knowledge of human weaknesses.

There is nothing external that does not immediately become internal in this intertwined and integrated world of ours. And vice versa. Thus domestic policies of the states serve as their foreign policies. Comparison of internal and external, consistency of actions, views and deeds, show not just the surface of events, but rather what happens behind the looking-glass. If this is true generally speaking, it is doubly true when checked against glasnost.

As has happened only too often in the twentieth century, glasnost is quite capable of performing the function of anti-glasnost, or of the screen which hides affairs, diametrically opposed to its info-propagandistic wrappings. We all know that, both from personal experiences and in no lesser measure from experience of world events, which every now and then take tragic turns because of two kinds of glasnost: for internal and external use, for the chosen and the rejected, as a result of a splitting of politics into visible and invisible spectres, the split personalities of the politicians themselves, and split morals.

'Glasnost is indivisible, glasnost is broader than the state borders,' said Eduard Shevarnadze on 8 June 1988 addressing the UN Disarmament Session. We do not restrict the Foreign Minister's thought to the limits of the information field. We are not indifferent to what is sown and grown there, a noble seed or a poisonous weed. In an epoch when the future of the mankind is hostage to the eternal captivity of reason, it is our mutual task to restore the indivisibility of truth.

Maxim Gorki believed that speaking the truth was 'the most difficult of all arts'. Maybe because there is nothing more universal, and more brilliant, than the truth. There is only one truth, but it will be enough for everybody, reads a wise proverb. The truth is the answer to all the challenges facing civilization. Upon one condition, though: that all are equal before the truth, so that on its way to the audience the truth does not get polluted by vicious hands or mouths.

Let us recall the Ems telegram: one forged word led to the Franco-Prussian War. There have been many cases when just one word, suppressed or uttered, has ruined not just an individual, but governments, parties, creeds, states. Now the image of the prophecy emerges as a reality: a word may ruin the world, a word of an order which will prove that darkness also may spread with the speed of light.

Shevarnadze pointed out in his letter to the UN Secretary-General (of June 1988) that the USSR attaches fundamental importance to moving from separate confidence measures, openness and glasnost in international relations, to large-scale policies in this realm. These policies are called upon to become an integral part of the comprehensive system of world security, a tangible factor of effective confidence-building, and upgrading the predictability of countries' actions – all part and parcel of the disarmament process.

In the framework of the process of real disarmament opened up by the INF treaty and the emerging 50 per cent cut in the Soviet and American strategic offensive arsenals, the issue of openness, the Soviet Minister emphasized, acquires a new dimension. The issue of real, not demonstrative, openness should not be limited by several states arbitrarily divided into 'open', and 'closed' societies. The Soviet Union proves by deeds that we do not find it a problem to be transparent in the military realm, and to take an active part in shaping the realistic ideas of military potentials, doctrines and intentions of states, because the USSR stands against disinformation and the creation of myths which only step up power confrontation and the militarization of ever new realms.

Accordingly, the USSR supports the Resolution of the 42nd Session of the UN General Assembly 'On Objective Information on Military Issues', and stands ready to join the UN supervised activities aimed at unifying the criteria of evaluations and accounts. When conditions are ripe for realistic comparison of data, the USSR will make them available to the world community.

It is worth mentioning that our efforts to discredit thinking in terms of power, and move on to practical disarmament, are part and parcel of the democratization of Soviet society, of its perestroika. They testify to the sincerity of our plans, and of our belief that the task put forward is practical: to liberate the world from the evil of militarism, and to help the triumph of common sense.

It should also be pointed out that there is openness and openness. There is talk of sabre-rattling, and destabilizing actions. But do those who hear it always realize that this sabre-rattling does not have to use the sound of tank tracks, the whining of battle aircraft engines, or images of the grey masses of warships overwhelming the victim for its effects? The military cacophony may include publishing doctored figures, advertising the murderous capacities of weapons systems, 'leaking' of a country's readiness to go the whole hog, and interviews with 'interesting' people. Is that kind of openness necessary? Is it permissible to use considerations of 'the utmost glasnost' to justify this 'psychological warfare' backed up with 'impressive' arrays of military appropriations, the placing of orders for 'state of the art' armaments, Rambo-type 'heroic deeds' and American-style mini-series on TV? Where is the distinction between commitment not to use the threat of force, and glorification of violence?

Now we have started, let's keep discussing the limits of glasnost. Russian literature has a parable of hospitality extended to absurdity and humiliation by just too much of a good thing. Are we still within the limits of glasnost when a person's mentality is all but crushed by the avalanche of information? Even if the avalanche is crystal clear? Formally, its components can pretend to be 'facts'; but taken together they will produce a false image, like a binary chemical cell, where two innocent components get mixed together and result in a deadly potion.

A fact, as rightly noted by Gorki, is raw stuff, from which the sense has yet to be distilled. The influx of information ought not to turn into annihilation by noise, into destruction of the personality, into polluting the spiritual environment. Physically, we all had the same creator – Nature. Morally, we all are the product of circumstances, and of our own, critical or unthinking, reaction to them – and not least to the information with which we are surrounded during our waking hours.

Of course, monologues and mono-opinions are alien to glasnost. Without pluralism any development will ossify, or go round in circles. From our cognizant experience of the Universe, philosophy has drawn the law of the struggle of polarities. Hopefully the philosophers won't mind if I venture to suggest that we should think not only in terms of fighting, but in terms of polarities working together, in terms of their dialogue.

So, glasnost means dialogues, and dialogues require a certain level of culture, tolerance and good will. A sense of humour will not hurt either, though one cannot get by on a sense of humour alone. But first of all a dialogue is adorned with honesty, which admits that one may be wrong, while one's opponent may be right, be that in high politics, or in daily existence.

Two newspapers, or two different TV channels, report similar but still different versions of events. That is a dialogue; but still not the entire dialogue, no matter how smartly presented. Why do the mass media (except the news agencies)

294

seek news (or create it themselves when they fail to find it), and spread sensation? Not for mutual enlightenment. They basically address themselves to public opinion. They maintain a dialogue with public opinion. But does this make the receiver of their information an equal partner in the dialogue? Of course, he can buy or not buy a newspaper, turn his TV set on and off of his own free will – he is even free to smash a TV set, if it pleases him. But still even the most demanding customer must be satisfied with the observing function only.

I won't boast that Perestroika has found the keyword for our writer–reader partnership. I'll limit myself to stating a modest fact: positive developments are obvious. Glasnost has expanded the rights and the duties of the Soviet mass media. The most significant one is the right to cover and report everything which is not restricted by law. No, they may not invade privacy, or disclose medical, military and certain other secrets. War propaganda is banned, along with propaganda of violence, national enmity, and pornography. Slanderous and deliberately false information is not allowed. That is normal, and it cannot be any other way. Otherwise, whatever is not banned is allowed.

I would cite democratization as a major achievement of our mass media along with letting their audience speak up with a more audible voice. Not the pre-rehearsed one, but the spontaneous voice of the people, which renders the sound of life truthfully. This goes together with the right to demand answers to criticisms of administrative, Party and social institutions. I believe that criticism without response loses a lot, and that the mass media cannot possibly set themselves up as the mouthpiece of the public and the means of efficient control over legality and justice in society and the State.

Admittedly, the new ways do not emerge all that easily, or without conflict. Still, there are quite a few officials, who view themselves as annointed by God, and those below them as the screws in some kind of inanimate machine. People of that kind, here and elsewhere, are always eager for the 'sweet glasnost' which pleases the palate and the eye. But they just can't swallow the bitter glasnost. In this country it took the Decree of the USSR Supreme Soviet 'On the Responsibility For Suppression of Criticism' to treat this phenomenon. It is high time we learned to really apply it in the courts of law, because in the first six months of 1988 only thirteen cases were started against those who suppressed criticisms, and only one person was prosecuted.

At the same time, the mass media have ceased to be a no-criticism zone too. No newspaper or TV programme may distort facts with impunity, or interpret them in an insulting way, or in contravention of existing laws. For example, only the court is entitled to pronounce a person guilty. If a journalist presumes to usurp this prerogative, he is liable to be made accountable, and if his actions involve bad consequences he is liable to be prosecuted. Publication of disputed or false information provides its subject with the right to demand a public apology. The 19th Party Conference Resolution on Glasnost registered the right of every citizen subjected to criticism to have a valid answer published in the same newspaper.

The way I see it, glasnost is not limited by the mass media. The important aspect of glasnost is the openness of officials and administrative agencies, their availability to the citizenry – what we call the undeniable right of every citizen to obtain complete information on any issue in public life which is not subject to State secrecy. The intention is to fix constitutionally the right of Soviet citizens to obtain information, to prepare legal acts specifying the rights and obligations of the State, officials and citizens in the execution of glasnost.

Lashing out, or the rapid obtaining and spitting out of information, cannot provide indicators for glasnost. Naturally, the gap between an event and its reporting creates confusion, rumours and disbelief. The rumours always snowball, often when there is no snow at all. When finally, people learn that nothing really happened, an unpleasant echo still sounds: why were we not told?

A legend exists among Soviet pressman that soon after the United Kingdom entered World War II, a meeting was held in London to discuss how to deal with enemy propaganda. The decision was made to be the first to report their own troubles. There is no way of knowing whether any such meeting was ever really held at all. But still, the idea is sound. The Soviet mass media accept it.

I write this confidently, though I know I shall immediately be taken to task over Chernobyl and the Yeltsin affair. How were they compatible with current glasnost, or do they indicate imperfections in the ongoing processes? It is stupid to try to break through open doors, and to deny the objective and subjective growing pains of the new information policies. The inertia of the old ways has not been fully overcome yet. The bank of positive precedents is only accumulating. I shall attempt to support this point with the known facts.

Chernobyl. When the fourth reactor failed, which happened late on the night of 25/26 April, the nuclear power station (NPS) administration wanted to play down the danger in the vain hope that they would be able to avert the worst. The chain of irresponsible actions which had preceded the explosion helped to determine the cowardly reaction of some NPS leaders to the catastrophe itself. This and many other things became known much later. But the failure to come up with a truthful report badly impeded the search for optimal ways to handle the extraordinary situation.

Were any opinions voiced in favour of an immediate public report of the accident during the first national-level discussion of the event? Yes, there were. Not because of the danger from radioactive pollution – such data were not available yet – but because of elementary logic. The accident had happened; there were no reasons to cover it up, and no ways to either. The opposing arguments also were founded on logic – the purely formal kind: if it wasn't known what had happened and why, there was no point in 'alarming people'. By that time fragments of fission material had started falling on the ground, and the evacuation of people out of the affected 30-km zone emerged as the most urgent task. The problems of information were put off for yet another day.

What can be said in retrospect? The reactions were no different from the pattern which had already been set by similar nuclear incidents elsewhere. The Three Mile Island explosion in the USA, and accidents in West Germany and England, set the precedent. On all these occasions attempts were made to postpone unpleasant explanations to the public and to avoid admitting that a serious accident had occurred – but the fact that everybody behaved the same way is no excuse, nor does it change the sad fact that the Chernobyl catastrophe was the worst yet.

But every cloud has its silver lining for those who are able to learn from their misfortunes. Chernobyl served as a revelation and showed in a way what will be in store for the planet if Man forgets himself for a second, and ceases to check his wishes against realities – even in his peaceful affairs, not to mention his military ones.

Chernobyl promoted the development and codification of nuclear glasnost. The international convention on compulsorily informing the IAEA of serious breakdowns in civilian nuclear plants was signed. Issues of nuclear power security became subject to public and scientific debate in the Soviet Union. The pros and cons of territorial placements of new nuclear power stations are evaluated more thoroughly than previously, and with broader participation from the public. A number which were in the design stage have been cancelled, and construction of some others has been abandoned.

Chernobyl drastically changed our approach to public coverage of accidents and disasters, especially those which involve loss of life. The Soviet press, radio and TV now report events such as the *Admiral Nakhimov* catastrophe, hijacking attempts, the Arzamas railway explosion, and so on, right from the spot, citing a lot of controversial opinions, and judgements. The influx of glasnost in this field creates an impression that democratization has led to slackness and disintegration of discipline, which is resulting in industrial and transportation catastrophes, and disasters in the streets.

Under the old way, people were calm partly because they were ignorant. The decline of crime in this country was reported so regularly that one was left wondering why any crime still existed here at all. It seemed there was no drug addiction in this country, no drinking problem, no prostitution, or homosexuality; everything seemed to be fine with invalids and orphaned children; public health didn't seem to be a problem; naturally, no problem existed in the realm of international relations, or social justice, or any other. All problems were typical of other social systems; if any popped up here they were only 'the spots' of the past. Thus, problems didn't exist as long as we didn't mention them. When we did start mentioning them, we were bringing into our 'pure' society alien decadent phenomena from outside.

Strange as it is, those moods are still quite widespread, and may be explained by information gaps only partially. I, for one, see here a symptom of a serious disease, which is a desire to close one's eyes to 'other people's' problems for the sake of one's comforts. This disease inevitably leads to discord and disunity, to the loss of ability to feel for others, to the loss of compassion. He who does not feel the pain of others cannot be really humanly healthy. Fyodor Dostoevsky said that all the happiness in the world could not compare with a single tear from a child offended by injustice. A society which remains indifferent to its neighbour's sorrows, and lives parasitically off his grief, isn't worthy of respect.

In several decades, human genius has achieved more than all previous generations, but civilization has gained little, if at all, in humanitarianism. The cruel twentieth century has roughened up our feelings, truncated decency, made our souls insensitive. We have seen an information explosion, the rise of journalism and openness, glasnost, but at the same time human communities are failing to climb out of their egocentric bondage, which inevitably forces people to see everything in terms of 'their own' and 'alien'. Politics has broken away from morals, and found itself chained to chariots of war. At certain stages politics displays servility to militarism, and functions as a continuation of war by different means.

There are things for all of us to think about. The unacceptable patterns are worth looking into, but mostly in order to avoid the mistakes others have already made. Also, and this is important, current problems only seem to resemble the old ones. In reality they are quite different in their nature and require original solutions. Man cannot change his environment without changing himself. It is not just that we have, physically, grown in size and stature over the last couple of centuries. It is not just that man becomes physically mature earlier. Man is overfilled with information, while his ability to assess things is often critically impaired, and his moral criteria leave much to be desired.

Another and dangerous global contradiction is obvious: the renovation cycle of the natural sciences keeps accelerating. Revolutions follow one another in rapid succession. We are on the verge of upheavals in biology, medicine, energetics. But how about politics, ideology and psychology? No visible movement there. Movement in what direction? Can we overlook the fact that justification and support for decrepit and even ancient criteria of the true and false persist even in the most contemporary and newest technologies? This contradiction has assumed antagonistic shapes in the realm of the military. In the realm of ecology we are close to the limit, beyond which the Earth will doom itself to withering. In the realm of demography mankind faces an explosion with unpredictable consequences. And in some strange way, everything locks up at the very end of the century, and the millennium, as if it is not a calendar date that lies ahead but some kind of Rubicon.

What is in store for civilization on the other side of the river? Is the shore steep, or sloping? What is it paved with? With fragments of dreams that never came true? Or do new shoots break through the frustrations, shoots of agreement between Man and his environment, and accordingly of his internal harmony? One can't live in a new way if one keeps on thinking in the old way, under any social régime.

But – *retournons à nos moutons*. How is glasnost compatible with the Yeltsin affair, if at all? I could wriggle out of that one by pointing out that the records of, say, the British Cabinet are not disclosed for thirty years, and that some remain closed even after a century. Why should the USSR be any different? But it is hardly worthwhile to dissemble, and thereby inflate the episode which occurred at the October 1987 Plenum of the CC CPSU. As Mikhail Gorbachev admitted at the 19th Party Conference, we chose the greater evil.

On the occasion of Boris Yeltsin's speech, both he and his opponents proceeded on the assumption that the Plenum debates would not be published, as this had been the established tradition. Mind you, Yeltsin was not discriminated against in any way at all. I'm not sure whether he would have approved of breaking with the tradition in this particular case either, as making his words public would have involved making the words of other Plenum members public, and they were not all that flattering to Yeltsin, to put it mildly. In recent comments Yeltsin has deplored his bad timing and poor wording. As a witness, I can hardly help agreeing.

A speaker who comes to the rostrum without a prepared text gains immediate attention. If he is also lucid and coherent, his words will be heeded. The audience may have reservations, but they won't pick each line to pieces. Few causes and few speakers are sufficiently inspirational to persuade an audience to share their views rather than their emotions. Yeltsin definitely was not among that number that day.

Leaving aside repetitions and pauses, Yeltsin's address took four minutes at the most, but he certainly packed those minutes. To the best of my knowledge, he did not put his diatribe down on paper after the Plenum either, nor did he authorize the shorthand record taken in the hall. Thus, a conflict of opinions was there, but no formal record exists – providing fertile ground for rumours.

What was his position, then, and what were the arguments?

Perestroika had lost momentum. This was his starting point. Society, which had eagerly looked up to the ideas of renovation, was alarmed. The failure to force reforms through immediately and in a drastic way was turning expectations into frustrations.

Basic reforms of the entire Party's work were the key, Yeltsin went on. In this context he voiced his frustration with the ways of the CC Secretariat, and drew a grim picture of his personal relationship with Yegor Ligachev, whom he accused of an undemocratic style of leadership. Yeltsin also felt that the Politburo could have functioned in a more business-like fashion.

Either he had insufficient experience of work in the highest Party bodies, or his short temper was to blame, but anyhow, Yeltsin concluded, he had failed to find his place in the Politburo. For that matter he didn't consider himself equipped to continue in his capacity as an alternate member of the Politburo, and he appealed to the Plenum to relieve him of those duties.

That was a record of his words as I put them down while he was talking. And I made a note on the same page: 'Looks like B.Y. decided to create Yeltsin's problem. Let's hope he fails to have Ligachev's one created.'

Addressing the 19th Conference, Yeltsin basically repeated what he had told the Plenum. This time he read a prepared text, quite a long one, which was later carried by *Pravda* and other newspapers. Strangely, Yeltsin glimpsed only direct or indirect proofs of his case in the report and discussions, but failed to see any hints of his own faults or imperfections. That is a pity.

The conflict of Yeltsin with Yeltsin was bound to break out, and did. Yeltsin the arch-reformist isn't compatible with Yeltsin the arch-conservative. One can't fight Stalinism by Stalinist methods, one can't forward democratization by anti-democratic means, one can't assert respect for individuals by displaying contempt. Vicious ways may compromise the noblest ends, just as demagoguery may kill glasnost.

B. Raushenbakh, a famous Soviet scientist, notes that there are two kinds of knowledge: rational and irrational. The former counts, the latter feels. Rational knowledge is alien to moral categories. Kilometres and kilograms, seconds and hours, dollars and roubles call the rational tune. Irrational knowledge puts forward culture, ethics, concepts of good and evil.

Where does the 'golden mean' lie? How does one stop a human being from turning into a computer? It goes without saying that the selective glasnost for one kind of knowledge only, which we come across every now and then, destroys the human soul.

What do we aspire to? What is our vision of civilization beyond the second millennium? Common denominators are difficult to find as no consensus exists among national communities and political systems. But those denominators are vital, if we want to avoid our civilization folding at its current page. I believe this is what glasnost and freedom of speech are all about – educating us in responsibility for our words and deeds, and exploring the real dimensions of time and space of our contemporary existence.

The face of the twentieth century is pockmarked with militarism. A prominent American researcher said some ten or twelve years ago that the policies of tomorrow are born on the draughtboards of military laboratories. Shifts for the better in Soviet–American relations, and the first concrete steps towards real disarmament, might have rendered his judgement less categorical today. I am ready to make a risky prediction: the future of the world community will grow ever more dependent on the quality of information available, and the level of information culture.

Every ocean has a shore, and glasnost cannot be without shores. Nor can any freedom, in a society which claims that democracy is conceivable as a function of a balance of a great many individual freedoms. Each régime will express this function in its own terms, will emphasize its own laws accordingly, and will not fail to have its social interests protected by exceptions. Whether the latter is admitted or not does not change the equation. Whether it catches the eye or not is of no importance.

The Soviet Union will not emerge available for the understanding of the world overnight. To be understood by others, we must first understand certain things about ourselves. We must decide for ourselves whom we deem worthy of our respect, and to whom we deny the credit of confidence; on what we base our optimism for the future, and why, and what feeds our hopes that that future will not pass us by. I think it is only too natural.

Of course, we hate to admit a lot of painful things. We would be only too happy if we could have certain facts and events crossed out of our history. But there is no getting rid of the truth. The greatness went hand in hand with the baseness, the glorious with the shameful. Mind you, we do not try to invent excuses. We are more concerned with the issues of where and why the evil emerged, and why the immunity of the system failed. We opted to avoid the conventional way of the prophets without honour in their own country; we did not rush to search for patterns, or at least for comfortable pretexts for our renovation. Accept it as a sign of the system's maturity, and an expression of its confidence in its own strength.

We have to go through purgatory, and do so with no reservations or cunning whatsoever. Everybody must be rendered unto according to deeds and merits. The true image of every single episode of Soviet history must be restored without any white-washing, or covering up. Where we cannot set the record straight, that is exactly what we have to admit: that we do not yet know, that we must seek witnesses and testimony. But under no circumstances must we create versions out of thin air. That can only be harmful.

Perestroika has already printed once-disgraced books in millions of copies, restored the stature of scores of cultural figures formerly anathematized for different reasons, or for no reason at all. Boris Pasternak and Andrei Platonov, Anna Akhmatova and Mikhail Bulgakov, Nikolai Gumilyov and Vladimir Nabokov have regained their places of honour in our literature. Films have left the dusty shelves they had sat upon for years. They struck notes discordant to the period of stagnation, but fall so naturally in step with democratization and glasnost that it is as if they have just been produced.

Huge advances have been made in the fields of science and technology, which contemporary generations are almost unaware of. Like Socrates in time immemorial, N. Vavilov was forced to drink the cup of sorrow along with hundreds of other scientists. Why? What did genetic science get in the way of? Whose displeasure did the theoreticians of physics provoke with their formulas? Any slander planted by home-spun envious rivals or foreign adversaries, any chimera of the 'cibernetics are idealism in science' type, was given more credence than a word of honour. Inconceivable!

Overall restoration of the way things really happened in 1917 and in the following years has started and keeps developing across the board. Stalin's show trials of Lenin's closest lieutenants, which virtually beheaded the Party on the eve of World War II, are now being re-evaluated on the basis of evidence and records. Nikolai Bukharin has been reinstated along with many other prominent revolutionaries. Their honour has been restored.

These changes are irreversible. Society has sky-rocketed high enough to see the whole picture, not just separate parts. Waking up isn't always a pleasure. It is tough admitting to yourself that you have wasted your life, while so many of your fellow countrymen were being destroyed by baseness, evil and stupidity. But we have to go beyond emotions. We will be successful here as soon as we cut short the shadows of the past, as soon as we fully restore to Socialism the truth stolen so perfidiously.

Criticizing the past is not an expedient way to justify or support the concept of perestroika. Accordingly, glasnost does not confine itself to giving descriptions and evaluations of what has been. Glasnost is the way things get done, and chart the course for the future. The 19th Party Conference, its very mood, its atmosphere of involvement, its high demands on standards of decision-making, provide what may well be the best proof of that.

Nobody is barred from perestroika *a priori*. The Party does not divide people into followers or opponents. Presumed virtuousness is a condition for normal relationships within a family, a society, a country, or between countries for that matter. Perestroika gives everyone a chance to fulfil himself, calls upon everyone to show what he is capable of. Conditions are created for everyone to openly and freely express his or her position in respect to the new Soviet revolution, which openly states its credo: to give Socialism back its real human face – so that people will not only be born equal, but will stay equal all their lives.

Metropolitan Alexiy

Metropolitan Alexiy started his church life, after leaving secondary school, as a psalm singer at the Tallin Cathedral and later at Kazan Cathedral. He received his spiritual education at the Leningrad Theological Seminary and Theological Academy, and over a period of eighteen years rose from deacon to Metropolitan.

He was granted the degree of Doctor of Theology for his *Essays on the History of Orthodoxy in Estonia*; has been elected an honorary member of the Leningrad and Moscow Theological Academies, and of the Crete Orthodox Academy (Greece); was Deputy Chairman of the commission which prepared the celebrations of the Millennium of the Baptism of Rus; and has been President of the European Church Conference, a member of the board of the Soviet Peace Fund, board member of the Rodina ('Homeland') Society and Vice-President of the Soviet–Indian Friendship Society. For his church, ecumenical, patriotic and peace-making activities, Metropolitan Alexiy has been granted the highest honours of the Russian and other Orthodox Churches, and awarded orders and medals of the USSR. At present he is the Metropolitan of Leningrad and Novgorod.

Looking Back after a Millennium

METROPOLITAN ALEXIY[1]

The celebration of the Millennium of the Baptism of Rus has become a nation-wide event. To be honest, not long ago it was impossible to imagine that via television the whole country would be able to hear the hymn 'How the Russian Land Faces God' performed in the Bolshoi Theatre by the joint chorus of Trinity Sergy Monastery and of the Moscow Theological Academy and Seminary; that millions of people would watch *The Cathedral*, a TV documentary, on their screens. That Andrei Gromyko, Chairman of the USSR Presidium of the Supreme Soviet, would meet the participants in the Jubilee festivities of the Russian Orthodox Church in the Kremlin and would pointedly speak about the prominent role of Christianity in the destiny of our fatherland. And that the work of the Local Council of the Russian Orthodox Church, the fourth one in the past seventy years, would call forth such a public response.

Of late we seem to be witnessing several discoveries of considerable significance for our life. A substantial part of our society has discovered that the idea of the Church being a harmful, doomed remnant in the backward consciousness of some of our citizens, an attitude predominant in the official ideology for many years, was an ignoble attempt to deprive the people of their historic legacy. Besides, it became clear that atheism at any price was not necessary, and moreover, it was harmful, because applying that principle was inevitably connected with violation of both the historic past of our country

---

[1] Metropolitan Alexiy of Leningrad and Novgorod, manager of Tallin and Estonian dioceses, chairman of the European Conference of Churches, Board member of the USSR Peace Fund.

309

and the freedom of conscience of millions of our compatriots. I believe that our society has realized that all of us, both believers and materialists, are heirs to our great spiritual tradition; and it was that very tradition which introduced the truth of goodness, charity and love into our life – the truth, which, if buried in oblivion, makes people pay dearly.

Our State power has arrived at definite conclusions. The pointedly attentive attitude to Pimen, the Patriarch of Moscow and all Russia, to us, members of the Holy Synod of the Russian Orthodox Church, to the participants and the guests of the Local Council, was not just due politeness, but a sincere desire to cooperate. To work hand in hand here on Earth showing concern for peace in the country's prosperity, for purity of human relations, for strengthening the spiritual basis of the life of society – the very manner in which these tasks have been formulated shows how mistaken were those who wished to deprive the Church of any activity, to cut off all the roads leading from the Church into the world. A new law on freedom of conscience, which will free the Church from petty tutelage, will be a determinant condition for such cooperation.

I suppose the local authorities who have not always respected the rights of the believers have come to serious conclusions now. Absolute respect for the individual, recognition of his inherent right to his own outlook – these are the democratic principles to guide the authorities, not only in Moscow, but everywhere. And this is where the example of the new thinking in this sphere of life, too, is extremely important, the very example given to us by Mikhail Gorbachev and Andrei Gromyko.

The Russian Orthodox Church took some very important steps during the celebration of the Millennium of the Baptism of Rus. 'The Charter on Russian Orthodox Church Management' seems to be a worthy result of the joint efforts of the 272 bishops, clerics and laymen who gathered at the Local Council. The discussion of the draft of the Charter and the speeches of the Council participants on other problems of Church life testified to a new freedom of thought among believers, to the defeat of old fears, to an awakening desire to put things in order in our Church home.

The Local Council was dedicated to the Millennium of the Baptism of Rus. This is why it appears to be necessary to look into our part to the best of our ability, to discuss the role of Christianity in the destiny of our fatherland, its role in the cultural and spiritual development of Russia.

As I am going to dwell on the Millennium of Russian Christianity, on its importance for the fate of Russia, I think it best to start with history, beginning from the year 988 in Kiev, from Vladimir Svyatoslavovich, the Prince of Kiev, from the Baptism of Rus . . .

Though many historians, Church historians among them, name some other dates in this connection, I am inclined to regard the year 988 as the time of the Russian baptism. Among secular and Church historians the question has not received a final answer which will satisfy everybody, and this is not likely to happen. But indeed, the exact date is not of absolute importance. What matters for us is that, as *The Word on Law and Grace* by Illarion, the Metropolitan of Kiev (eleventh century), tells us, Prince Vladimir 'wishes with his heart and soul to become a Christian'. Of course, our chroniclers, St Nestor among them, might have made a mistake. But in our discussions of the Baptism of Rus, we have every reason to regard the year 988 as the most reliable date from the point of view of history. I state that, not only as a representative of the Church celebrating the remarkable Jubilee this year; I also say it because modern science, having compared our chronicle with other Russian and foreign sources, gives us a number of serious confirmations of the date.

Let us review the events. In 986 or 987 (the exact date has not been proved) the two rulers of Byzantium, Emperor Basil II and Constantin, asked Prince Vladimir for military assistance. The proud basileiy had no choice but to ask for help from their former enemy and a pagan at that – things were going badly for them at the time. They had suffered a heavy defeat at the hands of the Bulgarians; Varda Foka, a prominent Byzantine military leader, had raised a mutiny and proclaimed himself Emperor; Arabs had invaded Calabria, the Italian province of Byzantium. A Russian detachment of

6,000 men which arrived from Rus in 987 (or in the spring of 988) saved the day.

The Russians had had one precondition for the agreement: for the Emperor's sister Anne to marry Prince Vladimir. The Byzantians agreed (though it was contrary to the rules of their arrogant court to allow barbarians to marry their princesses, even though they were Christians). A son of Otton I the Great, the King of Germany, had asked for Anne's hand but had been refused; but now they put forward their own condition: Vladimir was to be baptized.

He was baptized and it happened precisely in 988, which is proved, in particular, in *The History of Stepanos Taronski, Asokhik known as Taronazi* by an Armenian author of the eleventh century, as well as in *The Arab Chronicle* by Yakhya of Antioch. I omit the details of how the contracting parties quarrelled because one of the parties (Byzantine) demanded that Vladimir first get baptized and only then married, and the second party (Vladimir) insisted on Anne being sent to him first. Vladimir proved his right by force: he conquered Corsun, the Crimean Byzantine possession, and sent a threatening warning to Constantinople . . . 'If you do not let her (Anne) be my wife, the same will happen to your capital.'

It sounded much more expressive in Old Russian. I must deviate a bit, but I cannot help noting that a translation into Modern Russian (not to mention translation into other languages) loses much of the brevity and expressiveness of the Old Russian original. By refusing to translate the divine service into Modern Russian, the Russian Orthodox Church is not displaying sluggishness or blind attachment to form and letter. We have been keeping a thousand-years-old tradition, the great uniformity of form and content as we see it. Thus, Monk Grigory of the Caves, a major spiritual poet (at the turn of the twelfth century), the author of the service in the name of St Vladimir equal to the Apostles, a service which has been performed by the Russian Orthodox Church up to our time, has left us the following sincere lines: 'The town of Kiev, the mother of all towns, verily became Your kingdom, it was the place which glorified Christ and the Father and the Spirit, owing to your Grandmother and you.' The singer blessed

Kiev, Princess Olga baptized in 954–959, and her grandson Prince Vladimir himself. I am deeply touched by the following lines by the blessed Grigory: 'Our Lord Christ is performing a great and glorious miracle which words fail to describe: he is consecrating the whole Russian Land by holy baptism and is enlightening Prince Basil.' (During the baptism Prince Vladimir was given the name Basil.)

Russian singers caught up the richest traditions of Byzantine liturgical poetry and developed them on their own national soil, Russian liturgical poetry was especially bright and rich in images in writings by Roman the Sweetsinger (from the end of the fifth to the second half of the sixth century). 'Will those who hear shudder, will those who see it be terrified when Christ is drawn to torture, abuse and death?' – this is a quotation from his Kondak on Judas's treachery.

But let us, however, turn back to the events of Rus's Baptism. *The Tale of Bygone Times* tells us how hard it was for Anne to think of marrying an unknown prince from a remote barbarian country. 'This is like going into captivity', she cried: 'I wish I were dead.' She went to Corsun, however, and married Vladimir in the spring of 988. Our chronicle, including her story of Corsun captivity, and Vladimir being baptized and married, deserves to be trusted as a valuable historic source because its author, St Nestor, undoubtedly listened to the stories of those who had witnessed these events and wrote them down. Jeremiah of the Caves was 'one of those who have memory of baptism of the Russian Land'. To be brief, I assume that *the whole complex* of the data obtained by historians allows us to regard the year 988 as the date of the baptism of Prince Vladimir, of Kievans, as the date of the baptism of Rus.

The importance of the event for the history and the fate of the Russian people, of Russia, cannot be underestimated. I suppose our life today, with its tormenting contradictions and ardent search for the spiritual ideal, is closely interrelated with that summer day in 988 when Kievan Rus turned into Christian Rus. By the way, I know for sure that this point of view has acquired a lot of opponents recently. In their opinion, Christianity has distorted the true image of Rus, suffocated the growth of a truly Russian culture, and caused fatal losses in the spiritual development of the Russian people. To ponder about 'what might have been if . . .' seems to me to be a kind of historic temptation, historic speculation, a dangerous game of a lost mind. To moralize over a choice of historic development, after a thousand years to offer another direction for historic development, to try to prove another road to have been more direct and smoother, seems to me to be an occupation more suitable for small talk than for an earnest attempt to interpret the past.

This year has seen the book by Archpriest Lebedev *The Baptism of Rus* published by the Moscow Patriarchy. I am familiar with the book from its manuscript. A historian by education, Lebedev seems to be very convincing in showing that Russia was prepared to accept Christianity and that the year of 988 was a natural result of Russian spiritual development. The book contains many subtle and accurate comments, puzzling comparisons allowing for a fresh point of view on events which used to be taken for granted, and deep remarks. Look how the author interprets the unusual relationship between Russia and Byzantium (I am quoting from manuscript): '. . . Vladimir's attack ended in what "making passes" at the goodly neighbour might have led to – marriage (both in the direct and the figurative sense). Rus obtained Byzantium as a bride and through the action turned out to be the bride of Christ! This is where the spiritual and the historic meaning of 988 lies . . .' Besides, there were serious social, economic and political preconditions for Rus accepting Christianity. It had been ripening in the depths of Rus development. This is why some historians, and N. Gordienko, a scholar from Leningrad, among them, do not see enough reason for regarding the Baptism of Rus undertaken by Vladimir Svyatoslavovich as the first step on Russia's way to being Christianized.

When speaking about spiritual preconditions for Rus accepting Christianity, a historian belonging to the theological, Church community would inevitably make a point of the role of St Apostle Andrei the First-Called, described in *The Tale of Bygone Times*, if you remember it, in the following way:

. . . and he went upstream on the Dnieper. And it so hap-

314

pened that he came and stayed on the river bank under the mountains. And in the morning he rose and said to his pupils gesturing to the mountains: 'Do you see these mountains? They will be enlightened by the Grace of God, there will be a great city with many churches raised by God.' And he climbed the mountains, blessed them and set up a cross, and prayed to God, and went down the mountain where later Kiev was to be built, and went on his way up the Dnieper.

This is a tale which has reached us from the depths of history, its very existence testifying, as I see it, to its deep roots in the people's consciousness. Meanwhile, there exist some proofs of St Apostle Andrei actually having stayed in the Russian Land. Let us see, if Christ's pupils and apostles, true to the legacy of their teacher who had told them: 'Go ye therefore, and teach all nations, baptizing them in the name of the Father, and of the Son and the Holy Ghost' (Matt. 28:19), hurried to all parts of the world, why should not one of them have visited the Land of our forefathers while preaching the Gospel?

Proofs of that kind – and there are many of them: the Greek versions of the life of St Apostle, the fact of Holy Fathers and Christian Church zealots staying in the Russian Land being mentioned as far back as the third century, Roman coins of the epoch of Emperor Augustus, Trajan and Marcus Aurelius found by archaeologists in the Kiev area – all of them taken together may be quite a sound basis for resolving some of the issues of our history. The art of a historian often consists in his ability to reproduce a whole picture of the past out of some hints, details, or trifles.

But if we are to speak of less remote preconditions for the Baptism of Rus, we can find many of them in the social and economic, as well as in the spiritual, life of our forefathers. Let us take trade, for instance. In order to conclude bargains with partners from Christian countries – and we must remember that in the ninth and tenth centuries Christianity became predominant in the countries of Central Europe, and that in the countries of Western and Southern Europe, that had happened still earlier – Russian merchants simply had no other choice but to give up their paganism. Otherwise their 'pagan' goods might not have found any buyers in Christian countries. Ibn-Hordadbech, an Arab geographer, in his *Book of Roads and Countries*, wrote that Russians did trade with Byzantium and the countries of the Arab East.

One more detail. Constantinople Patriarch Foty testifies in his *Circular Message* to some Rus people being baptized as far back as the sixth decade of the ninth century, that is, a hundred years before the baptism of Vladimir, which, as some historians want us to believe, was to become the very beginning of Russian Christianity. In fact, it was not the beginning, it was the continuation and the first summation of a process embracing the whole Russian Land. Evidence of the same kind may be found in the biography Constantin VII Porphyrogenous wrote of his grandfather, as well as in some Greek chronicles. At the time of Prince Igor (he was known to be a pagan) there was in Kiev a 'Sobornaya' church (the main church) bearing the name of St Iliah. This gives us an occasion to think there were other Christian churches in Kiev in that period (i.e. the fourth decade of the tenth century). And let me remind you once again that Vladimir's grandmother, Princess Olga, was baptized, too. Marriages between dynasties were also very important during that period, in that they guaranteed the loyalty of the parties to an agreement. Which of the European kings would have allowed his daughter to be married to a Russian pagan prince? It was mentioned earlier, with reference to *The Word on Law and Grace*, that the baptism was a summation of the mighty spiritual process developing in Vladimir's soul. Such process towards God was free of any political, economic, or other considerations and calculations of any kind. But life is so varied that there was room for combining the personal spiritual urge of Prince Vladimir with his intention to marry Anne. It is quite possible that the possibility of such a marriage and its necessity for Russia as a state finally spurred Vladimir to be baptized. A contemporary Church historian remarks in this connection: 'To combine the problem of personal salvation with great blessing for his native Russian Land, both spiritual and political – this is where we see the true wisdom of the great Prince equal to the Apostles! This spiritual, state and patriotic wisdom is the best reason for us to glorify our Baptizer!'

A millennium ago Russia faced a great historic choice. It is important to point out that it was *its own* choice, without any direct interference or pressure from outside. And again, all the development that had preceded it had predetermined the choice. Christianity, and not Judaism; Eastern, and not Western, Christianity.

This is a problem of a vector of interests. Russia at that time did not have a negative attitude to Western Europe, but Byzantium was spiritually closer. It was with Byzantium that Russia intensively exchanged ideas and people. The Lord said: 'Whereunto shall I liken the kingdom of God? It is like leaven, which a woman took and hid in three measures of meal till the whole was leavened' (Luke 13:20–21). Christianity turned out to be the very leaven which was accepted by the Russian Land with gratitude and on which – and I hope there is no room for argument here – both Russian culture and Russian thought were founded. Because, no matter which of the great Russian writers and thinkers of the past or present we look at, we can see the same 'leaven' in them.

Of course, we should not picture the situation as if, as soon as Vladimir had Russia baptized, the whole Russian population eagerly reached out to the new faith. In the summer of 988 a wooded Perun was whipped and thrown into the river, but paganism was consistent in its struggle for influence for a long time afterwards. And even after it finally died as a historic remnant (though it left some traces in our memory in the form of some of our living traditions), the millennium that has expired cannot be proclaimed an epoch of total concord inside the Church.

The Russian Orthodox Church from the very beginning had to face *dissent*. Generally speaking, the fact of dissent, of another opinion, of a different point of view, makes up the richness and the beauty of life. There have always been and will always be personalities who regard the existing order as imperfect, not moral enough, lacking concern for Man. Their attempts to reconstruct the world and immediately to bring heaven to the Earth so to speak, are fraught with great disaster and great bloodshed, though I am not dwelling on that now. I should like to remind you of the so-called *heresies*.

At the very beginning of the fourteenth century exposers of those of the clergy who did not live righteously raised their voices. 'Your breath smells like an open coffin. You have fallen so low and abuse is so evil!' And again: 'It matters not whether you are a monk at a monastery, it matters if you actually do good as a monk should do' (Ivan Cherny, a professional scribe, a church choir master).

Generally speaking, all these heretic movements were nothing less than a kind of reformation, the spiritual, political and economic results of which are so evident in Europe . . . But not in Russia.

Russia did not know religious wars. The First Peasant War under Ivan Bolotnikov merely reflected the ideas of those Russian heretics who were against feudal oppression. So, the Russian Reformation left us only with ideas – but profound and bright ones. Besides Ivan Cherny, I can name Theodor Kuritsin, the author of the famous *Laodician Epistles* (the end of the fifteenth century); Matthew Baskin (the first half of the sixteenth century) who, referring to the Gospel, demanded that serfdom and slavery be done away with and, as a personal example, tore up the deeds to those people who were dependent on him; Theodore Kosoy, a very serious believer, but one that did not accept either the Church or its hierarchs.

Perhaps such fighters could not be denied personal honesty and a desire to make the world better than it is. Especially when among the clergy there were people worthy of denunciation and giving reason for angry exposures. But who can be sure that a Protestant Church under Kosoy (and his religious thinking was Protestant in essence), had it appeared in Moscow, would have been totally free from those drawbacks he found in the Russian Orthodox Church of his time? And Lev Tolstoy, who was the same kind of Protestant in his thinking, made a point on his last pilgrimage of first visiting the Orthodox monasteries of Optima Pustin and Shamordino first. Without going into the details of the bygone clash of the heretic faith and thought with the canonic Christian faith and ideas, I should like to point out that the great religious might of the Russian people has brought to life quite a number of monasteries (there were 1,097 of them at the beginning of this century), it has given birth to outstanding saints and pious men, such as Nil of Sora, Joseph of Volotsk, Dmitry of Rostov, and, of course, Sergey of Radonezh with his innermost idea of love overcoming the hate of a divided world – this religious might finally defended the truth of the Russian Orthodox Church.

The last flare-up of this heretic movement, if I may call it such, occurred in the 1920s and 1930s. I mean 'obnovlentsy' ('renovators'), or, as they called themselves, 'zhivotserkovniky' (Church revivers). I must say that in their struggle against the Russian Orthodox Church, they used a weapon very popular at the time – they accused the Church of being counter-revolutionary. In his philosophical autobiography *Self-Cognition*, Berdyayev wrote: 'My attitude to an "enlivened" Church was negative, because its representatives had started from denunciation of the Patriarch and his Church. Reformation is not carried on in such a way . . .' I suppose the time will soon come when the whole truth will be out about the deeds of the 'zhivotserkovniki'. Now we can merely state the fact they are hardly remembered by anybody. And, finally: I love John Chrysostom, and not only love him – I revere him, and I remember one of his ideas which would be appropriate here. 'Nothing can produce so much darkness as the human brain, which argues about things in an earthly manner and does not accept heavenly enlightenment.'

But let us return to the Millennium. It will be no exaggeration to say that it is our national celebration. Thinking about the events of 988, we cannot avoid the outstanding role of the Russian Orthodox Church in promoting and consolidating Russian statehood, its participation in the victories of the Russian people in the horrendous Time of Troubles and in the Great Patriotic War of 1912, its moral and material help during the years of the Soviet people's fight to the death with German fascism. I should like to point out particularly that on the very first day of the war, on 22 June 1941, Metropolitan Sergei addressed the clergy and the believers with a message to be immediately dispatched to all the dioceses. He wrote in particular: 'This is not the first time the Russian people have had to withstand such an ordeal. With God's help they will be victorious again and will disperse the enemy. Our Orthodox Church has always shared the fate of its people. It has stayed with the people both in trouble and in joy. And it will not leave its people now. It blesses the heroic deed to be undertaken with God's blessing.' During the war the Church was known to have given money to provide a squadron of airplanes and a column of tanks, later named after Alexander Nevsky and Dmitry of the Don, respectively. By the end of 1944 the sum of money given by the Church for the defence effort amounted to 150 million roubles.

I cannot help mentioning the peace-loving work of the Russian Orthodox Church. Let me remind you of the World Conference of Religious Workers 'For the Preservation of the Sacred Gift of Life from a Nuclear Catastrophe' which took place in Moscow and brought together over 600 representatives of different religions from ninety countries. The call of the religious workers to free the world of nuclear weapons has played an important role in the common desire of all humankind to do away with the threat of a disastrous military clash.

We must also point out the role of the Russian Orthodox Church in the development of national culture. 'A leap into the world of literature took place at the same time as Christianity and the Church came to Russia, which required a written language and Church literature', Academician Likhachev wrote. *The Tale of Bygone Times*, *The Prayer* by Daniel the Prisoner (Captive), *The Life* by Archpriest Avvakum, *The Story* by Abraham Palitsin – these are just a small portion of Old Russia's literature which anticipated the great Russian literature of the nineteenth century. I am not going to pass final judgement, but Russian literature, no matter which historical period it belongs to, seems to have a complex of Christian ideas. It would be a bit trivial to mention Fyodor Dostoevsky in this connection. But all his writings are full of anxious love for Christ!

I shall give another illustration. I was deeply impressed with *The Quarry* by Andrei Platonov. I suppose this work, so small in volume, weighs so much on the scale of artistic truth that I do not even know what to compare it with . . . The style is reminiscent of the best pieces of Russian icon art – the image seems to be devoid of perspective, but at the same time it is so deep. And he surely has been influenced by Nikolai Fyodorovich Fyodorov – it is never expressed directly, but it sounds in the intonation and in the choice of words, especially in the passages on death. And as a student of the history of Russian philosophy points out, Fyodorov felt an exceptionally strong attachment to the Kingdom of God and deep repulsion to anyone who had come to believe there could be no heaven on Earth. His insatiable search for the Kingdom of God as for completeness, as for life 'with everybody and for everybody', was not merely an idea, but a motive force of his inner progress, an ardent stimulus for his search – for his critical attitude to the world around, for his pondering on how to bring nearer, 'how to achieve, the Kingdom of God'. And we can add – it was also a nutrient medium for his idea of restoring to life all the past generations. In my opinion, it is in this hidden but strong connection between Platonov and Fyodorov that we can look for the source of the mysterious creative force of the author of *The Quarry*, a force pointed out by S. P. Zalygin. And what about *Doctor Zhivago*? The Christian principle of the novel stands out quite clearly both in the novel itself and in the culminating verse.

Russian painting has also been nurtured by Russian Christianity, which, I suppose, is especially evident when we look at the works of Victor Vasnetsov spiritualized by the idea of Russian art being strong enough to acquire, and to express, the world comprehension of the ideal of goodness and beauty. His wall-painting at the Vladimirsky Cathedral in Kiev is a marvellous specimen of truly religious art! And this is what he wrote about himself and his work: 'Being an Orthodox Christian and a truly believing Russian, I could not but help sacrificing at least a small candle to our Lord. The candle may be simple and rough, but it was offered sincerely, with all my heart. We were born in the bosom of the Church, and God help us die Orthodox Christians.'

In this connection I should like to make another point. Culture comes from cult. The art of word, architecture and painting – everything was once submitted to cult requirements, to religious needs. Pavel Florensky elaborated on that

point with his typical depth and wisdom: 'Fine arts are historically nothing more than loose links in the chain of a more
serious and more creative art, the art of creating the image of
God, or Theurgia.' He was of the opinion that the liturgy
contained unearthly beauty, the same beauty which, according to Dostoevsky, was supposed to save the world.

Speaking of Christianity and influence upon culture, I cannot avoid mentioning the Bible and its sacred spiritual meaning in the cultural and educational tradition of the world. I
am not going to dwell on its significance as the Holy Spirit of
God's presence. For me, a true believer, it is there beyond a
shadow of a doubt. But even those who think differently cannot but agree that it is the Eternal Book of humanity because
it is bottomless. It gave food to the creative genius of Shakespeare, Dante, Dostoevsky; it inspired Rublyov, Michelangelo,
Raphael; without the book there would have been no Church
of the Protecting Veil on the river Nerl, no Chartres
Cathedral, no St Basil's Cathedral . . . And how much wisdom
can be found literally on every page in the book! The inspired
psalms of David, the formidable statements by the Old Testament prophets, the Apocalypse so full of deep mystery, the
Four Gospels which for nearly two thousand years have been
bringing to us the Commandments of our Lord Christ – I am
sure that, irrespective of world outlook or religion, a person
with a soul and a mind will always be listening to the voice of
the Bible with ecstatic emotion. 'Neither do men light a candle
and put it under a bushel, but on a candlestick, and it giveth
light unto all that are in the house' (Matt. 5:15). Unfortunately
our people cannot buy the holy scripture yet. We have been
stealing from ourselves – I have no doubts about that. Because
only a naïve or a very silly person could think that a mass
edition of the Bible would lead to an increase in believers. A
mass edition of the Bible would lead to a rise in the general
level of culture – that is evident. One can become a believer
without having a Bible and, on the contrary, it is possible to
remain an atheist after reading the Bible all one's life.

Our literature is now paying its debts – to Platonov, Pilnyak,
Zamyatin, Kluyev, Grossman, and other masters of Russian
prose and poetry whose works were earlier banned. To my

mind the process should develop, become wider and deeper, and embrace the works of the Russian thinkers in some way connected with the Christian tradition. Our readers must have free access to the works of Vladimir Soloviev, N. Berdyayev, S. Bulgakov, S. Trubetskoy and E. Trubetskoy, P. Florensky, K. Lentyev, V. Rosanov, L. Shestov, and so on. Only an ideological bureaucrat could be afraid that that would undermine the position of scientific materialism and that, if somebody reads Berdyayev, he will become an active advocate of his system, which is, as one scholar aptly noted, an original amalgamation of Christian ideas and non-Christian principles. And Gorki said of Rosanov: 'He was such an interesting person, a true man of genius.' Such an estimation of Rosanov did not prevent Gorki from disputing with him on many points of principle concerning the world outlook. This is exactly what a truly creative attitude to a heritage is, when to know does not necessarily mean to accept. Culture thrives on variety. And it is a must for us to return everything that enriched Russian thought to our heritage. Fyodor Abramov, our contemporary and marvellous writer, has said: 'The nation is incomplete without me.' In truth, he is very right. But who decided that our nation was complete without Sergei Bulgakov, for one, and when did they decide that? Why is it that we behave as if we have renounced him? His was an incredible life, intellect and spirit. He died in Paris in 1944, and he deserves to have our nation know about him. At first he was a social-democrat close to Kautski, Babel, Leibknecht, the author of many articles and essays on political economy which are of interest even now, a professor at Kiev University. Then, after a crisis in his world outlook, he arrived at a religious way of thinking and became a clergyman in 1918. In his writings he tried to combine science, religion and philosophy; and cannot we decide for ourselves what his attempt resulted in?

Our striving for full historic truth, the powerful motive force in our life which has now received the name of glasnost, has resulted, and will persist, in restoring many names undeservedly forgotten, workers of the Russian Church included. I presume the person of Patriarch Tikhon (Belavin), the first

Patriarch after the Patriarchy was restored, deserves objective study. He was the flesh of the flesh of the Russian pre-revolutionary clergy, generally conservative. It was very difficult for him to accept the Revolution. But it is known that even Maxim Gorki and Korolenko and Kuprin and Skitalets did not accept it immediately, either. Yes, Patriarch Tikhon issued an appeal against the Brest Peace Treaty. But it was voted against by many prominent Bolsheviks, Felix Dzerzhinsky among them. This is why I think we must study what Patriarch Tikhon did, taking into account the peculiarities of his time and of his personality. Or let us take Archbishop Luka (Voino-Yasenetsky) . . . In 1946 Luka, the Archbishop of Tambov, a professor of surgery, received the Stalin Prize. But before 1945, before the Stalin Prize, he had to suffer arrests, prison and exile. In 1921 Valentin Felixovich Voino-Yasenetsky, a surgeon and the head of the faculty of surgery and topographic anatomy at the State Turkestan University in Tashkent, became a clergyman. He did not leave surgery and teaching – he was to serve medicine while he had strength enough. But alongside this service, until his death in 1961, there was another kind of service – to God. In 1923 Father Valentin, a priest, became a bishop named Luka; the same year he was arrested. And he was not alone – many priests and bishops were being arrested and tried in courts all over the country. Bishop Luka spent three years in exile in the most remote corners of the Krasnoyarsky Territory deep in Siberia; upon his return to Tashkent in 1930, he was arrested again . . . And in 1937 he was arrested for a third time and after two years of prison sent again into exile into Krasnoyarsky Territory. But no matter where he was, Luka went on healing people as a medicine man and helping them as a spiritual pastor. During the years of the Second World War, hundreds of wounded Soviet officers and soldiers gratefully repeated the name of Bishop Luka, Professor Voino-Yasenetsky, the major consulting surgeon of the Krasnoyarsk hospital.

His fate reflects the fate of the Russian Orthodox Church in many aspects. In the 1920s and 1930s the Church suffered a lot, it lost many of its servants . . . Father Pavel Florensky, a prominent theologian, philosopher, art specialist and engineer, died in the labour camps. And 1937 saw the execution of Metropolitan Constantin (Dyakov) of Kiev and Metropolitan Seraphim (Alexandrov) of Tver. Archbishop Andrei (Ukhtomsky), a most gifted person, perished . . . Hundreds of churches were closed or destroyed. The film *Give Us More Light*, shown recently, tells us how the Cathedral of Christ the Saviour was blown up in Moscow – and how many more explosions were rending the air and human hearts at that time!

In the war years, the attitude to the Church changed somewhat. We know that one night early in September 1943, in the Kremlin, Stalin saw three leading hierarchs of the Russian Orthodox Church: they were Metropolitans Sergei, Alexiy and Nikolai. Stalin said: 'You are in a bad way with personnel. You must prepare personnel.' After the two preceding decades, things really were bad with personnel. Then the Metropolitans started speaking about modest courses, but Stalin said, as if having forgotten about the past, that courses were a small thing, a trifle, that they needed theological academies and seminaries. That night it was decided to publish a magazine called *Moscow Patriarchy* and to call together the Local Council for the election of the Patriarch. After a short time with some breathing room, the Church had to live through another difficult period. There were about 15,000 Orthodox churches functioning in the country. Nikita Khrushchev ordered that the number be cut in half. The Kiev-Pechery Lavra, the oldest holy place of the Russian Orthodoxy, was one of those closed.

Our society is still feeling the consequences of that extremely undemocratic and unconstitutional act. I don't think it is only a question of the local authorities being persistently unwilling to observe the Soviet laws; laws themselves and the respective rulings are far from perfect.

There is one more thing to be discussed. This year will see the seventieth anniversary of the Decree 'On the Separation of the Church from the State and of the Schools from the Church'. Lenin's decree asserted the Marxist and Leninist understanding of freedom of conscience as a dialectic unity of the freedom of faith and of atheist convictions. Back in 1905, Lenin wrote: 'The State must have nothing to do with religion, religious communities should not have any connections with the State power. Everybody should be free to follow any religion or to accept no religion at all, i.e. to be an atheist . . . Any mention of a citizen's faith must be destroyed without question.' The Decree adopted in 1918 was based exactly on these principles, imbued with the spirit of democracy and respect for the believer's sentiments. Our society has paid dearly for forgetting these principles and for directly violating them later on.

The 'Ruling on Religious Communities', which regulates the relationship between the State and the Church and which is still in effect, was issued in 1929 and slightly altered in 1975. The real practice of State and Church relations has gone well beyond its framework. This has often been discussed in our press.

During his meetings with Pimen, the Patriarch of Moscow and of all Russia, as well as with members of the Holy Synod of the Russian Orthodox Church, Mikhail Gorbachev pointed out the necessity of restoring the Leninist norms to the attitude towards religion, the Church and believers. The restructuring of our society presupposes a democratic attitude to the Church and respect for the sentiments of believers. Take, for example, the Church's social activity, philanthropy, in particular. To be philanthropic, in other words, 'to do good' – this is what it means literally in Russian – is one of the main purposes of the Church, which has the mission of spreading goodness and charity on the Earth. It does its best to perform its duty: it donates considerable sums of money to the Soviet Peace Fund, it is ready to answer any call for help from any corner of the Soviet Union. The Russian Orthodox Church has done its bit in the mass campaign of support for the people who suffered as a result of the Chernobyl accident. Likewise, it did not remain on the sidelines where the sacred task of rendering help to the victims of the natural calamities in Georgia was concerned. In other words, the Church has the right to do good in general, by participating in the humanitarian activity of social organizations or by rendering help to the population of whole regions.

But in my opinion the social mission of the Church cannot

be restricted to philanthropy of this kind only. Why, for instance, cannot a church parish give a helping hand to an aged, sick parishioner or to a parishioner in trouble? Why cannot this charitable deed so much needed by the people be done openly, without fear that it might lead to accusations of violations of the existing instructions? Charity is both the duty and the mission of any true Christian. And I think the restrictions now preventing the Russian Orthodox Church from carrying out its mission and its duty should be removed.

One more thing. I have discussed the Bible here, its importance in world culture, and the unfortunate fact that it remains beyond the reach of the vast majority of our country's citizens. But we must also realize that sensible Bible reading is not such a simple thing, it requires some training, some teaching, if you like. It means that while publishing the Bible, we must put out a substantial scientific commentary to it – so that for the diligent reader there would be no dark and mysterious spots in the Eternal Book.

Besides, as I mentioned earlier, we cannot forget that practically all members of the Russian Orthodox Church were born and grew up in our Soviet times and many of them simply had no chance to penetrate the depths of Church service to God. Some things are inherited from tradition, others can be learned in church, still others can be read – but this is evidently not enough. This is why I think talks with the priest in the church would be quite in accordance with the present restructuring of our social life, talks which would enable the priest to explain the foundations of the Orthodox Church or certain aspects of the service and would allow him to strive to educate the parishioner in the spirit of peace and love for his fellow men. By the way, the 1918 Decree 'On the Separation of the Church from the State' provided a possibility for people to teach and to be taught religion in private. Parents had the right to invite a clergyman home to teach children the fundamentals of religion.

As I see it, *at the present time* there are no problems concerning the Russian Orthodox Church and the State which would be impossible to solve. There are no irreconcilable contradictions. On course, there are still many sharp edges to be smoothed away. But at the same time, here are some of the latest facts: a new cathedral has been built in Murmansk, a number of church buildings have been returned to the Church – Danilov Monastery, Optina Pustin, the Tolgsky Nunnery in Yaroslavl, the Trinity Church in Kirov, and the list goes on. This is why I am full of hope, optimism and enthusiasm for perestroika. I say: we have celebrated the seventieth anniversary of our State. That means that the life of even the oldest Church members has passed during the Soviet years. They have been brought up in the land of soviets, they are the Soviet people in the true meaning of the word, conscientious and honest workers. A vast number of believers are veterans of labour, veterans of the Great Patriotic War. How is it possible, as often happens, to regard them as second-rate citizens, to treat them with suspicion? Today all the believing and non-believing citizens of our country work hand in hand for the benefit of their fatherland, for the preservation of peace on our planet. They are eager to participate in perestroika, in making our society more democratic. This is why it is especially important to stress Mikhail Gorbachev's idea that the depth of differences in world outlook is no obstacle to cooperation, that believers are Soviet people, working people, patriots, and that it is their right to express their beliefs.

I believe the Church has something to tell people today. The Christian tradition is oriented on the human personality in all its uniqueness with all its moral responsibility. The expansion of mass culture may be countered by the Church with the richest spiritual legacy of many a century; consumer attitudes with an appeal to people to give of themselves for the good of their fellow men; the cult of violence, cruelty and war with the preaching of mutual love and peace throughout the world.

A *Chronology of Perestroika*

11 March 1985   The plenary meeting of the CPSU Central Committee which, following the death of Konstantin Chernenko, elected Mikhail Gorbachev General Secretary of the CPSU Central Committee.

23 April 1985   The plenary meeting of the CPSU Central Committee where preparations for the 27th Party Congress were discussed. It was to become a symbol of the 'April changes' which would start the period of perestroika and acceleration.

7 May 1985   The CPSU Central Committee resolution 'On Measures of Preventing Drinking and Alcoholism' was adopted – the first decisive attempt at influencing public consciousness. It was generally approved.

11 June 1985   A conference in the CPSU Central Committee on the problems of speeding up progress in science and technology. The conference had far-reaching consequences. The report by Mikhail Gorbachev 'On the Main Problems in Party Economic Policy' gave pointed and self-critical analysis of stagnation in the economic sphere and in industrial management.

12 July 1985   The Resolution of the CPSU Central Committee and the USSR Council of Ministers 'On Broad Application of New Economic Methods and Increasing their Influence on Progress in Science and Technology'.

19–21 November 1985   The first summit meeting between Mikhail Gorbachev, General Secretary of the CPSU Central Committee, and Ronald Reagan, President of the United States of America, in Geneva.

16 January 1986   Mikhail Gorbachev's statement on a programme for total elimination of nuclear arms in the world within fifteen years, ending in the year 2000.

18 February 1986   A plenary meeting of the CPSU Central

329

Committee discussed the political report of the CPSU Central Committee for the 27th Party Congress, summing up the results of the broad Party discussions on the forthcoming changes in the USSR Programme and the Charter. Boris Yeltsin was elected a candidate member of the CPSU Central Committee Politburo, after becoming First Secretary of the Moscow City Party organization. Vladimir Grishin, who had occupied the post, was relieved of his duties.

25 February to 6 March 1986 The 27th Congress of the CPSU. Mikhail Gorbachev, General Secretary of the CPSU, delivered the report.

6 July 1986 The Good Will Games started in Moscow under the motto 'From Friendship in Sport to Peace in the World'. For over ten years American and Soviet athletes had not met in major international competitions. Now the joint effort of sports organizations, business quarters and the public ended the rift.

11–12 October 1986 The second personal meeting between Mikhail Gorbachev, General Secretary of the CPSU Central Committee, and Ronald Reagan, President of the United States of America – the Reykjavik talks.

20 October 1986 The first session of the 'Issik-Kul' forum where Chingiz Aitmatov, a famous writer, welcomed prominent workers of world culture to his native Kirghizia. James Baldwin, Arthur Miller, Peter Ustinov, Y. Kemal, Claude Symin and others who liked the 'new thinking' were present. The first session ended in a meeting with Mikhail Gorbachev.

13 January 1987 A Decree of the Presidium of the Supreme Soviet of the USSR and a Resolution of the USSR Council of Ministers were adopted, allowing joint ventures and amalgamations on USSR territory.

27 January 1987 The CPSU Central Committee held a plenary meeting to discuss personnel policy under perestroika, the necessity for consistent and steadfast development of the base for Soviet democracy as opposed to the braking mechanism and conservatism.

14–16 February 1987 The international forum 'For a Non-Nuclear World, for the Survival of Humanity', which gathered in Moscow prominent workers in culture and science and representatives of religious and social movements from all over the world.

28 May 1987   Mathias Rust, an amateur pilot from West Germany, violated the Soviet line and landed his plane by the Kremlin gates near Red Square. Further serious reason critically to evaluate the system of departmental management, this time in the 'authoritative' military department. The Defence Minister of the USSR and the Commander-in-Chief of Air Defence were dismissed.

23 June 1987   The World Women's Congress opened in Moscow. Its motto was: 'No Nuclear Weapons by 2000'.

25–26 June 1987   A plenary meeting of the CPSU Central Committee discussed the tasks of the Party in connection with radical economic restructuring, and the question of how to combine plan management and personal and group interests most effectively.

30 June 1987   The USSR Law on State Enterprises (Associations) was adopted. Economic levers for enterprises' independence began to operate.

21 October 1987   The CPSU Central Committee was discussing preparations for the seventieth anniversary of the Great October Socialist Revolution at a plenary meeting. Boris Yeltsin spoke out and was ruled out of order by the participants at the meeting.

2 November 1987   Ceremonial meeting devoted to the seventieth anniversary of the October Revolution.

7–10 December 1987   The third meeting between Mikhail Gorbachev and Ronald Reagan. The visit of the General Secretary of the CPSU Central Committee to Washington. The treaty on the elimination of intermediate-range and shorter-range nuclear missiles was signed.

4 February 1988   The plenary meeting of the Supreme Court of the USSR repealed the penalties against the victims of the Stalinist repressions of 1937–8. The executed comrades-in-arms of Lenin – Nikolai Bukharin, Alexei Rykov, Grygory Zinoviev, Lev Kamenev, Yuri Pyatakov, Karl Radek, Cristian Rakovksy and other comrades – were among those rehabilitated.

11–20 February 1988   The beginning of the Nagorny Karabakh disturbances connected with a demand for the region to leave the Azerbaijan SSR for the Armenian SSR.

15 May 1988   Soviet troops started their withdrawal from Afghanistan in compliance with the Geneva agreement.

29 May to 2 June 1988   The fourth meeting between Mikhail Gorbachev and Ronald Reagan – the visit of the US President to Moscow.

June 1988   During the festivities dedicated to One Thousand Years of Christianity in Russia, Andrei Gromyko, the Chairman of the Presidium of the Supreme Soviet of the USSR, met leaders of religious organizations from nearly 100 countries.

19 June to 1 July 1988   The 19th National Party Conference outlined plans for future restructuring and democratization in Soviet society.

18 July 1988   The Presidium of the Supreme Soviet of the USSR met for a heated discussion of the ethnic problem in Armenia, Azerbaijan and Nagorny Karabakh, of measures affording real help to the population of Nagorny Karabakh and improvement of their living conditions. The Resolution 'On the Decisions of the Supreme Soviets of the Armenian SSR and Azerbaijan SSR on Nagorny Karabakh'. Speaking at the meeting, Mikhail Gorbachev called the discussion a crucial moment in the process of perestroika.

Bibliography

M. S. Gorbachev, *Collected Speeches and Essays*, 5 volumes (Moscow, Politizdat, 1987–8). This collection covers twenty years of Party and political activity by the General Secretary of the CPSU Central Committee, beginning with the time when he was the head of Stavropol regional organization. The important landmarks of the period are the March (1985) plenary meeting of the CPSU Central Committee which elected Mikhail Gorbachev General Secretary; the April (1985) plenary meeting where the policy of perestroika and acceleration was proclaimed; the 27th Congress of the CPSU; and the seventieth anniversary of the Great October Socialist Revolution where the basic principles were formulated which reflected a general view of the history, achievements and mistakes of the Party, of the present tasks of perestroika and democratization of Soviet society.

Reports from the 19th All-Union Conference of the CPSU (Moscow, Politizdat, 1988).

On Practical Steps for Realization of the Decisions of the All-Union Party Conference, Documents of the July Plenary Meeting of the CPSU Central Committee (Moscow, Politizdat, 1988).

The Visit of M. S. Gorbachev, General Secretary of the CPSU Central Committee, to the United States of America, 7–10 December 1987. Documents and Materials (Moscow, Politizdat, 1987). This collection includes materials on the Washington talks of the Soviet and US leaders, the documents on the elimination of intermediate-range and shorter-range missiles which were signed there, and the leaders' speeches for the public and the press.

The Soviet–American Summit Meeting. Moscow. 29 May to 2 June 1988. Documents and Materials (Moscow, Politizdat, 1988). Materials on the visit of President Ronald Reagan of the USA to Moscow, his talks with General Secretary Mikhail Gorbachev of the CPSU Central Committee, the meetings of the two countries' leaders with the public and the press, and events promoting the development of Soviet–American relations.

A. A. Gromyko, *Memorable* (Moscow, Politizdat, 1988). A two-volume book of memoirs by this major statesman, Chairman of the Presidium of the Supreme Soviet of the USSR, about his life and political career, starting from his childhood in a hardworking peasant family at the very beginning of the twentieth century. The rest is the story of a diplomatic career mostly based in the USA, and his reminiscences of a large number of contemporaries prominent in the field of politics, business, science and culture.

Yegor K. Ligachev, 'On the Progress of Perestroika in Higher and Secondary Education and on the Tasks of the Party in this Connection. A Report to the February [1988] Plenary Meeting of the CPSU Central Committee', Pravda, 18 February 1988. The secretary of the CPSU Central Committee and Politburo member analyses the situation in higher and secondary education in the country, talks about training specialists in various spheres of economics, science and culture, and stresses the urgency of raising standards.

A. N. Yakovlev. 'To Work, to Think, to Be Responsible', PRAVDA, 3 December 1987. A speech by the secretary of the CPSU Central Committee and Politburo member before central and republican media people and workers in science and culture on developing the course of glasnost, democratization and cardinal economic reform.

On the Radical Restructuring of Economic Management. A Collection of Documents (Moscow, Politizdat, 1988). Those who wish to know about the progress of Soviet economic, scientific and technological development and economic relations will find all the documentary sources here, from the USSR 'Law On State Enterprises (Associations)' to separate resolutions by the CPSU Central Committee and the USSR Council of Ministers.

'Mighty Measures for Perestroika', PRAVDA, 13 November 1987. A detailed report on the plenary meeting of Moscow City Party Committee which resulted in the collective denouncement of Boris Yeltsin and his dismissal from the high post of the capital's Party organization leader.

N. Shmelyov, 'Advances and Debts', Novy MIR, No. 6, 1987; 'New Anxieties', Novy MIR, No. 4, 1988. These articles by a professor of economics and well-known writer caused a considerable stir because of their pointed approach to the problems and hardships of Soviet economics, and to the search for new methods for its recovery.

Chingiz Aitmatov, 'The Price of Enlightenment', OGONYOK, No. 28, 1987. Some ideas of the world-famous Kirghiz writer on the urgent problems facing Soviet society.

Yu. Shcherbak, 'Chernobyl', YUNOST, Nos 6–7, 1987. A journalist investigates the gravest accident of our time: the fire at the Chernobyl atomic power station. Why did it happen? How did people behave?

A. Gurkov, 'Supreme Court Trial of a Flight', Moscow NEWS, 13 September 1987. What awaited Mathias Rust, the young West German amateur pilot who landed his sports plane near the Red Square? And a trial at last . . .

Yu. Karyakin, 'Is It Worth Stepping on a Rake?' ZNAMYA, No. 9, 1987.

' "Zhdanov Liquid", or Against Slander', OGONYOK, No. 19, 1988. Sharp, implacable polemics with the still-flourishing heirs and supporters of the Stalin-Zhdanov dogmatic enslavery of culture. Is it fair that to this day collective farms, streets, a university and a whole town still bear the name of Zhdanov, a Stalin associate who sent dozens of Party workers, scientists and workers of culture to their death?

F. Medvedev, 'He Wished to Alter Life Because He Loved It', OGONYOK, No. 48, 1987. A typical essay restoring the names and the memory of the victims of Stalin's terror. Nikolai Bukharin – Lenin's comrade-in-arms, 'the favourite of the Party' as Lenin put it – was executed on Stalin's orders half a century ago. His story is told by Anna Larina, his widow, who memorized the testament of the martyr revolutionary. Such articles and research stories cover many names – Mikhail Tukhachevsky, Alexei Rykov, Fyodor Raskolnikov, Nikolai Shlyapnikov and others – and have become typical of the Soviet press.

A. Nikishin, 'Recovery', DRUZHBA NARODOV, No. 9, 1987. Another case of analysis of the mass nationalist disturbances in 1986 in Alma-Ata, the capital of Kazakhstan. Answering journalists, Nursultan Narzambayev, the Chairman of the Council of Ministers of the Kazakh SSR, discusses some painful aspects of national policy deviations and ways of overcoming them.

N. Andreyeva, 'I Cannot Give Up My Principles', SOVETSKAYA ROSSIYA, 13 March 1988. A peak in political discussion – a large article which shocked the public by its frank appeal to be true to conservative ideas, to Stalin worship. Interpreted as a manifesto of anti-perestroika forces, it aroused suspicions as to whether there was somebody from top Party spheres behind a modest university teacher . . .

'Principles of Perestroika: Revolutionary Thought and Action', PRAVDA, 5 April 1988. The editorial board of the main newspaper sharply criticizing the letter of N. Andreyeva as a hostile attack on perestroika and democratization. It evoked a wave (if not a storm) of 'anti-Andreyeva' statements throughout the Soviet press.

D. Granin, 'A Transient Phenomenon', OGONYOK, No. 6, 1988. V. Balyazin, 'Return', OCTYABR, No. 1, 1988. A. Vaksberg, 'Processes', LITERATURNAYA GAZETA, 4 May 1988; 'The Mystery of October 1941', LITERATURNAYA GAZETA, 20 April 1988. Typical essays and memoirs on victims of repression and persecution; people such as Nikolai Vavilov, the great scholar in genetics who died in prison because of pseudo-scientist Lysenko; Alexander Chayanov, the world-known agricultural agronomist who was shot as an enemy of the people; the Soviet writers Mikhail Koltsov, Joseph Babel and Mikhail Zoshchenko, producer Vsevolod Meyerkhold, and prominent Soviet military leaders, all executed at the beginning of the war.

G. Popov, 'No Way Back', SOVIETSKAYA KULTURA, 7 April 1988. A. Gelman, 'Time to Gather Efforts', SOVIETSKAYA KULTURA, 9 April 1988. Growing polemics around the forthcoming 19th National Party Conference. A radical economist, one of the 'heralds of perestroika', analyses the correlations of progressive forces and conservatives in perestroika . . . A famous playwright rejects the habitual eulogies to the Party and speaks about its responsibility before the people for having created such an unacceptable system of society and economic management.

V. Legasov, 'My Duty Is To Tell People Everything . . .', PRAVDA, 20 May 1988. Academician Valery Legasov, a prominent nuclear physicist, at the peak of his career committed suicide. What was behind it? A few days later PRAVDA published his notes on clearing up after the Chernobyl accident . . .

'Afgantsi', ZNAMYA, No. 7, 1988. A sincere, frank story, by young soldiers devoid of false enthusiasm, about military action in Afghanistan.

V. Novikov, 'Staying Alive', OCTYABR, No. 1, 1988. After a long period of suppressing the name and the works of Vladimir Vysotski, a poet, singer and actor who died in 1980, there came a wave of eulogies. Novikov's is one of the few articles on Vysotski which stands out for its quiet and thorough style.

V. Dudintsev, *White Robes*, NEVA, Nos 1–4, 1987. A novel depicting the persecution of scholars in genetics in the epoch of Lysenko's supremacy in biological science, and of the Stalin-Zhdanov dogmas in ideology and culture.

A. Rybakov, *The Children of the Arbat*, DRUZHBA NARODOV, Nos 4–6, 1987. The bestseller of perestroika, written twenty years ago and published now for the first time, a novel attempting the exposure of Stalin's tyrannical psychology.

A. Platonov, *The Quarry*, NOVY MIR, No. 6, 1987; *Chevengur*, DRUZHBA NARODOV, Nos 3–4, 1988. The novel was finally published after fifty years on the black list. About sharp spiritual problems at a time of vulgarizing and distorting revolutionary ideas.

B. Mozhayev, *Peasant Men and Women*, DON, Nos 1–3, 1987. V. Belov, *The Eves. Chronicles of the Late 1920s*, NOVY MIR, No. 8, 1987. Writers known for their deep acquaintance with country life dispel official stereotypes of the period of total collectivization and depict in their novels the tragedy which befell the Russian peasantry as a result of Stalin's dogmas.

A. Akhmatova, 'Requiem', NEVA, No. 6, 1987. A martyr in Russian poetry who survived her husband being shot, their son being arrested and imprisoned, who was persecuted by Stalin and Zhdanov, she has left us a poem expressing her thoughts and feelings. This is the poem's first publication.

M. Bulgakov, *Adam and Eve*, OCTYABR, No. 6, 1987; *Purple Island*, DRUZHBA NARODOV, No. 8, 1987. Probably these were the last forbidden Bulgakov plays to have seen publication. It hardly seems possible that there is nothing more to be discovered, nothing more of what was secretly copied and passed on.

J. Brodsky, *From Nowhere with Love*, NOVY MIR, No. 12, 1987. Poems by the Nobel Prize-winning poet in New York. Even two years ago nobody would have believed it.

A. Galich, *From his Literary Legacy*, OCTYABR, No. 4, 1988. Neither would anybody have believed that the publication of tragic and satiric songs by Alexander Galich who emigrated under Brezhnev would become possible.

M. Shatrov, *On . . . and On . . . and On . . .*, ZNAMYA, No. 1, 1988. The most controversial play out of Shatrov's Lenin cycle. An imagined dispute between Lenin and Stalin on the ways of revolution development.

B. Pasternak, *Doctor Zhivago*, NOVY MIR, Nos 2–4, 1988. It does not require any annotation: the novel most famous because of its vicious persecution by dogmatics has at last been published at home . . .

V. Grossman, *Life and Destiny*, OCTYABR, Nos 1–4, 1988. Fine artistic glimpse into the dark period. The manuscript of the novel was 'arrested' by the KGB in the mid-1960s. It is a wide-scale epic of people's life, victory, and suffering during the fight for Stalingrad, with tremendous historical and social background.

Index

337